Learning the Library

Learning the Library

Concepts and Methods for Effective Bibliographic Instruction

Anne K. Beaubien
Sharon A. Hogan
Mary W. George

R. R. Bowker Company
New York and London, 1982

To our parents

Published by R. R. Bowker Company
1180 Avenue of the Americas, New York, NY 10036
Copyright © 1982 by Xerox Corporation
Printed and bound in the United States of America

Library of Congress Cataloging in Publication Data
Beaubien, Anne K.
    Learning the library.

    Bibliography: p.
    Includes index.
    1. Library orientation—Handbooks, manuals, etc.
2. Searching, Bibliographical—Handbooks, manuals,
etc.
I. Hogan, Sharon A.   II. George, Mary W., 1948–
III. Title.
Z710.B37   025.5′6   82-4262
ISBN 0-8352-1505-9   AACR2

Contents

Preface

This book is intended for several broad audiences: practicing librarians, regardless of previous experience with bibliographic instruction; library science students and faculty; school, academic, and library administrators; and educators, researchers, and students active in various scholarly disciplines. *Learning the Library* details an academic bibliographic instruction program, offering a comprehensive examination of concepts, techniques, and applications. The book is a step-by-step, "how-to" guide for successful program development; and as such, it is a companion volume to *Theories of Bibliographic Education: Designs for Teaching*, edited by Cerise Oberman and Katina Strauch (Bowker, 1982), which applies education theory to bibliographic instruction and explores the education principles underlying the teaching method. With these two volumes, the librarian, educator, administrator, researcher, and student have access to both parts of the bibliographic instruction whole—an understanding of the theory and principles and the practical knowledge to apply them successfully.

Increasingly throughout the 1970s, practicing librarians were called on to provide "something more" for users than the traditional orientation tour of the library. Reference librarians, perhaps more than others, assumed the bulk of instructional responsibilities, whether at their own initiative or by circumstance. What at first appeared to be a simple extension of the logic and skills operating at the reference desk quickly turned out to be a large project in terms of focus, choice of content, format options, and implementation.

Indeed, starting from scratch is daunting. So, too, is the process of expanding or modifying an existing instruction program to meet user needs more effectively. Based on a combined experience of more than 20 years in instruction, reference, and other public service activities, the authors have attempted to extract and synthesize those factors—ranging from theoretical and political issues to step-by-step procedures and helpful hints—that are most critical to the design of a successful instruction program. For practicing librarians, then, this book will function as both a self-instructional text and as a reference manual, whether they are just beginning a program or revising one.

Increasingly also in the 1970s, vacancy announcements for professional library positions have specified instructional duties, leading library schools to respond by either incorporating a segment on instruction into a standard masters course in library science or by creating a separate course on the principles and practices of what has come to be called "BI" (bibliographic instruction). This book is intended to provide background material for the former case and to serve as a basic textbook for the latter. Library school faculty teaching general reference and subject bibliography courses should find individual chapters, especially those in Part II, Understanding the Research Process, useful for suggesting alternative approaches to the presentation of tools by title or type. Doctoral or continuing education students can readily apply these same theoretical chapters to literature searching in virtually any field, thus becoming more efficient and more versatile in their work.

Administrators of library- and education-related organizations form another audience because they are asking questions about the nature, costs, and impact of bibliographic instruction in a larger context. Library directors, school principals, and academic deans are all legitimately concerned about the information-gathering abilities (the so-called library literacy skills) of their staffs and the people they serve. Insofar as these managers seek to discover alternative, innovative, and ever-more-effective ways to realize the missions of their institutions, the discussions in Part IV, Implementing a Program, and Part V, Impact and Conclusion, should be informative as an outline of administrative considerations adhering to bibliographic instruction and the benefits that ensue.

Finally, a model of how knowledge is generated, captured, communicated, and codified in related fields is addressed. Also suggested is the possibility of modifying this model and incorporating it into the methods courses already being taught so that students new to a discipline can quickly grasp the intellectual framework it took educators years of specialization to acquire. It is our belief that educators are sincerely interested in conveying to students a sense of "what it's like" to do research in their field. Our efforts are aimed at fostering the corollary position, helping students learn systematically to discover research that has already been done.

It should be noted that the focus here is on higher education, from the community or vocational college to the research university. This focus is most evident in the chapters dealing with subject-specific bibliography; however, the same principles of the organization of information and procedures to identify and retrieve it are valid in all other situations as well, whether school, public, or special libraries. The ability to adapt concepts and approaches to the level and needs of a given user has always been a particular talent of librarians.

Similarly, attention centers on the potentials of the classroom presentation and its extension, the one-to-one tutorial. Together these modes, or formats, account for the majority of bibliographic instruction currently in use: the single course-related or course-integrated lecture; the full, formal or informal course; and the tutorial itself. Although there is discussion of other recognized modes of BI—printed materials, point-of-use explanations, programmed instruction, and computer-assisted teaching—those particular aspects are adequately covered by the literature in the field of education; any or all of them may effectively contribute to a well-conceived classroom presentation. However, it is the classroom presentation itself that is the chief concern here.

The arrangment of this book reflects the usual order of BI on those many occasions when a program has developed from the inspired initiative of one or two "grass roots" librarians acting on their own. That order puts the situation first, followed by substance and procedures, and then by administration and repercussions. This book is ordered accordingly: preliminaries, content, presentation, organization, and impact. Although this order may be common, it is not sacred. Librarians who have taught BI at an institution where there is already an established program may not need suggestions on preparing for a lecture, but might well be uncertain about how to make initial faculty contacts if they were to move elsewhere to set up new programs. Readers are encouraged to pick and choose material here to suit particular needs and curiosities.

Regarding terminology, there has been an attempt throughout this book to reflect a broad perspective by generally referring to the consumers of bibliographic instruction as "users." In certain chapters, however, most notably those devoted to the one-hour lecture and BI courses (Chapters 9 and 10), the term "students" is used most frequently. Similarly, the BI practitioner is generally referred to as "BI librarian" in contrast to "faculty." This is not intended to devalue the faculty status or role of many academic librarians, but is an attempt to apply a common terminology in order to clarify distinctions.

A word about the evolution of this book: since the 1972–1973 academic year, the three authors have collaborated constantly on all aspects of their BI presentations. Although each has had differing experiences and has dealt with different disciplines, this book was derived jointly, usually as a result of one author's insight as amplified and validated by the other two. The culmination of combined efforts was the opportunity to teach, as a team (known by the acronym SAM), Library Science 608 (Special Topics: Bibliographic Instruction) in the School of Library Science at the University of Michigan, Ann Arbor, a very stimulating challenge that has been undertaken annually since the spring of 1976.

As for the development of this book, the parts and chapters were arrived at by mutual deliberation and agreement. If the result of this work is a text that influences the direction and impact of BI, then the authors' common personal and professional goals will have been achieved.

As is the case with any work evolving gradually from experience, we are indebted to numerous individuals for their stimulation and support: Dean Russell Bidlack and his colleagues (University of Michigan, Ann Arbor) and the nearly 100 students who served (and survived) as our BI test ground, helping ideas to germinate and blossom; Jackie O'Jack and Mary Shaw Bates for skill and patience in typing the many drafts of the manuscript; Evan Farber, Tom Kirk, and Carla Stoffle for their continually challenging insights; Michael Keresztesi for unlocking the first of many theoretical doors; Irma Johnson for her persistent, and ultimately persuasive, advice to publish; and Connie Dunlap who as an administrator understood our dream and let it grow.

Anne K. Beaubien
Sharon A. Hogan
Mary W. George

Introduction

Bibliographic instruction, or BI, is like mountain climbing in that its justification lies in its challenge, in this case the challenge of making others aware of the full range of information resources. That challenge has always existed, of course, but until recently relatively few people needed recorded information—and that on a fairly limited array of topics—and few sources existed for them to consult. The educated individual could reasonably claim a knowledge of the classic authors and of the basic texts and tenets of several disciplines; reference sources were primarily encyclopedic in nature; language and leisure were not limiting but broadening factors; keeping current in all fields meant following a handful of journals and academic proceedings.

In the last two decades of the twentieth century, what is the situation? More people, both generating and seeking information on absolutely every subject with more sources and more types of sources, appearing every day. Ironically and tragically, however, the average level of education has decreased as the number of "schooled" individuals has increased, leaving an ever-widening gap between those who should know how to find information and those who in fact can. Writers who use the term *library literacy* when referring to the ability to identify, articulate, and solve information needs are accurate; like the traditional three R's, a certain fundamental research acumen is essential to responsible citi-

1

zenship, if not also to survival and success, in today's world.

But to return to the mountain-climbing simile. Those who participate in either mountain climbing or bibliographic instruction do not view their involvement as recreation or as a sport or a game; both pursuits lack precise rules and officials. Both activities require individuals who are naturally skilled and excellently trained, who share a spirit of adventure and commitment, and who can cooperate as a team. Every bibliographic instruction situation, like every mountain, is unique and unpredictable; so equipment and experience replace sure knowledge of the terrain.

Differences between the two activities are also telling. Every mountain has a known height, a certifiable peak, while bibliographic instruction shares with other areas of education the imprecision of intellectual pursuits—when does anyone truly know something? The purpose of mountain climbing is the experience itself, the expansion of the climber's being in all dimensions. Carry-over to other pursuits is, of course, significant, but scaling a certain mountain does not make one necessarily any better at handling daily human life. Bibliographic instruction, on the other hand, continually enhances the talents of the instructor; librarians who unfold their "mysteries" to others come to understand those same mysteries better themselves, and in the process (a key notion in the pages that follow) they become wiser professionals—better at the reference, selection, cataloging, automation, and, not least of all, administrative components of the profession. A mountain once climbed does not change. A person once introduced to the concepts underlying library research is never again the same, for the effort results in multiple transfers in the course of life—across time, place, and disciplines.

What about the dangers involved in failure? The threat of instant death or grave injury following one false step by the mountain climber cannot be equated with the imminent danger recognized by BI librarians, that without their efforts the force of the inquiring mind, the competent scholar, the able researcher may well die out within a few generations. Last, and most sad, the praise accorded the successful mountain climber is denied the successful bibliographic instructor, just as it is to anyone who revives an art that society does not acknowledge to be dying.

So why try? Not just because the challenge is there, although that is the initial motivation for most BI efforts at this point, but also because for anyone devoted to the public service aspects of librarianship, there is no better way to expand one's own knowledge and talents. Bibliographic instruction, well conceived and well executed, reinforces the reference, selection, and online skills that are typically part of the public service responsibility. In turn, those activities lead to more effective instruction as users are made aware of the whole complex system of information organization and retrieval. Other reasons have to do with local situations such as faculty status or tenure requirements, but they are in the long run incidental to the motive of teaching for learning's sake, which is the essence of BI.

During the 1970s, BI programs of all shapes and sizes sprang up in the United States and in other advanced countries. As do the participants in any grass roots movement, librarians came to BI from their own experiences and observations, often as reference librarians weary of repeating the same information to innumerable individuals on the one hand and, more significantly, probing seemingly simple questions on the other hand, only to discover that the questioners—often faculty—had not the vaguest notion of the complexity of their undertakings, the wealth of information and information sources that exist, or how to structure a search strategy in a logical, efficient, and thorough manner.

If one were only bent on solving the endless repetition-of-basic-facts nuisance, then a manual on the various mass modes of BI—workbooks, printed guides, audiovisual presentations, computer-assisted instruction, and the like—would be sufficient. In fact, the 1980 book by Beverly Renford and Linnea Hendrickson,[1] together with the many articles in both library and education literature, the proceedings of national and regional BI conferences, and the material available from various BI clearinghouses such as LOEX,[2] would be adequate. Although we will also discuss the characteristics of each major BI mode, it will be with a different end in view. Our aim in the chapters that follow is to concentrate primarily on the theoretical underpinnings of bibliographic instruction, on the concepts, thought processes, and intellectual decisions that the efficient library researcher must make in order to function freely in the world of limitless knowledge, however deeply buried it may be. Thus, even when we discuss the practical matters of presentation, organization, and impact of a BI program, it will be from the perspective of an effort geared to transmitting logic and judgment in the search for information.

Our belief (no longer merely a suspicion), based on contact

with colleagues in BI from around the world, is that very few librarians involved in bibliographic instruction have had training in or exposure to the principles of knowledge creation, growth, and proliferation; their attention has focused instead on the control of knowledge. Since BI concerns the systematic identification and location of recorded information, it is imperative that everyone who attempts BI have a basic understanding of the reasoning behind these processes and of how reference tools relate to the information they contain. Our intention is to provide this background, relating the dynamics of information origin and transfer to the dynamics of research at whatever level it is conducted. Only when BI librarians grasp the substantive intellectual basis for what they have themselves been doing all along at the reference desk will they be able to teach their students to extrapolate to ever higher levels of complexity.

Notes

1. Beverly Renford and Linnea Hendrickson, *Bibliographic Instruction: A Handbook* (New York: Neal-Schuman, 1980).
2. *Library Instruction Clearinghouses: 1981—A Directory*, rev. by Barbara Wittkopf (Chicago: Association of College and Research Libraries, 1981). The address of LOEX, the national bibliographic instruction clearinghouse, is Eastern Michigan University Library, Ypsilanti, MI 48197 (telephone 313-487-0168). Carolyn Kirkendall is the director of LOEX at the time of this writing.

Part I
Preliminaries

A t the heart of this book are concepts, theoretical frame-works, and mental processes that guide sound library research. A librarian who chooses to base an instruction program on universal principles rather than on arbitrary titles or tricks "students ought to know" will soon discover that all other considerations—budget, staff requirements, and administrative structure, to name only the most obvious—will be dictated to a large extent by that choice. Content determines approach in bibliographic instruction just as it does in any other area of education. Therefore, Part II of this book, concerning content, precedes discussions of presentation, organization, and impact (Parts III–V).

The purpose of Part I is to cover matters that influence content and that demand unique decisions on the part of each library before more specific planning can proceed. These matters are the library's environment with particular regard to the potential audience for instruction, the library's goals for itself and its audience in providing instruction, and the selection of a particular method or methods of instruction to achieve the stated goals for the given audience. Chapters 1–3 discuss each of these topics.

A word of definition and of distinction should be added at this point regarding the term *orientation* as opposed to "library or bibliographic instruction." At one time, *orientation* referred to all types of user education. Even into the early 1970s, the word *orientation* was the only approach to material on library instruction to be found in *Library Literature* and other printed indexes. With the resurgence of the user education movement in the early 1970s, librarians in the vanguard agreed among themselves to use orientation to mean "introducing users to the physical facility, policies, and procedures followed in a particular library." That is, orientation refers to navigation around a site. The phrases "library instruction" or "bibliographic instruction" denote more specific, often more in-depth, user education focusing on specific types of reference tools and in particular on search strategy, the way those types of tools fit together to make an efficient, effective research process. The *Bibliographic Instruction Handbook* defines orientation as "service activities designed to introduce potential library users to the services, facilities, and organization of a particular library. The primary purpose is to familiarize the user with the library as a system."[1] That same publication treats bibliographic instruction and library instruction as synonyms and defines them to

refer to any planned activities, outside the reference interview . . . designed to teach the library user how to locate information efficiently. The essential goals of this process are an understanding of the library's system of organization and the ability to use selected reference materials. In addition, instruction may cover the structure of the literature and the general and specific research methodology appropriate for a discipline.[2]

Virtually every publication relating to BI makes a distinction of the same sort between orientation and library or bibliographic instruction. BI subsumes orientation, although the reverse, of course, is not true. Whether orientation is accomplished by the traditional guided group tour conducted by a library staff member or through another method, it is important to incorporate familiarity with a particular library in any form of instruction. This can be achieved in many ways, for example, by requiring all students to have completed a basic orientation component before the beginning of any additional instruction. In a multisession BI program, it is possible to devote the first hour or less to conducting a tour of the library for the class. Some librarians find it helpful to spend the final five minutes of an instructional period pointing out to students the actual location of the various reference tools they have just discussed in the classroom. However orientation is handled, it must convey a sense of the unity of the library, of the interaction of its various components—reserve, reference, circulation, and the like.

Perhaps the most effective means of ensuring that users are comfortable in a library building is to provide multiple orientation components. These might include, in addition to the guided tour, a self-guided walking tour recorded on a cassette or written on paper, specific graphics or signs throughout the building, perhaps with paths along the floor from point to point so that at each station users are informed of the purpose and policies of that particular service, or a repeating or on-demand slide-tape or videotape production, usually available in the lobby, so that new users can acquaint themselves with the building the first time they enter it. In the not-too-distant future, it may be possible to issue a brief computer program from the circulation or reserve desk so that new users can learn about the library on their personal computers.

Although orientation is not mentioned except in passing in the rest of this book, it should be understood that it is assumed to have occurred prior to any library instruction.

Notes

1. *Bibliographic Instruction Handbook* (Chicago: Association of College and Research Libraries, 1979), pp. 58–59.
2. Ibid., p. 57.

1
Analyzing
the Situation

Modern management literature stresses the importance of assessing the environment before undertaking any major projects. This holds true as much for library instruction as for any other endeavor. It is no more possible to design a successful bibliographic instruction program based on an off-the-cuff analysis of user needs than it is to design a spacecraft based on speculation about the properties of the ionosphere. Without careful attention to the realities of the situation, the former is as likely to crash as the latter.

Situation analysis is an investigation of factors that are not subject to change and with which the library and any of its services must contend. These factors include society, community, institution, library, staff and user populations, and others discussed in this chapter. Every step in analyzing the situation prior to the design of a bibliographic instruction program should be carefully and specifically recorded, whether by individuals investigating a particular aspect of the situation or by a group of librarians brainstorming on the implications of what they have found. The importance of hard data at all stages of program planning is discussed in Part IV, but it should be obvious that detailed notes or minutes regarding the library's environment will be needed to support specific conclusions about the appropriate form of library instruction. An outstanding example of meticulously researched situation analysis has been published by the University of Texas at Austin.[1]

Society

Society is the largest and in many respects the most influential context in which libraries exist. Society supports the library and expects certain benefits in return. Politics, economics, and sociology all play important roles in determining what society expects from the library by way of innovation or traditional services.

It might be argued that it is futile for librarians to spend any time at all considering political, economic, or social conditions of the world at large when they intend, in fact, to set up a highly specific instructional program. On the contrary, it is all the more important to understand the expectations of society at such a time. It is possible to design a library instruction program that will meet the needs of societal groups larger than the immediate clientele. For example, in the academic world the institution might be looking for ways to attract new student populations, and the library could be a key element in the delivery of those programs, such as a community college reaching out to groups that need alternative education or to local high school students. It is a function of looking beyond those who come to the reference desk for service.

It is essential that all librarians understand where the community or educational institution may be headed; this is particularly crucial in a tight economic situation where such a move might provide some additional financial resources. At a minimum, public relations will be affected—positively, one hopes—by any attempt of the library to institute a new service such as library instruction.

The Community

An analysis of the community in which the library exists can be more specific than the necessarily broad view of society. The "community" is the political and geographic entity in which the library—public, school, or academic—finds itself. In the world of public libraries, analyzing the community is a standard practice; a variety of books on the topic range from how to do a community analysis to marketing an I and R (information and referral) service.[2] A community analysis is not as common in an academic or school setting. User studies abound, but they rarely encompass a broad range of factors, concentrating instead on users of the card catalog, a particular library branch, or a library service such as reference. However, in order to set up an instruction program, it is beneficial for either a school or an academic library to consider the larger community.

Any type of library should take note of what other libraries exist in the area. Are there high school libraries, public libraries, colleges, research institutions, or special libraries? One might consider cooperative programs, or at least include awareness of these resources in the planning for and ultimately the execution of a particular presentation. A public library instruction program for a garden club might refer to a local herbarium that has a dried flower collection and many specialized books. The availability of local resource-sharing agreements or a local union list will promote the accessibility of materials.

Demographic statistics on the population, as well as social and economic characteristics, may influence the type of program that is developed. What is the nature of the business community? Is it retail, wholesale, manufacturing, heavy industrial, or the research and development facilities of major corporations? Such an analysis will lead to a prediction of educational level, library awareness, and general research expertise of a certain proportion of citizens. The general tenor of support for library and educational issues can be gauged from past election results as well as from enrollment statistics in local adult education or continuing education courses. The age and ethnic profile of the residents can be an important indicator of potential interest in innovative library programs.

Although admittedly an analysis of this type provides only a bare sketch of community expectations and needs, it will prepare the planners to anticipate such factors as the reaction of nontraditional students or the community to a new program. Any and all information, whether based on hard data or coming from knowledgeable members of the community, can assist BI planners at an early stage, helping them to design a program that best meets the needs and expectations of the community at large.

The Institution

In a school or academic situation, planners should focus on the institutional environment, that is, on the specific characteristics of the school system or the academic setting. Does the stated philosophy of an institution match reality? For example, a school system may aim at directing a large percentage of students toward additional education, but in fact, only a small percentage of graduates might choose vocational or further academic schooling. A liberal arts college may claim that its primary purpose is to provide outstanding undergraduate instruction in the arts and sciences, but it may in fact have shifted emphasis toward preparing students for some specific advanced or professional degree. Talking with school officials or reading the college catalog should establish the image that the institution conveys.

In higher education the national reputation of an institution is hard to gauge and, furthermore, it is likely to vary from discipline to discipline. But, if BI planners are able to identify a particular strength nationally of the college or university, they can build on that strength in the program they design.[3] If, for example, advanced research is one of the major distinctions of an institution, it would make sense to gear a library instruction program at graduate students who are also research assistants, pointing out that the more they know about efficient, effective library research methods, the easier their lives will be. If, on the other hand, undergraduate teaching is commonly cited as the major strength of a school, instruction might focus on working with faculty to integrate library research skills into their courses or with undergraduates to ensure basic research understanding. A community college that seeks to be a resource for the whole community may wish to cosponsor library skills programs with the high schools. If service to the state or nation is regarded as the principal goal of an institution, as it sometimes is in the case of medical, law, or other professional schools, library instruction that enhances the ability of public servants to do research would seem an appropriate way of gaining support.

Most institutions have, however, a mixture of teaching, research, and service strengths; so it is impossible to identify primary characteristics. Instead, planners can investigate the number and nature of research institutes, academic departments, interdisciplinary programs, the specific degrees awarded and how many in each program or discipline, or whether the pattern of courses required by students in any given field is sequential.

More specific and more easily determined data about a

school system or an academic institution of higher education involve three core groups: the teaching faculty, the administration, and the student body. A brief look at some variables that affect each of these groups will clarify their importance for library instruction planning. The discussion covers a higher education setting, but parallels for elementary and secondary school systems are obvious.

The teaching faculty

Regarding the faculty, the factors to study are the following: where the members themselves have been trained; how long they have been at the institution or how long they can be expected to stay there; and what their other involvements are in their own discipline or in the community at large.

Understanding the educational and career backgrounds of faculty will help BI planners to predict the faculty's own research needs and also to predict faculty reaction to programs planned for their students. Faculty who received their own undergraduate and graduate training at prestigious institutions with major research libraries undoubtedly will have certain expectations for themselves and for their students and for your institutional library. Although your institution may be relatively small, isolated, and newly established, it may employ assistant and associate professors from major institutions. If so, they will be used to having the majority of their research materials at their fingertips and will think of using interlibrary loan only for a minority of their sources. They will logically expect your institution to have a free hand in ordering new journals and monographs, however expensive they may be in their particular field or discipline. They may not understand the importance of union catalogs and other locational tools because these people became accustomed in the past to having virtually any source they were able to identify in their home collection or readily available in the immediate geographic area.[4] As a consequence, faculty with such backgrounds will likely be somewhat frustrated if your collection does not have the wealth and depth of material they are used to.[5] Drawing on that frustration, it is possible to design a bibliographic instruction program aimed either solely at the teaching faculty or at majors or graduate students in a discipline where the faculty may be expected to attend the same sessions, and they too will be learning the techniques that will improve their research efficiency.[6]

It should be possible to determine the tenure and nontenure ratio of faculty from lists in college course catalogs. Another factor is the number of new faculty hired in any given academic year. Often the newly hired assistant professors are the most amenable to the suggestion that the library work with their students. Younger faculty are usually all too conscious of their recent struggles in the course of completing their own dissertations or other postgraduate work, often without the benefit of research assistance other than suggestions from major advisers or doctoral committee members. Although these new faculty may feel competent in their areas of specialization, they are often anxious and somewhat uneasy when it comes to advising students about the best reference tools to consult in a larger or an interdisciplinary area in which they have been assigned to teach survey courses. In their eagerness to begin or continue publishing in order to qualify for tenure, they are the most receptive of the faculty to library instruction addressed to them as a group.

One should also be aware whether some of the junior faculty at the institution are concurrently doctoral students at other institutions, and if so, in what disciplines and from what institutions. Their dual role will color their perceptions of the institution's library and its services and will likewise make them more personally eager to further instruction. In the same regard, it is useful to determine the ratio of teaching faculty to students in general and, specifically, the average number of students per course, or per section within a course in fields that are first addressed with instruction. Often a regular faculty member is responsible for a large lecture, but the actual give-and-take is conducted by teaching assistants who are themselves graduate students at the institution. This group of potential BI students has a dual role as they are themselves more receptive to instruction and, insofar as they are teaching younger students, are most likely to pass along library research methods.

The sacred professorial trinity of research, teaching, and service must be understood by BI planners in the context of their own institution. That is, what is the relative emphasis placed on research, teaching, or service or a mix thereof by the administration and by the traditions of the institution? It is important to design publicity regarding instruction to emphasize the primary thrust of the faculty.

For those institutions in which research is critical, changes in the library, such as acquisition of new bibliographic tools, implementation of online systems, and participation in local, regional, or national networks or cooperatives could have potential impact for a researcher-scholar and can serve as the basis for faculty "updates" on library resources. It is important to have a sense for the nature of faculty research commitments and the extent of grants or other outside funding on which faculty research may rest. An active library instruction program that emphasizes the strengths of the collection, builds toward research needs of the faculty, and offers special reference services such as database searching will not only aid the faculty member preparing the grant request, but will reinforce the role of the library as part of the research environment of the institution.

In some cases a library research component may be added to the objectives of the grant. An application for money to extend a basic literacy program to college freshmen might also include a component involving library research methods addressed to the group, or a grant to develop a new interdisciplinary program might include funding for the development of a library research module.

The service aspect of the faculty responsibility is also served well by library instruction. The faculty will have more time to devote to counseling and other commitments to the university, as well as to sharing their talents with a larger community, because library instruction frees them from spending time outside of class nursing students through the mechanics of simple research projects.

Faculty in professional fields such as law, business, and medicine, who have an outside practice in addition to their teaching commitments, can be identified as a separate group by library instruction planners. It is possible to design a program that will benefit the faculty's outside professional interest, at the same time assisting their students to a fuller appreciation of the potentials of the library. As more and more students combine disciplines, work in interdisciplinary areas, and change professions and careers throughout their lives, it becomes imperative to design a flexible BI program that will carry over from one field to another and will assist graduates in the practical as well as the scholarly aspects of their work.

A usable profile of the faculty may be constructed in several ways. Obviously, it is impossible to investigate the background and career of even a handful of faculty members. It might be better to choose certain key departments, perhaps one in the humanities, one in the social sciences, and one in the sciences. (If a decision has already been made to focus on certain fields, it would, of course, be important to focus on the faculty in those areas only.) If the chosen departments are small, a quick study of all the faculty in those areas is feasible. Using the *Comprehensive Dissertation Index* and any easily available biographical works, such as *Contemporary Authors*, the *Directory of American Scholars, American Men and Women of Science*, or the *Biographical Directory of the American Psychological Association*, it is possible to note the institutions and years in which current faculty worked on their degrees and whether their dissertations have been published. If the institution compiles an annual list of faculty publications, it should be consulted to determine the frequency and areas of publication.

Most institutions periodically issue a list of grants received, subdivided by recipient; a glance at this list will allow you to compile your own list of grants and fellowship awards to members of a specific department. Outside activities, such as consulting or advising political bodies, are more difficult to document, but press releases out of the university's administrative offices, which might be deposited in a pamphlet file or institutional archives or indexed by a local newspaper, are possible sources of such information.

In the last analysis there is no substitute for personal acquaintance with as many faculty as possible in the targeted departments. These people can help establish any additional characteristics of the department as a whole. In short, it is important to construct a profile that is accurate and meaningful, although the effort involved should not detract from continued planning of the content of the instruction program.

The administration

The most important aspects of the institution to understand, in broad terms, are the constraints (political and sociological) imposed by economic realities. For example, let us say that library instruction planners recommend a term-long course to be offered to undergraduates with library credit. First of all, it may be beyond the library's prerogative to suggest credit for a course, especially if money is allocated on the basis of credit hours offered by the department; second, if a course would be considered by a college or university administration, the suggestion of a credit course given by the library might be threatening to the financial stability of departments and might be strongly resisted. Unless the financial implications were understood by the library instruction planners, it would seem on the surface that the departments were resisting BI, when in reality they were resisting the approach that was chosen. The institution's administrative structure should be examined with existing political and sociological realities in mind, and the BI program should be charted to avoid dangerous shoals. Library instruction planners should design a program that will enhance, not detract from, the overall tendencies of the institution.

If enrollment is shrinking and tuition is rising, is the institution making a conscious effort to recruit new types of students, whether minority, nontraditional, or with subject backgrounds that were not previously prevalent among students? Any time that library instruction planners can spot a potential student audience, they can target it and reinforce the effort of the institution.

When a new department or program is established, the library as a whole must respond by increasing its rate of collection in the newly emphasized area and by extending bibliographic access to the material via card catalogs, reference tools, and specialized reference services. BI planners should consider focusing efforts on a new program if only because interdisciplinary programs ordinarily give students and teachers more difficulty, since many of the usual bibliographic tools may not yet exist in the field.

Sources for profiling university administrators are somewhat similar to those used for profiling the faculty (see under the Teaching Faculty, above). Various directories list higher education administrators, such as *College and University Administrators Directory, Directory for American Scholars,* and *American Men and Women of Science.* These provide the biographical data, career ladders, and scholarly interests of the various administrators. To get an idea of the current thinking of university administrators, look at the statements they make to the news media. Access to these sources of information would be through press releases or an index to a local newspaper.

In addition to biographical sketches and policy or direction statements, annual reports from various levels of the institution's administration are valuable, specifically those of the president, the provost or vice-president for academic affairs, and the office in charge of grants and funding from outside sources. These reflect more the tenor of a particular administration than does the immediate planning effort, since annual reports generally show what has already happened rather than predict the future.

Because the sources that are available to library instruction planners reflect past actions, the most important key to current institutional planning may be the contact between the library administration and that of the college or university. This contact is usually the director, or it may be the director and officer for budget and planning. They have direct contact with those offices that are considering shifts or future directions for the college or university, and thus they are privy to discussions that concern expanding or new departments, planning for space facilities, targeting new student populations, or decreasing support for a particular program or department in the university. If the library instruction planners do not have access to this thinking, somehow a link must be established in order to provide long-range planning information. Being aware of the reputation and response of policymakers and senior administrators will help BI planners construct programs that will reinforce the goals of the entire institution.

The student body

Students are perhaps the most important group to be understood at the time library instruction is instituted. A whole range of data can influence a library instruction program, from the gross number of students at an institution to the individual student's motivation for attending the school.

It is important to understand, as much as possible, the socioeconomic and geographic background of the student body. Do undergraduates come from specific feeder schools in the area, and hence have a homogeneous background, or do they come from around the state or nation? What are their national test scores or their average place in high school? Have they attended public or private high schools, and if private, parochial or the so-called prep schools? Does the institution favor an open enrollment program? Does the institution encourage nontraditional students, either older students coming back or students who are attending part-time? Is there a large foreign student population? Any of these groups might demand a unique approach in planning a library instruction program to meet special needs, whether advanced or remedial. At the very least, a mixture of teaching styles would be appropriate. For example, foreign students may be versatile in written English but have trouble with an oral presentation; on the other hand, students may come from schools where reading skills are not particularly stressed, but their verbal presentations are quite good. There could also be a wide variety in educational values and in the need for books and learning among groups, particularly those from different cultural or ethnic groups. Information-seeking habits acquired as children vary and have an impact on how one continues to seek information in an educational environment.

Other factors to consider about the student body include the number enrolled in each class—freshman, sophomore, junior, senior; the number in professional schools or whatever graduate levels are being considered; the number of students taking classes in a given department; and the average size of lecture and recitation sections within each department. The potential numbers of students to be reached with a BI program is critical. If a student body consists of 8,000 undergraduates, you can assume that approximately 2,000 are incoming freshmen. If you decide to give a one-hour lecture in a required course, such as freshman English, which everyone must take, that action will have a tremendous effect on staff time and materials. Assuming 2,000 students at 30 students per class, there will be 66 sections to teach. If only one or two librarians are available to give lectures, they will do little else. You may decide that another mode would be appropriate given the constraints on staff time.

Average class size will influence whether the librarian can bring students to the library for instruction, include a tour, provide a handout, or use group discussion techniques. You may want to target a specific level of student, department, or program to make the numbers of students reached more reasonable for the type of instruction decided on.

Also critical is the ratio of part-time to full-time students and whether students tend to take classes during the day or in the evening. What percentage of the student body is residential? What part commutes? This is critical because then one asks, Which library is the users' library? If the student commutes to a community college that is 30 miles from home in the suburbs and also works in a downtown urban area, several libraries are available—the one at the community college; public libraries in the college town, the suburb where the student lives, and in the downtown areas; plus other local college libraries. Even if most students live on campus, a number of libraries might be available, for example, dorm libraries, seminar collections in departments, the main library, or various branch libraries. Whether the student population is commuter or resident, you are not orienting users to one library, but instructing them in how to use the literature or how to access information generally, regardless of format or location.

How many students hope to go on to professional schools? How many expect to do graduate work in the arts and sciences? How many regard the bachelor's degree as the end of formal study? How many are in a vocational program and will be certified after two years? The answers to these questions may well reflect the motivation of the student population. If many students are going on to graduate work, the motivation to learn research methodology should be quite high. If students see the end of their formal education occurring in four years, perhaps the necessity to understand the ins and outs of a particular scholarly discipline may be less clear to them, but a need to gain access to information generally might be more attractive.

Are there many transfer students? If so, from what institutions and at what level? How large is the dropout rate? How many transfer to other institutions? If one is trying to establish a comprehensive freshman-level instruction program, a large percentage of transfer students either out of or into the institution may make a comprehensive program impossible. It may demand a multilevel approach or a different kind of instruction program to include incoming transfer students. A large dropout rate might mean that the motivation to learn from an instruction program will not be as high as it might be in a sophomore- or junior-level class once students have made a firm commitment to the institution.

How many students are financing their education through a work-study program or are otherwise employed? A large percentage of work-study or employed students may mean that they will have a high motivation for working efficiently, but they will not have much time for a separate library instruction course because of pressures from job, career, family, and/ or school.

Is the college or university involved in an exchange program or in a one-semester-away-from-campus work program? In some cases, the numbers of these students might not be large, but such programs might seriously interrupt a library instruction course set up as a sequential series of contacts.

Most data on students is available from various institutional offices, such as the registrar's office, the office of student affairs, the placement office, and the admissions office. Admissions officers can be especially useful in helping library instruction planners understand the background of the student body since they work with the figures and characteristics on a day-by-day basis. General characteristics can also be found in any number of current national educational directories. Information about departmental or professional school enrollment or course distribution can be gained either from the departments involved or from an overseeing office such as an office for academic affairs.

The Library

Once library instruction planners have a sound grasp of the various "people" groups with which they will be dealing (namely the faculty, the administration, and the students of the institution), they need to survey the library's own resources that will be used to support an instruction program. These include the collection, staff, and other resources, such as money available to support the program, space, equipment, present library services and operations, and the library's involvement in local or regional cooperative networks.

Collection

The heart of any library instruction program is really based on the collection of the library itself. "Collection" in the broadest sense includes books and bibliographic access to them, journals, materials in other formats, and information in other formats, that is, access to various databases. Going beyond the various standards that suggest the ratio of numbers of volumes to numbers of degree-granting programs at the bachelor, master, and doctoral level, look at the various parts of the collection and not just the totality. Statistics such as an approximate volume count in certain subject areas of the collection, the number of periodical and serial standing orders (again, as they relate to certain classification areas in particular sciences and social sciences), and the extent of auxiliary materials such as audiovisual and documents are all important. In each case the statistics indicate the depth and breadth of the collection and whether it is able to provide the support necessary for teaching, graduate programs, and faculty research.

Beyond sheer numbers, however, you must look at the collection policies for various areas. Is your collection at a basic, intermediate, or research level? If you understand the collecting levels and how they have evolved over time, it will be much easier to interact with specific disciplines in helping to explain to them the strengths of a particular collection. The collection policies of all reference areas are also important to know, since most instruction programs draw heavily on the reference collection and/or associated bibliographic access tools. The strengths of the special libraries on campus that may also serve students and faculty involved in research should be understood, as well as their relationship to the main and/or branch libraries. If you are teaching access to information, you must explain the availability of that information wherever it is housed and in whatever format, even though it is perhaps beyond the walls of the particular building in which an instruction program is developing.

Accessibility to a collection may be crucial to building a library instruction program. The fact that there is no access to the in-process file must be understood when developing an instruction program with a department that relies heavily on current material. If there is a large storage collection, physical access to material may be slowed down by either erratic or untimely delivery of the materials coupled with restricted bibliographic access. A large decentralized system will be confusing to the user who does not understand why all fine arts material is divided among three libraries or why all chemistry material is not together, and in today's world of interdisciplinary studies, this could in fact be a problem for almost any researcher.

Physical access may be a problem even in a single library if the floors are separated, stack areas are far from public service points, or the building is divided along social science, humanities, and science lines, again introducing the problem of exactly where a particular subdiscipline or topic might be located. Whether there is sufficient information/book collection to support the instructional programs or whether the library's collections could support the programs but are not used by students to the extent they could be (perhaps because of commuting, nonresidential students), one must think about developing the library instruction program to include or compensate for the collection, however it exists or however it is used.

Library staff

Probably the key factor in assessing the type of instruction program that one will develop is the availability of staff, and this includes staff at all levels. How many librarians, public service and/or technical services, might be involved? Are there support staff? What sort of clerical support might be devoted to the program? Are there staff with special talents who can assist in designing materials for the instruction program? The number of staff members available and the talents that they have or are able to draw on are directly related to the number of students that can be reached by the instruction program and the mode of instruction that can be attempted.

The question of how many staff are involved, at what level, and with what percent of time is related to the question of how the library instruction program is to be set up administratively. What units will be primarily responsible for an instruction program and whether it is a separately funded entity or an add-on to existing duties are related to the goals of the library and the way an instruction program evolves within a particular library setting. (See Chapter 11 for a discussion of organizational options.)

Library resources

Directly related to the number of staff involved in an instruction program are the allocated financial resources. The library instruction program that is supported by the institution as far as staff resources may nevertheless not have access to other funds. Extra money may not be available for handouts, for printing guides, or for developing slide/tapes. However, other kinds of resources may be available; for example, if the library and the audiovisual center are under the same administrative office within the institution, it might be possible for the library to draw on the resources of the center to help in constructing materials. An in-house computer or a system of minicomputers might be utilized in a library instruction program. The resources to support a program are not necessarily related strictly to money, but may involve services and easy availability of resources elsewhere on campus.

Space is certainly a consideration in designing a library instruction program—space to teach, space to keep materials, space to counsel students, space to display point-of-use or other audiovisual aids. It is not necessary to construct a separate classroom facility within a library in order to have a teaching area, but it is wise to locate it away from a public use area so that the noise from a class does not disrupt other students. (A teaching area at the University of Michigan is a table placed in the back of a combination microform and documents storage area. It is on a level with the other services in the building and is easily reached by students once they know the way to the teaching room.) Of course, it is not necessary to teach in the library at all. The literature is filled with the argument about whether it is better to teach in the classroom where one upholds the tradition of a teacher in a classroom or whether one should teach in a library near the tools that students are expected to use. Also, one does not necessarily need any teaching space, if the mode of instruction is a computer-assisted program, a workbook, or an audiovisual presentation. In such cases, however, space must be made for access to computer terminals or to the audiovisual machinery.

There must be space to keep materials—bibliographies, extra copies of indexes, guides to the literature, cards or worksheets from which to construct handouts or workbooks, transparencies, and so on. The space may be large or small in relationship to the instruction program, but some space must be provided.

Space that might not normally be considered when planning an instruction program is the need for space to talk to students. If you are involved in a workbook program, you may need no more than space at the reference desk where you can talk at length about a specific problem, or the space needed may be a private office where you can talk to a student in a bibliographic instruction course who needs quite a bit of counseling. If a library instruction person's "office" is in an open public area or surrounded by a number of other librarians, the counseling of students or the coming and going of students might annoy other people and could be a psychological deterrent for those who would like to ask for help.

Another factor to be considered when evaluating resources for a library instruction program is the availability of various kinds of audiovisual equipment, including overhead transparencies, slide projectors, audio cassettes, video machines, and computer terminals. Is such equipment available in the library? Is there a budget to procure such equipment? Are there facilities on campus that can provide this equipment in a reasonable fashion? Is there enough space for the equipment? Is there enough electrical power in the building to handle such equipment and are power outlets located near the usage area? Are repair and maintenance people or facilities nearby so that the turnaround time for down equipment will be reasonable? It would be disastrous to build a library instruction program on videotape only to have the video repair service 60 miles away and the turnaround time a week or more.

It may not be readily apparent that other services and operations of the library should be considered when planning a library instruction program, but such a program could have an effect on other parts of the library, or conversely, operations in other parts of the library may have a major effect on a library instruction program. Factors affecting the library collection, such as budget, acquisitions and cataloging rate, storage and special projects, for instance, retrospective conversion of any part of the collection to an online catalog or backlogs created by a switchover to new cataloging rules or a new computer system, must be taken into account to avoid creating a program that will strain a certain part of existing library activities. If interlibrary loan is already overburdened, an increase in such requests from students who have a BI session that includes materials not in the local collection may cause a problem. If shelving already has a long turnaround time, the additional books to be reshelved as a result of students doing a workbook assignment would only cause greater unhappiness on the part of both students doing the assignment and other library patrons.

It is important to study the present pattern of staffing public service points, particularly staffing the reference desk. Are professionals available at all hours? Are support staff or students available some of the time and if staffing is by students, are they undergraduates, graduate students, or library science students? Since the basic level of interaction is between the public and those persons in the library who staff public service areas on a daily basis, it is important that all staff members understand the intent of the library instruction program and the possible impact it would have on service at this desk. Although numerous studies show that the majority of questions asked at any particular reference desk are of a directional nature, studies also indicate that as library instruction expands on campus, the nature of the questions begins to change.[7] No matter how positive or rewarding a particular library instruction session, if it is not reinforced by a positive experience at a public service desk, the instruction and contact will have gone for nought.

You should inventory the current programs that explain the library and its resources. For example, do brochures and other printed materials already exist? How is orientation handled, and how successful has it been? Are any people other than librarians currently offering research method courses, and if so, which library or library facilities do they draw on? Does the library currently have any special programs for specific campus groups, for example, minority students or bilingual or continuing education students who may be new to the campus? Any one of these can provide the beginning of an instruction program or in fact may be ground that does not have to be covered again.

Are new programs developing, such as automation of the library's catalogs or the availability of free bibliographic database searching, which will have significantly changed use patterns of the library by any particular group on campus, and if so, how important is it to construct a BI program that will assist the user's transitions to these new technologies? It is necessary to project and analyze any demands on the library staff and the collection that might result from the initiation of a bibliographic instruction program so that the best possible program can be designed.

Library User Needs

All of the points for analysis discussed so far are concrete factors that need to be understood by planners before a particular form of instruction is undertaken. Other considerations, however, must be determined at this point, either by observation or by survey. These include the apparent need of the target group for BI. That is, if the planners have decided, for instance, to focus on a particular undergraduate or graduate audience, or to concentrate on all students in a particular department, what are the library research needs of that audience? Is orientation necessary? Do students need an introduction to the research vocabulary and concepts of their disciplines? Do they need a sense of what types of research and reference tools exist? Do they need specific titles for their discipline? To what extent should you concentrate on search strategy, on interdisciplinary crossovers, or on moving from theoretical to practical applications? Do students have time constraints or needs regarding research that they are assigned in their ordinary courses? Will the instruction be separate from any curriculum demands? Do you need to discuss alternative search strategies for disciplines or research areas that have no developed bibliographic access? Are there timing considerations with respect to the instruction needs, for example, orientation first, basic search strategy for underclassmen, then discipline focus the last two years?

These are all, of course, open-ended questions, but there are ways to go about answering them. First, you can observe directly from the reference desk the types of questions being asked, the types of research needed for papers, whether the papers are of primary or secondary sources, what kind of information might be required for an assignment on role-playing, and whether the students have any idea of how to approach the tasks. You can decide whether the need is for basic orientation or whether the particular assignments require a discipline focus or a type-of-tool approach. Another way is simply to look at the college catalogs or at various syllabi that are usually available through specific departments. Are there honors courses that require in-depth research? Are there many interdisciplinary programs that would require a facility in several disciplines? Are methodology courses already being taught in specific departments?

A third way of determining user needs is a direct opinion survey. Such surveys should be constructed to include not only those who come into the library, but nonusers as well. Descriptions of such surveys exist in the literature along with evaluations of the results.[8]

A fourth approach might be direct testing. Earlham College

(Richmond, Ind.) tests incoming freshmen to determine their level of library competence. Based on the scores of a simple library test, students are channeled into a library course that is intended as remedial or catch-up for those who come less prepared to college. Several current library tests are in the literature, some of which have been validated.[9] A determination of the users' needs, however acquired, will have a significant impact on the design of the instruction program.

Target Group

Now the most critical decision must be made by the library instruction planners, namely, what is their target group. Having carefully analyzed the institution and its resources and having assessed the probable library instruction needs of students as a whole, it is time to target a specific subgroup of the potential audience for BI on which to concentrate the new program. This decision ultimately must be made in view of the library's own mission and long-range goals, together with the current budget situation and library staff.

The saying "Where there's a will, there's a way" applies in many respects to bibliographic instruction. If only one librarian is available part of the time to develop a new program, however, it is irrational to assume that you can teach 3,000 freshmen in the course of an academic year, no matter what mode of instruction you select. It is far better to concentrate on an identifiable and relatively small group of students, at least in the beginning, so that the library staff, students, and teaching faculty who are first involved in the program can work together to improve it before it is expanded to a wider audience.

No magic formula indicates the best initial target group, although many colleges and universities have tended to begin with freshmen in a required course such as English Composition. Another possible beginning is to offer an introductory session explaining bibliographic databases to faculty and/or students. It is an attractive topic, and while you have a captive audience, you can explain the concepts of indexes and subject headings. The only group that should definitely not be chosen as an audience for BI is one that has no immediate library research needs, for example, beginning chemistry students who are not involved in any library assignment. It could be argued that these students also need instruction in accessing information, but the absence of an immediate research need on their part would result in low motivation and could discourage beginning library instructors.

The size of the target group is also important. It is often necessary to concentrate on a subgroup of a potential larger audience, for example, 10 sections out of a possible 40 sections of the same undergraduate class, or 1 section of a course for humanities honors students. Only after the target group has been selected can the planners proceed to write objectives and decide on the best possible way in which to accomplish those objectives.

It is assumed in the chapters that follow that the library instruction planners have a thorough grasp of the given factors and of the needs of both the institution and the target group. As a result, their subsequent decisions will be made in response to the realities of the situation and will meet the actual needs of individuals.

Notes

1. University of Texas at Austin, General Libraries, *A Comprehensive Program of User Education for the General Libraries* (Austin, Tex.: The General Libraries, 1977). Another comprehensive plan is available in Jay Martin Pool et al., *Preliminary Paper Toward a Comprehensive Program of Library Instruction for the Libraries of the State of New York at Buffalo*, ED 092 137 (Buffalo, N.Y.: SUNY Buffalo, University Libraries, 1974).

2. American Library Association, Library Community Project, Headquarters Staff, *Studying the Community* (Chicago: American Library Association, 1960).

3. Jack Gourman, *The Gourman Report: A Rating of Graduate Professional Programs in American and International Universities* (Los Angeles: National Education Standards, 1980); Jack Gourman, *The Gourman Report: A Rating of Undergraduate Programs in American and International Universities* (Los Angeles: National Education Standards, 1980); and "How Professors Rated Faculties in 19 Fields," *Chronicle of Higher Education*, January 15, 1979, p. 6, are recent surveys. A discussion of school ratings and a bibliography of surveys appears in David R. Gerhan, "Graduate, Professional School Ratings: Facing the Need-to-Know," *Journal of Academic Librarianship* 5, no. 4 (September 1979), 215–221.

4. The university-library syndrome is discussed in Evan Ira Farber, "College Librarians and the University-Library Syndrome," *Academic Library: Essays in Honor of Guy P. Lyle*, ed. by Evan Ira Farber and Ruth Walling (Metuchen, N.J.: Scarecrow Press, 1974), pp. 12–23.

5. Dagmar Horna Perman, *Bibliography and the Historian* (Santa Barbara, Calif.: Clio, 1968), pp. 10–15, reports on the research patterns of historians. The profile of the historians surveyed showed that they had been trained in institutions with large research libraries or that they had access to such libraries. They uniformly commented about the lack of both research materials and of specialized bibliographic reference works in their present academic settings. A profoundly pessimistic view of the research expertise of historians is Margaret F. Stieg, "The Information Needs of Historians," *College & Research Libraries* 42 (November 1981): 549–560.

6. Descriptions of such programs are found in Margery Reed and Sarah Katharin Thomson, "Instructing College Faculty in the Bibliographic Resources of their Subject Field: A Case Study," *Educating the Library User*, ed. by John Lubans, Jr. (New York: R. R. Bowker, 1974), pp. 191–201, and Anne Grodzins Lipow, "Teaching the Faculty to Use the Library: A Successful Program of In-depth Seminars for the University of California Faculty," *New Horizons for Academic Libraries*, ed. by Robert D. Stueart and Richard D. Johnson (New York: Sauer, 1979), pp. 262–267.

7. Billy R. Wilkinson, *Reference Services for Undergraduates* (Metuchen, N.J.: Scarecrow Press, 1972), p. 336, and John Lubans, Jr., "Mediated Instruction: An Overview with Emphasis on Evaluation," *Drexel Library Quarterly* 16 (January 1980): 27–40.

8. John Lubans, Jr., "Library-Use Instruction Needs from the Library Users'/Non-Users' Point of View: A Survey Report," *Educating the Library User*, pp. 401–409, and his "Evaluating Library-User Education Programs," *Educating the Library User*, pp. 232–253, discuss surveys for user needs.

9. Masse Bloomfield, "Testing for Library-Use Competence," *Educating the Library User*, pp. 221–231, discusses major tests with examples and includes a bibliography of published tests.

2
Setting Objectives

Librarians are, unfortunately, not usually in the habit of writing down their objectives for most operations. Many changes within a library occur for internal reasons of cost saving or efficiency, or in the public service area they are an attempt to meet perceived user needs, which are often not measurable because of the random nature of the contacts between librarians and library users. But the lack of objectives in most library operations does not mean that this should be the standard practice. On the contrary, long-range planning suggests the setting of goals and objectives as the basis for all organizational actions; it should most definitely be required for new program development.

In the BI literature, references to objectives have taken on two slightly different meanings: (1) a general understanding of program objectives and, (2) the more specifically designed educational objectives. The two are not unrelated, but the general objectives are rather loosely constructed definitions of audience size, level, and institutional public service philosophy, and the more specific objectives have been derived from the field of educational psychology, following a rigid terminology. Chapter 1 discussed how to designate those elements of a program that must be identified for long-range planning. Chapter 2 discusses overall program objectives, concentrates on the more specific articulation of learning outcomes through the formulation of behavioral objectives, and ends with a brief discussion of evaluating objectives.

Determining specific multidimensional objectives during the early planning stages defines the outcomes expected of the program, provides a context for evaluation, serves as a basis for adjusting the program as it proceeds, and ultimately gauges the program's overall long-term impact on both the user community and the library itself. For objectives to be useful to planners, they must be carefully thought through, written, and formulated prior to all other decisions.

Types of Objectives

Objectives for the BI program as a whole will be especially useful when presenting the program in an annual report or when preparing a funding document for the library administration or a grant proposal for an outside agency. It could be argued that once a target audience has been selected for a bibliographic instruction program, the planners should immediately decide on a specific mode or modes of instruction to reach that audience. Each instructional mode, however, has its own limitations (discussed in Chapter 3) and costs (discussed in Chapter 13); so by choosing a mode of instruction before writing objectives, planners are restricting their thinking and doing a possible disservice to their target group. If, on the other hand, educational objectives are drawn up immediately after the primary audience has been defined, it becomes possible to mix and match various ways of presentation to reach the objectives. The time and effort spent constructing meaningful objectives is less likely to hamper and more likely to enhance the total program when it is done at this stage, since planners can concentrate on their ideal goals without becoming sidetracked by the problems inherent in any given mode.

The development of program objectives is based on the long-range planning terminology devised by organizational psychologists and management theorists. Bibliographic instruction librarians turned to the field of educational psychology for the definition and construction of objectives to be used in teaching and learning. The popularity of instructional technology and behavioral psychology in the late 1960s and early 1970s influenced a whole generation of teacher training, and librarians, uncomfortable with classroom techniques, adopted the terminology and approaches wholeheartedly.

The Task Force on Library Instruction of the Association of College and Research Libraries (ACRL) set about defining objectives for undergraduate programs; conferences were held on the topic of objectives, and workshops were designed on how to write them. Many different adjectives are used to modify "objective"—for example, behavioral, competency, and criterion-based. All these adjectives imply that an objective is specific enough to be measured in quantitative terms. Three specific levels help planners focus their attention on the end product, that is, the library user: general objectives, terminal objectives, and enabling objectives. Only the last of the three is truly behavioral in nature in that it consists of a subject (the user)—an action to be performed, a time frame for the performance, and last, one or more criteria on which the performance will be judged. Such specificity is essential to the construction of evaluation instruments that will gauge the success of each student's absorption of the presented material and, taking a group of students as a whole, that will determine whether the bibliographic instruction program has improved their ability to deal effectively and efficiently with library research.

The three degrees of objectives for library instruction can be illustrated by the general, selected terminal, and enabling objectives published in the ACRL *Bibliographic Instruction Handbook*. The complete set of objectives in the *Handbook* may serve as a model on which any individual library can base its objectives.[1] The following is the general objective for bibliographic instruction in an academic institution: "A student by the time he or she completes the program of undergraduate studies should be able to make efficient and effective use of the available library resources and personnel in the identification and procurement of material to meet an information need."[2] Terminal objectives relating to this general objective might be as follows: "T3. The student is familiar with or has knowledge of the library resources that are available to him."[3] "T4. The student can make effective use of the library resources available to him."[4]

Although these terminal objectives for a bibliographic instruction program are not objectively measurable, they do represent specific aspects of the overall general objectives, and in turn they lend themselves to a highly specific and measurable breakdown into the enabling objectives. Some enabling objectives are the following: "Given a map of the library the student can correctly identify the location of the reference department and its catalog in a specified time period."[5] "In a specified time period the student can identify major reference tools in an unfamiliar field using a guide to the literature such as Sheehy's *Guide to Reference Books*."[6] "In a specified time period the student can list five periodical titles and the indexes which cover them in an unfamiliar field using a directory such as *Ulrich's International Periodicals Directory*."[7] Each of these enabling objectives has four basic elements: the subject (that is, the student), who is both the doer of the action and, of course, the recipient of the instruction; what the student is expected to do; the intended time frame in which the student is expected to act; and one or more criteria on which the student's behavior will be judged. The location of the activity, namely the library, is either omitted, and hence understood, or a specific location such as the reference department is mentioned.

None of the enabling objectives indicates *why* an action is to be performed. When it comes to wording an enabling objective, however, the "why" of the action is generally not specified but is subsumed in a larger general objective, that is, "to make efficient and effective use" of library resources. The "why" of the enabling objective is efficient and effective use, furthered by the time constraint, since one can argue that students cannot be efficient unless they can accomplish a finite task in a reasonable period of time. Other examples of objectives for bibliographic instruction programs may be found in the literature or borrowed from LOEX or one of the other regional and state clearinghouses. However, some particularly well-written and comprehensive objectives are those of the University of Texas at Austin, an excellent example of general systemwide planning for several levels of students, and the School Library Media Center of the Prince Georges County Public Schools, Maryland, showing identification of specific skills at each grade level K–12.[8]

In addition to using the ACRL, Prince Georges County Public Schools, or one of the other published sets of objectives as models to be adapted at one's own institution, highly specific educational objectives can be found in manuals put out by education departments of most states and addressed to teachers in the public school system. In some cases these objectives are intended as guidelines for a school district or ideals of performance for students in a given grade or at a given age level. In other cases they are mandatory and have the force of regulations, such as that students must accomplish a certain percentage of the objectives before they can be promoted to the next grade level.

If the audience targeted for library instruction is within a specific subject discipline, it is also good for the planners to consult any curriculum guidelines issued by the national professional association. Sometimes these guidelines are used in evaluating academic departments throughout the country in that field.[9] Guidelines for writing behavioral objectives are available in the educational literature. One of the most widely used descriptions is Robert Mager's *Preparing Instructional Objectives.*[10] A discussion of writing behavioral objectives in the context of bibliographic instruction is available in *Writing Objectives for Bibliographic Instruction in Academic Libraries.*[11]

Common pitfalls in writing objectives for a bibliographic instruction program include shifting the perspective from the student or learner to some other subject. It is important to keep the learner as the subject of the sentence and the doer of the behavior being measured. Another frequent problem concerns vagueness about the conditions under which the behavior is to occur; vague conditions naturally make for a vague conclusion as to whether or not the student has accomplished the task. A third pitfall is the choice of a weak verb; "the student will locate" is much more clear than "the student will know." If objectives for a bibliographic instruction program are drafted by a committee of planners, committee members may disagree about the goals or be unable to agree on the precise wording of enabling objectives. If this occurs, a single individual should undertake to write objectives and then let the committee react and modify them. If the library instruction is intended to mesh with an existing course in the curriculum, the goals written by the librarians for their segment of the instruction may not correlate with the overall plan that the teacher or faculty member has for the course. This needs to be worked out in advance so that there are no misunderstandings, which could lead, at best, to ambiguity about the effectiveness of the library instruction and, at worst, to very bad relations between the library and members of the academic department in question.

Behavioral objectives have not met with enthusiasm in all quarters—many academic librarians and others in the field of higher education scoff at measurable statements in behavioral objectives, believing that quantitative descriptions are not sufficiently comprehensive to deal with the complexities of learning that take place in the college classroom.[12] To refute this view, one need only consider that any new project, whether undertaken by an individual or by an institution, requires initial justification before obtaining resources.

Both the construction of behavioral objectives by the ACRL as well as other bibliographic instruction programs during the 1970s and the more recent criticism directed at these objectives reflect the historical context of the late 1960s and 1970s. The popularity of behavioral psychology as pioneered by Watson, Guthrie, and Thorndike, which was expanded and adopted widely after the work of B. F. Skinner in 1968, influenced the development of behavioral objectives for bibliographic instruction in the 1970s.

The behavioral objectives approach of instructional development to education results from three influences: behaviorism; systems theory, which was developed during World War II by the U.S. Air Force as a managerial procedure; and educational technology, which grew out of the use of audiovisual aids during the post–World War II era. The systems approach allowed for a step-by-step task analysis to design an educational procedure, an approach that was easily adapted to educational technology. However, the systems approach often seems rigid and inflexible and has been criticized as not being valid in the context of the humanities. Educational technology itself has not been readily adapted by those in higher education, who view the audiovisual media only as adjuncts to the major teaching approach—the lecture or discussion. Only in the fields of certain professional schools, such as medicine, dentistry, and engineering, where specific training procedures are being taught with a view toward an end product, has instructional development in the use of educational technology flourished.

As behavioral psychology and educational technology began to fall into disfavor in the mid-1970s, they were replaced by a new approach to learning theory. Such instructional development theorists as Gage and Harmon extended the earlier work of Chomsky, Brunner, and Osteval in developing an approach to try to account for the individual learning that takes place on the part of a student user. The cognitive psychology approach assumes that each individual has stored a unique set of factual information and retrieval mechanisms, so that any new knowledge is received, evaluated, and assimilated in the context of what is already known. This would differ from individual to individual and help to account for the more complex learning processes. The switch is from looking at external manifestations of learned behavior—in a behavioral objective sense, what the person can do in a specific amount of time—to looking inward at the learning process itself.

Benefits of Objectives

The shift in emphasis in the educational world away from behavioral objectives does not nullify the need for objectives. A systematic approach to instructional design is still needed, since it will provide a framework from which to build and evaluate a program. A number of positive results of objectives can affect both the bibliographic instructor and the student.

The teacher/librarian benefits in many ways from having specified objectives:

1. Objectives help the instructor select and structure the content to be presented. By always keeping in mind what the student should be able to derive at the end of the program, the instructor is better able to devise means to that end.

2. Articulating objectives improves the effectiveness of the instructor. Not only will the material to be presented be more focused, but the instructor's approach to the material will become more effective. The instructor is likely to attempt innovative teaching methods or to experiment with new examples or assignments to achieve an end he or she has carefully defined. Similarly, the instructor will be more inclined to modify a traditional mode of instruction, for example, the classroom lecture, with other approaches in order to stimulate more thorough and faster learning.

3. Objectives are very useful when the usual instructor is

absent and a colleague must substitute for a session. A complete set of objectives for the entire program, together with lesson plans or scripts or drafts of printed materials, depending on the method under consideration, will help a substitute understand exactly what effect is intended for a particular segment.

4. Objectives help the instructor to justify a BI program to the library administration. Well-constructed objectives are a strong argument that the proposed program has been thought through carefully. They also lend themselves to several possible evaluation techniques, and since library administrators are likely to ask questions about evaluation at an early stage, the presence of objectives in the proposal will only strengthen the case. Later on, after the instruction is completed, reference to the original objectives, together with documentation as to the extent to which they have been met, will help the instructor and the administration plan for the future in terms of budget, personnel, and possible program modifications.

5. Objectives lend themselves to the construction of evaluation instruments. At the end of an instructional program, some form of evaluation should be coordinated with the original objectives. Thus, objectives can help isolate problems or rough spots in curriculum design. For example, if the majority of students in a given group are unable to meet certain enabling objectives at the conclusion of instruction, it is possible that the material presented, or the method of presentation, did not convey the information intended. If the objective is to be retained, the presentation must be modified; if the presentation stays the same, the objective that was not met must be modified or omitted.

6. Objectives, once formulated, can be readily transferred to similar situations, that is, to like audiences for a different discipline. Also, if the instructor moves to another institution and becomes involved there with bibliographic instruction, the same objectives can be modified to suit the new situation and the newly identified audience.

7. Objectives validate the instructor's work to other librarians and to professionals in other fields. The original list of objectives, together with documentation on how well those objectives were met, allows any other librarian, faculty member, or scholar in a given discipline to appreciate

the work that was done and the work that the student should now be able to do.

Students also benefit from specified objectives.

1. Objectives presented to students at the beginning of any form of instruction permit them to know the direction in which the instruction is headed.

2. Objectives increase students' motivation because they are aware of what the instructor expects them to learn at any given point in the course. By providing ready reinforcement, objectives stimulate students to learn faster.

3. Objectives make study time more effective because the students have a definite direction in which to proceed, and they realize that they can achieve the objectives on their own without the assistance of other students.

4. Objectives allow students to evaluate their own progress throughout the course of instruction. Thus it should be possible, in the case of the self-paced modes of BI, for students to complete the entire program of instruction in much less time than may have been originally planned. This is especially true if the mode of instruction is the workbook; students have been known to complete all exercises in record time, motivated by the challenge of finishing quickly, knowing that their answers were correct.

The Future of Objectives

Although the specifics and the niceties of formulating clear objectives for a library instruction program may be debated, it is impossible to deny the wisdom of determining the ends of instruction before developing the means to achieve those ends. In many ways, objectives statements are like policy statements. They are only needed when a problem arises, but then they are most welcome indicators of an appropriate direction to take, indicators that all can understand.

Much work is yet to be done in the area of learning theory. The change in approaches from behavioral to cognitive psychology since the mid-1960s indicates the evolution of theoretical thinking about teaching and learning. That a direct relationship exists between the anticipated learning outcome and the choice of teaching methods is evident, but the best teaching methods for a particular outcome are not yet clear. Methods such as discovery learning or the Socratic method of problem-solving seem to match more closely the thinking behind cognitive psychology. In the field of bibliographic instruction, we must yet categorize the particular learning outcomes associated with such things as search strategy, discipline structure, or analyzing the reference questions, the kind of conceptual, theoretical basis that is discussed later in this book. The behavioral objectives that exist thus far in instruction begin to point the way toward the kinds of learning sequences that are expected. It is one thing to know how to use *Readers' Guide*—knowing the specific way it is arranged, knowing how to look up a subject heading. These learning behaviors fall into the category of rote or memorization learning. It is less clear, however, how one goes about describing what happens in knowing that an index must be used at a particular point in search strategy. One can approach an index such as *Readers' Guide* in at least three different ways: (1) through knowing how to use a particular index, in this case, *Readers' Guide*, (2) through understanding what an index is and that *Readers' Guide* is a specific example of that type of tool, and (3) through understanding what an index is and when to use it as a part of a complex search strategy. These seem to be three different levels of learning and are probably best taught by three different methods.

The work in bibliographic instruction that involves looking at learning theory and the instructional objectives we choose to teach is being carried on in both the United States and Great Britain. In the United States it is a decentralized endeavor, with certain librarians scattered around the country experimenting with different teaching styles. In Great Britain, however, this aspect is being examined closely by a central office of the British National Library.[13] If instruction is to move ahead, this area must be examined thoroughly by librarians and educational psychologists working together to find the best solutions for the desired learning outcomes.

Objectives and Evaluation

A major goal for bibliographic instruction in the 1980s is to establish baseline criteria from which objectives and corresponding programs can evolve so that evaluation can be meaningful.

Evaluation can have several objects, including evaluating information for the librarian, for the students, for library staff and/or the library profession as a whole, for the library administration, or for an outside funding agency.

To improve the quality of the BI lecture or course, the instructor should ask certain questions; the answers can provide a basis for modifications. Should the order or sequence have been different? Should the approach to the material have been different? Was the material covered appropriate? Were there serious omissions? Did the instruction meet the needs of the students?

Evaluation can be used as a teaching aid. When the BI librarian returns a test or assignment, there is an opportunity to discuss problem areas that emerged or common difficulties of students, without singling out any one student. An effective test indicates whether students are learning what the teacher expects and the extent to which they understand the teacher's presentation.[14]

Tests can be used for evaluating a student's knowledge. A pretest or diagnostic test may be used to determine weak, as well as strong, areas and which students may need special assistance. Tests can also be administered to motivate students by setting short-term goals toward which they can work. Evaluation for students is ultimately a test to determine their mastery of knowledge. Both students and instructors need to know what students have learned, especially if it is necessary to grade students.

Evaluating library instruction can serve the library staff and the library profession. A librarian who learns more about what constitutes an effective presentation for a given situation can share that knowledge with other staff members, who, in turn, will be able to learn from mistakes, successes, and insights. Dialogue about creative and innovative approaches to bibliographic instruction contributes positively to the professional growth of all concerned, and such dialogue encourages a peer-support system. Evaluating instruction can lay the basis for further research on the reasons for the relative success of alternative approaches and techniques. The findings and materials that are developed in the course of evaluating BI can be shared with others by submitting them to the Library

Orientation and Instruction Exchange (LOEX), the national bibliographic instruction clearinghouse, to develop the literature on bibliographic instruction.

Evaluation has another purpose besides helping students to assess their mastery of material and helping BI librarians determine whether or not they have met their objectives. The information gathered in the course of evaluation can be useful to administrators in allocating future resources and drafting long-term plans.[15]

By focusing on specifics, such as those in the following checklist, the instructor can tell if learning is effective and therefore if the instruction has been effective.

1. Number of pages of handouts used.
2. Number of students reached.
3. Number of hours of preparation time divided by number of students reached.
4. Number of hours of class time.
5. Number of departments reached.
6. Number of levels of students (or faculty) reached.
7. Effect on reference statistics; did the number of directional statistics or statistics on research questions go up or down?
8. Effect on the circulation and use of materials: of entire collection and of reference materials (indexes, bibliographies, etc.).
9. Change in bindery statistics.
10. Is Inter-Library Loan (ILL) up or down?
11. Amount of time spent in followup (for example, did students who have had instruction return to the librarian/teacher for additional direction on the same project or another project?).
12. Amount of time spent generating interest in BI (selling the program to the faculty or students).
13. Number of organizational meetings to attend in order to promote BI or the library in general.
14. Amount of time spent on other forms of public relations for the library.

15. Amount of support staff time, e.g., typing handouts, photocopying and collating handouts, pulling books for the class, making transparencies, slides, etc.

16. Cost of materials (photocopying, staples, etc.).

Evaluation data may be collected to convince an outside funding agency that a grant should be awarded or renewed. Much of the data referred to in the preceding checklist may be appropriate in such a case. The guidelines of the grant application should be read carefully to see if specific and/or additional points of information should be gathered.

Through the process of ongoing evaluation, we can begin to discover what users need to know about library research, how they learn, and how we can improve our instructional efforts.

Notes

1. *Bibliographic Instruction Handbook* (Chicago: Association of College and Research Libraries, 1979), pp. 35–45.

2. Ibid., p. 37.

3. Ibid., p. 38.

4. Ibid., p. 39.

5. Ibid.

6. Ibid., p. 40.

7. Ibid.

8. University of Texas at Austin, General Libraries, *A Comprehensive Program of User Education for the General Libraries* (Austin, Tex.: The General Libraries, 1977), and Prince Georges County Public Schools, School Library Media Center, *Basic Research and Communication Skills K–12* (n.p.: Prince Georges County Public Schools, Md., 1977). Other references are cited in Deborah L. Lockwood, *Library Instruction: A Bibliography* (Westport, Conn.: Greenwood Press, 1979).

9. National Association of Schools of Music, "Membership for Baccalaureate and Graduate Degree-Granting Institutions," December 1980, and American Assembly of Collegiate Schools of Business, "AACSB Accreditation Council. Policies, Procedures, and Standards," 1977–1978.

10. Robert F. Mager, *Preparing Instructional Objectives*, 2nd ed. (Belmont, Calif.: Fearon Publishers, 1975).

11. *Writing Objectives for Bibliographic Instruction in Academic Libraries: A Summary of the Proceedings of Sessions of the Midwest Federation of Library Associations*, Detroit, October 1–2, 1975 (Kenosha, Wis.: University of Wisconsin, Parkside, 1976).

12. Gregory A. Sprague, "Cognitive Psychology and Instructional Development: Adopting a Cognitive Perspective for Instructional Design Pro-

grams in Higher Education," *Educational Technology* 21:24 (February 1981).

13. Library User Education Conference, Trinity College, Cambridge University, September 1979. The proceedings were published as *British Library Research and Development Report* no. 5503.

14. See James Rice, "Testing and Evaluation," *Teaching Library Use: A Guide for Library Instruction* (Westport, Conn.: Greenwood Press, 1981), pp. 97–129.

15. See Thomas Kirk, "Bibliographic Instruction: A Review of Research," *Evaluating Library Use Instruction*, papers presented at the University of Denver Conference on the Evaluation of Library Use Instruction, December 13–14, 1973, ed. by Richard J. Beeler, Library Orientation Series, no. 4 (Ann Arbor, Mich.: Pierian Press, 1975), pp. 1–29; and Nancy Fjällbrant, "User Education Evaluation," *Directions for the Decade: Library Instruction in the 1980s*, ed. by Carolyn A. Kirkendall, Proceedings of the Tenth Annual Conference on Library Orientation for Academic Libraries, Library Orientation Series, no. 12 (Ann Arbor, Mich.: Pierian Press, 1981), pp. 71–89.

3
Choosing a Mode

Once the local situation has been analyzed, a target group has been selected, and appropriate objectives have been written, it is time for the BI planners to choose the best possible mode of instruction. By "mode," we mean a teaching method or format that will transmit the content of a library instruction program to an audience.

In this chapter, we describe seven common modes, discuss factors on which a table of pros and cons for each mode is constructed, and suggest ways in which such a table can function together with the previously determined factors—the situation, the audience, and the objectives—to aid planners in selecting the best approach, or combination of approaches, to achieve their overall goals.

Seven Common BI Modes

Modes can be defined by the technology involved (audiovisual presentations), by the location where they function (point of use), or by the technique they use (programmed instruction). The seven commonly recognized BI modes are the following:

Printed materials.

Audiovisual presentations.

Point-of-use explanations.

Programmed instruction.

Single lectures.

Formal courses.

Tutorials.

See Table 3-1 for a brief summary of pros and cons for each of these modes.

Table 3-1 Modes of Bibliographic Instruction: Pros and Cons*

	Pros	Cons
Printed Materials		
General (information sheets, how to find . . . , how to use . . . , self-guided tour)	Can cover orientation topics Effectively convey a specific tool Available to users all hours the library is open User does not have to ask for help Could complement a class Once prepared, saves constant repetition of core information Relatively inexpensive to produce Relatively easily updated Require little space to display Do not need faculty approval Reach a wide audience Good advertising for the library Can place in freshman packet or send to other user groups	Seldom convey question analysis, search strategy, discipline growth, nature of types of tools, bibliographic structure, or transferability to other topics or disciplines Not flexible to user needs User may conclude this is everything User must be motivated to use Might not be used May need copyright permission Difficult to evaluate effectiveness No librarian contact
Bibliographies and discipline guides	In addition to above: Can explain the concept of types of tools Can be subject specific or format specific Are readily adaptable from one library to another Provide tools selected by professionals	In addition to above: Provide little guidance unless annotated
Pathfinders	In addition to above: Convey a search strategy to follow Are efficient for users Commercially available with possibilities for local adaptations	In addition to above: Topics are necessarily narrow, so many needed to reach all groups of users
Audiovisual Presentations (videotape, audiotape, film, slide/tape)	Can cover orientation topics Can effectively explain a specific tool, the process of question analysis, and the nature of a type of tool	Seldom convey search strategy, growth of the discipline, bibliographic structure, or transferability to other topics or disciplines

*This table is an updated version of the one that originally appeared in *Bibliographic Instruction Handbook*, Policy and Planning Committee, Bibliographic Instruction Section (Chicago: ACRL, ALA, 1979), pp. 46–55.

Table 3-1 (cont.)

Pros	Cons
Audiovisual Presentations **(cont.)**	
Can combine orientation and instruction	Not flexible to user needs
Available when needed	Must be high quality to compete with expectations built up by commercial television
User does not have to ask for help	
Could complement a class	User may be embarrassed to use
Once prepared, saves constant repetition of core information	Some people intimidated by AV equipment
Can make multiple copies for showing in different locations	Might not be used
	May need copyright permission (especially for background music)
Do not need faculty approval	Require many technical skills
Repeatable	
Commercially available	Equipment is expensive and requires expert maintenance
	Need considerable space, outlets, special lighting
	Difficult to evaluate effectiveness
Point-of-use Explanations **(printed or AV)**	
Effectively convey a specific tool, nature of types of tools, and orientation	Seldom convey question analysis, search strategy, growth of a discipline, bibliographic structure, or transferability to other topics or disciplines
Available all hours the library is open	
User does not have to ask for help	Difficult to keep detailed and concise
Could complement a class as a transparency or handout	User must find the tool first
	Not flexible to user needs
Once prepared, saves constant repetition of core information	User must be motivated
	User may be embarrassed to use
User can reread or repeat as often as necessary for comprehension	Some people intimidated by AV equipment
Do not need faculty approval	Might not be used
Commercially available with possibilities for local adaptations	May require valuable space
	Difficult to evaluate effectiveness
Reach a wide audience	

(Table 3-1 cont. on p. 48)

Table 3-1 (cont.)

	Pros	Cons
Programmed Instruction (workbooks or computer-assisted modules)	Can convey concept of types of tools, a specific tool, search strategy, and question analysis Available when needed Done at user's own pace and convenience User does not have to ask for help Immediate reinforcement of progress Can utilize a unique set of questions Could complement a course Reach a wide audience Commercially available with possibilities for local adaptations Evaluation built in	Seldom convey question analysis, growth of a discipline, bibliographic structure, or transferability to other topics or disciplines Often based on discrete bits of information rather than broad concepts User must be motivated Not flexible to user needs Time-consuming to prepare initially Must be carefully pretested Require revision Tools containing answers will wear out faster Also, for CAI: Users must be trained to work the machine Users may play with system Instruction is not portable Computers have downtime Some programs do not require handling of reference tools Specialized programmer required Equipment is expensive and requires expert maintenance Computer time is expensive
Single Lectures	Convey concept of types of tools, question analysis, search strategy, growth of a discipline, bibliographic structure, or a specific tool Flexible pace for user needs Tailored to user level Allows personal interaction between librarian and user Can be given when needed Librarian is visible in academic community Reach a relatively wide audience	Seldom convey transferability to other topics or disciplines Motivation slow unless there is an assignment or innate interest Require teaching skills Require many repetitions to reach total audience Time-consuming to prepare initially Scheduling problems with librarians' time May require creation of classroom in library

Table 3-1 (cont.)

	Pros	Cons
Single Lectures (cont.)	Repeatable with modifications Can be course-related or course-integrated	If course-integrated, need faculty cooperation Difficult to evaluate effectiveness
Formal Courses	Can teach search strategy, growth of the discipline, bibliographic structure, a specific tool, the process of question analysis, the nature of a type of tool, or transferability to other topics or disciplines Reinforcement of learning possible through exercises, projects, etc. Tailored to user needs and pace Allow personal interaction between librarian and user Librarian is visible in academic community Team-teaching possible Flexible after initial preparation Evaluation easily incorporated	Users could become dependent on librarian Require teaching skills Require curriculum design skills In academic setting, need formal approval Scheduling problems with librarians' time Time-consuming to prepare initially Limited audience
Tutorials	Can convey types of tools, a specific tool, question analysis, search strategy, growth of a discipline, bibliographic structure, and transferability to other topics or disciplines Can be given when needed Based on user's own needs Allow personal interaction between librarian and user Allow instant feedback Level of sophistication readily adjusted No special space or equipment is needed No faculty involvement needed in academic setting	Users could become dependent on librarian Require interpersonal teaching skills Require in-depth discipline knowledge Scheduling problems with librarians' time Very limited audience

Printed materials

Printed materials are the most traditional and the most common means of disseminating information about the library. Typically, printed materials are used to explain orientation data; they include maps of the floor plans of the building, charts showing what classification ranges are on what floors or what symbols above a call number indicate a special collection. Handouts are also frequently available to explain special policies of the library, for example, interlibrary loan, circulation, and database-searching policies, or to describe special services within the library, for example, the documents division or microform collection. A more formalized collection of such information is the library handbook. Many libraries have also created specialized instruction sheets focused either on the method by which a user can find certain types of materials, for example, periodical articles or book reviews, or on topics of interest to a wide range of users, such as how to find information in the library on Native Americans.

The printed material may be in the form of a bibliography (sometimes annotated) on a particular subject. These usually do not indicate to the user a method to find more material on a subject; rather they spell out some appropriate reference tools, monographs, journals, or particular articles within journals that cover that topic. A variation of the bibliography sheet is a compilation listing newly acquired materials in a certain field, often headed "New Books Received in ____."

A different type of printed handout, which combines the bibliographic listing with the methodology, is the so-called pathfinder, originally published by Addison-Wesley. The traditional pathfinder appears on both sides of a standard 8 1/2-by-11-inch sheet and takes the user from general to specific reference tools by which he or she can find what material the library has on a relatively restricted topic, for example, puritanism in American literature. The idea behind the pathfinder is to give the user a workable search strategy for that specific field, moving from overview sources, such as encyclopedias and dictionaries, to the appropriate headings in the card catalog, to indexes. Some librarians have continued the pathfinder idea by generating additional pathfinders for topics of heavy interest on their own campuses. Others have purchased commercially available pathfinders and made copies available to their own users.[1]

The main advantage of printed materials is their flexibility, that is, their adaptability to local needs and local demands. The major drawback to any printed material, whether it is found in the classroom, in the library, or distributed on a street corner, is that people will often not read the information contained in it, or if they do read it, they will dispose of the material before they have the opportunity to learn from it. In our paper-glutted society, even the most spectacularly attractive and vividly graphic productions often become additions to the wastebasket collection rather than facilitate use of the library.

Audiovisual presentations

The most common AV approaches to bibliographic instruction today are the slide/tape presentation, the audio cassette used for a self-guided tour, film, and videotapes. Overhead transparencies are often important adjuncts to classroom teaching. Video recorders and videodiscs will doubtless become important BI techniques for the future.[2]

Point-of-use explanations

Point-of-use instruction involves the location of either printed or audiovisual explanations adjacent to a particular reference tool, for example, a complicated index. Users are presumed to find it helpful to read or listen to a step-by-step exposition of exactly how to use the particular title once they have one book in hand.

Programmed instruction

Programmed instruction, either printed as in the programmed workbook or computer assisted, is an educational method that allows the user to proceed at his or her own pace, absorbing the information and then being tested on small, discrete segments of data before proceeding to the next section. It is especially appropriate for highly detailed and closely sequenced content that can be broken down into individual units of information. Programmed instruction would, for example, be appropriate to explain the complex filing rules for a large dictionary card catalog. It might be less effective in explaining the intricacies of search strategy since that varies so much from discipline to discipline.

Single lectures

The single BI lecture, often referred to as a one-shot, may take place in the library or in the classroom, and it may be more than one hour, but its distinguishing feature is the single contact with a given group of students. Often the term "course-related" or "course-integrated" is used to modify the word *lecture*. "Course-related" implies that a faculty member has contacted the library for a single presentation on a library topic related to a standard course in the curriculum. Course-related BI lectures may or may not be tied to a particular assignment, and if they are, they may or may not occur at a time in the term when students need them most. "Course-integrated," on the other hand, implies that the faculty member has intentionally incorporated the library lecture as a significant feature in the course, usually planned in conjunction with the librarians, who assist students in completing a library research assignment.

Formal courses

A formal BI course is exactly that, a separately planned and separately presented series of lectures together with appropriate homework assignments, a final project, and/or an examination, either taught by a single librarian or team-taught by a librarian in conjunction with a faculty member. The opportunity to present, in an orderly and continuous way, the theoretical underpinnings of research, together with details as to specific types of tools, alternative orders for using the tools, and titles of each type for a particular discipline, as well as allowing time for reinforcement and feedback, is impossible in most other forms of instruction.

Tutorials

The BI tutorial is a one-on-one mode in which the user consults at length with the librarian about a specific research topic. It is an extension of the reference interview, but is conducted over a period of time as the project progresses. Examples of effective tutorials range from a librarian serving as a research consultant to a graduate student throughout the course of research on a doctoral dissertation, to librarians and carefully trained student assistants working individually with freshmen.[3] The "term paper clinic" is a form of tutorial because it takes place away from the reference desk and it allows more time and attention to be focused on the project at hand than is ordinarily possible at a busy reference desk. Many academic libraries sponsor paper clinics at appropriate times during the school year. Obviously, the tutorial mode reaches fewer students per librarian-contact-hour, although for those involved, it is usually an eye-opening experience.

These seven modes of bibliographic instruction are the most commonly recognized, but not the only, methods in use today. The seven may also be used in combination, and new ones will undoubtedly appear in the future. Using guided exercises in conjunction with lectures simply combines the pros and cons of single lectures and parts of workbook exercises, although often such a blending compensates for the disadvantages that may be evident in one mode alone. (Exercises provide motivation for learning and reinforcement of the content.) Regard Table 3-1 as a guide to BI planners in attempting to select the best possible mode or combination of modes for each situation.

Factors in Choosing a Mode

The advantages and disadvantages of the BI modes shown in Table 3-1 are derived from the following factors: the audience, the staff involved, level of instruction intended, faculty involvement, scheduling, equipment and space needs, ease of revising or updating the program, and visibility of the library or librarian (public relations). Many of these factors have obvious cost implications, indicated in the following pages. (The costs associated with each mode are detailed in Part IV of this book, especially Chapter 13.)

The audience

The extent and nature of the target audience will in large part determine which BI mode or modes are most appropriate to attain the objectives. The following are some questions to consider: How large is the audience in absolute numbers as well as in terms of users to be reached per time period (that is, are 300 freshmen to be contacted at various times throughout the course of an academic year, or only within a two-week time period before midterms)? Is the mode appropriate to the age and educational level of the intended audience? An audio tape point-of-use in one language in a multilingual community public library might not be the best choice. Is the mode likely to be acceptable to users based on what is known about their demographic characteristics? For example, in an Ivy League school students might resist the workbook mode or the more advanced audiovisual techniques because they are traditionally classroom oriented.

Is the mode flexible enough to meet the needs of various users, especially if the audience is drawn from many disciplines? Is it too rigid to be adapted to more specific needs that may arise? Is the mode available when the students need it? Can it reach out to assist students who will not ask for aid but who need the information? Can the mode be adapted to the user's own pace? Can the mode be individualized? Can it be repeated if the user so desires?

How efficient is the mode in terms of user time? How convenient is it for a variety of course schedules and life-styles? Will the user become dependent on that mode and not be able to transfer the information to another topic? What would be the user's motivation; that is, is it related to an assignment that requires library research, or is it just idle information users do not need at the time? Does the mode require prior knowledge of a computer in the case of computer-assisted instruction, or of the reference book in the case of point-of-use instruction? Will the mode be effective in terms of student retention? What discipline knowledge is required to be given to the audience that is targeted to receive instruction? Will the mode embarrass students at all, either because they have to ask for the instruction, because they are put off by the machinery or equipment involved, or because they feel somehow embarrassed to be seen needing instruction? Does the mode require that they be interrogated by the librarians before instruction is offered? How portable is the instruction? Can it move from a dormitory to a classroom to a site in the library?

These are just some of the many questions regarding the audience that must be thought through before a mode is chosen.

The staff

The staff factor is no doubt the most important because it is the most expensive consideration with regard to choice of mode. Do people currently on the staff have the skills needed for instruction or must outsiders be brought in? Some modes, especially printed materials and audiovisuals, require talent that can usually be provided by other than professional librarians, such as technicians, support staff, and clerical workers. If staff must be brought in from outside to accomplish special projects, that may influence the cost.

What kinds of skills are necessary for each mode—teaching, writing, or technical skills, computer programming or searching skills, audiovisual familiarity, or others? Will the mode that is chosen need to be prepared only once and then merely updated as conditions change, or will a total overhaul and revision be needed frequently?

For the face-to-face or classroom mode, team-teaching is possible, and teams can be made up from a group of librarians, librarians plus faculty members, or some other combination. One must look at the extent to which support staff can be utilized in the preparation of the mode, in typing, producing slides, correcting workbooks, and so on. Student employees or library science students working to gain experience may be used in lieu of full-time support staff for these kinds of tasks.

Usually these questions about staffing can be readily answered by the BI planners, but sometimes they will need to investigate resources elsewhere in the institution to see what is available to them and at what cost. Sometimes it is also necessary to take an informal talent or skill survey of the existing full-time staff to see who has the necessary subject background, teaching experience, or technical expertise. If you plan to write a grant proposal to obtain funding for the BI program, it may be possible to specify the needed skills in the document. If this is not possible and if the requisite talents are not readily available, it may be necessary to select one or more individuals for special training or have them attend continuing education courses to provide in-house specialists in the areas needed.

The longer the time frame for planning, the more possible it is to send staff members for additional training. In any case, enthusiasm and commitment for a BI program only partially make up for a lack of essential skills. Highly motivated librarians have often been able to work wonders to prepare single lectures, handouts, or whole programs on topics about which they did not themselves feel familiar simply by spending a lot of time getting ready before they undertook the project. Such dedication is, of course, the best possible form of self-education, but it cannot and should not be the only means of providing staff for a BI program. Superlibrarians who are continually asked to overextend themselves are only going to burn out faster than similarly committed colleagues who are allowed to work in their own areas of specialization.

Level of instruction

Another factor with a bearing on the choice of mode is the level of instruction intended. If orientation is the only goal, printed maps, walking tours, or perhaps simply a slide/tape presentation might be appropriate. On the other hand, if orientation and instruction together are the goal, a different combination of modes is called for, one that will highlight the tools to be presented as well as their location in the building. If concepts underlying the various types of tools and the construction of a search strategy are the primary focus, or if specific skills are to be presented, such as the step-by-step procedure for consulting a periodical index and then finding a particular article, very different modes are needed. A workbook, for example, might be able to teach a specific skill, but it is less able to teach the concepts underlying the choice of a particular title, the idea of selectivity among similar titles, or the creativity involved in trying alternate approaches to solve a single research problem.

The following are other critical questions regarding the level of instruction as it pertains to the choice of mode: How selective or comprehensive are the objectives (for example, are you trying to teach how to read a citation to *Readers' Guide* or search strategy)? How specific or how general is the subject approach?

All these considerations exist regardless of the grade or age level of the intended audience. It is just as important to ask whether a freshman class that is to receive instruction is focusing on a particular area of psychology as it is to ask whether a seminar of graduate students needs to learn about the common features of the various Wilson indexes. A common error in many bibliographic instruction attempts is to assume that the user's level of library expertise and educational level are comparable. One is much more likely to overestimate the research sophistication of users than to underestimate it. The best way to compensate for this is to rely on the fact that the more advanced the users are in their own field, the faster they will pick up the elementary concepts that still need to be presented. As a consequence, rather than varying the level of content of instruction to match the supposed level of the students' background, it is better to vary the presentation to cover what is perhaps very basic material without insulting the intelligence of the audience. Of course, if a mode allows more than one interaction between the BI program and the same group of students, it is possible to use the first contact to determine the exact user level of need and then structure subsequent contacts based on that information.

Faculty involvement

Different modes of bibliographic instruction entail different amounts of faculty involvement, so it is important for BI planners to base a choice of mode, at least in part, on past experience with the faculty. Course-integrated instruction (and to a large extent course-related instruction) involves close cooperation with the teaching faculty. Printed materials and audiovisual presentations located in the library may require no faculty involvement at all. Most faculty contacts are on a one-to-one, informal basis between the librarian and the individual faculty member, but sometimes the BI program may have to be formally approved by a faculty or college committee, especially where required workbooks are involved or courses are under the auspices of a department. Although this step may prove very helpful in the long run in terms of involving the entire campus or part of it in the program and calling attention to its existence, it can also be filled with political difficulties. It is wise to consider possible repercussions of faculty involvement when selecting a mode.

Another question the planners might ask is to what extent they would like faculty to be a part of their target audience. It is common in the case of one-shot lectures for the faculty member to attend the BI session along with his or her class. This can on occasion prove to be a disaster, especially if the faculty member continually interrupts the presentation (or indicates by manner that the information is boring or irrelevant), but more often the presence of the faculty member is the best possible reinforcement of the importance of the material presented. Bibliographic instruction librarians have also been known to target groups of advanced students, whether undergraduate majors or graduate students in a discipline, as their initial audience.

Scheduling

Scheduling the presentation of BI is a problem for modes that must be offered at stated times. These would involve primarily the face-to-face or classroom modes—the one-shot lectures whether nonintegrated (the library offers a lecture on the use of technical reports); term paper clinics, course-related or course-integrated; the multisession formal course; or the tutorial. All these are based on special appointments made in advance and may cause problems in terms of other commitments of the library staff (especially at times of heavy use), other commitments of the students, competition for space, or conflict with faculty priorities in terms of class time. Attempting to short-circuit these problems by scheduling BI sessions in the evenings or on weekends is likely to have the predictable ill effect of reducing attendance substantially. There also may be special constraints at institutions where the majority of the students commute to classes and do not remain on campus any longer than necessary once their classes are over. Although most scheduling conflicts can be resolved, it is important to foresee them early in the planning process and to think through their implications at the time the mode is selected.

Equipment

Equipment and supplies are an expensive aspect of a bibliographic instruction program. By equipment we mean not only the hardware involved in the production of AV material or the facilities necessary to prepare a computer-assisted program, but also such things as the added capacity that may be necessary if many handouts are to be reprinted, or background environment needs, such as increased lighting in a certain area of the library. Supplies include the usual paper and paperclip type of materials, but also additional copies of reference works, which may be used for demonstration or may be needed because the original copy wears out from student use during assignments.

The following are important questions to ask with regard to equipment and supplies: What must be purchased? What can be rented? What can be borrowed or used elsewhere on campus? Must insurance or maintenance contracts be considered? Is special training required to use the equipment? Are the electrical outlets and/or modems (for computer terminals) sufficient? Are illumination, heating, or soundproofing adequate wherever the instruction will take place? Must a blackboard or projection screen be moved into a location that does not ordinarily serve as a classroom? Will the equipment involved have a detrimental effect on the intended audience? Some students find computer terminals for computer-assisted instruction so complicated to use that they are put off from the instruction; others become so wrapped up in how to use the terminal that they never learn the content of the presentation.

Space

In terms of space, the obvious factors enter in—adequate room and seating in a comfortable location to accommodate all the students in a group, if a group mode is chosen. For other modes, one should consider whether display space for printed materials is adequate and whether room adjacent to specific titles is sufficient for point-of-use instruction to be effective without also being in the way. Is space for audiovisual or computer equipment sufficient so that it is properly ventilated and so that the people operating it or the students interacting with it have room to be comfortable and to be able to take notes on their experience?

Revision or updating

With any mode a concern is ease with which a presentation can be revised or updated. The time and costs involved in changing a presentation, whether to modify just a small portion or to redo all or most of the original, varies from mode to mode and can range from a minor nuisance and expense to a complete doubling of the original cost. Generally, the more involved the technology, the more expensive to revise, at least at this point. Printed materials and classroom presentations or tutorials, because they can be updated by an individual in a traditional fashion, take less time and are hence less expensive to revise. As librarians and students become more and more facile with computer technology, revisions in computer-aided instruction should also be easily handled and not exceedingly expensive.

Probably every librarian's dream is to produce the perfect BI program, which can be used over and over and never need revision. Unfortunately, in reality the features of even the most common tools change. For example, the *Readers' Guide* at certain times has carried book reviews as a separate section and has then omitted them altogether. The necessity of keeping the program current with changes means that even universally applicable instruction packages need to be modified.

Evaluation

Evaluation is the most difficult aspect of any educational program, but this is especially true of most BI modes, which involve but a single interaction between the audience and a presentation without any time for formal or informal evaluation of objectives or even subjective feedback to the planners. Administrative demands for an evaluation method can thus have a direct bearing on the choice of mode, as can the planners' desire to reinforce student exposure by means of a quiz or exercise.

To what extent do the planners want to require faculty members to participate in an evaluation, and if they do, can they expect cooperation? How much time is available in a given mode to pretest students or to posttest them at the conclusion of the presentation? Is it important to determine whether everyone who picks up a printed guide, for example, actually uses it, and if so, how might this be measured? If informal feedback is sufficient for the planners, perhaps this is not a consideration in the choice of modes. It is, however, a factor to consider at the inception of a program.

Public relations

Public relations are bound to be affected by whatever mode is selected. Will the BI program be part of the user's first experience of the library, as with a slide/tape presentation located in the lobby? How important to users at your institution is human contact? To what extent will people be put off if instruction occurs only through print media or a computer terminal? To what extent are faculty the opinion setters in the institution? If they are important, how will they be involved in the planning or evaluation of the instructional program? Are new programs within the library regularly reported in the student newspaper? Can the planners count on word of mouth, that is, the so-called locker room effect among students as a means of publicity about their program? Granted, the public relations aspect of whatever mode is chosen may not be the most important, but it is still bound to have an impact on the ultimate reception of whatever program is designed, and so it should be considered as an element in the initial decision-making.

Costs

The cost implications of the various modes include such things as staff time (prorated according to the salaries or hourly wages of the various individuals involved); materials (printing and printing supplies, computer time including storage, online time, and editing time, purchase of multiple copies of reference works, blank AV tapes, and the like); update and revision costs; equipment; remodeling; costs for space; purchase of guides and prototypes describing a particular form of instruction for use by the planners; copyright costs or the purchase of commercially available tools such as pathfinders; costs involved in possible vandalism or theft of equipment and materials; and costs expressed in terms of the number of students reached per contact hour. For example, the costs involved in the preparation of an AV presentation can be spread over thousands of students.

There is no golden rule by which BI planners can select the best mode of instruction for the situation, the audience, and the objectives they have identified. Of those three considerations, the objectives are probably the most important for pinpointing an appropriate mode. The objectives indicate the thrust of the content of the proposed program. One must then look at how effectively each mode would carry out the objectives of the program. Often the cost factors, the staff factors, or the available equipment will themselves determine the choice of mode. Whatever the constraints, the mode must deliver the content and then lead to meeting the objectives defined for the program. If the only possible mode, given limitations imposed on the program, is not able to produce the effect described in the objectives, the BI planners should reevaluate the scope of the program. The mode is, after all, only the delivery vehicle of the content, and if the content is delivered appropriately, the objectives should be attained. If the mode, on the other hand, is unable to deliver the intended content, the objectives will not be realized. Alternative approaches to modify the scope of a BI program could include change of audience level, change of group size, different staffing configurations, and so on.

Reading the voluminous literature of BI for case studies of

institutions similar to your own, and their particular choice of mode and experience with it, can be enlightening at this stage. Enough has been published since the 1960s to permit virtually any combination of situation, audience, and objectives to have appeared in the literature. Hannelore Rader's ERIC document, resulting from her Council on Library Resources scholarship, is an examination of ten outstanding bibliographic instruction programs in the late 1970s and should be studied for the examples it provides.[4]

Obviously, there are several factors, as discussed in this chapter, to consider when determining the advantages and disadvantages of various BI modes. Remember that the most important factors depend on the perspective. The categories listed below might be considered the most important for each viewpoint. Usually there must be trade-offs between users' needs, costs, and staff time.

Administrators
Audience reached, wide or limited?
Staff time.
Image of the library.
Cost of materials and equipment.
Special staff skills necessary for the mode (such as programming).

Users
Availability/accessibility when needed.
Relevant to individual needs.
Ease of use (for example, logically organized or machine simple to use).
Efficiency of user's time.

Librarians
Objectives of instruction.
Scheduling (staff, students, space, class time of faculty).
Skills necessary for the mode to be of high quality.
Staff time for initial preparation and revision/update.
Staff time necessary to give the instruction.
Faculty involvement.
Audience reached, wide or limited?

Objectives
Orientation only?
Orientation plus instruction?
Teach bibliographic structure and growth of disciplines.

Teach search strategy—why use one reference tool before another?
Teach research problem analysis.
Teach selectivity? Alternative approaches?
Discuss titles or discrete bits of information.
Subject specific or general?
Primary material or secondary material?
Teach transferability to other disciplines?

The content described in Part II of this book is highly theoretical in that it underlies the existence of the various types of tools, specific titles, and varying search strategies in all present and future disciplines. We believe that this can best be conveyed in a classroom situation. The one-shot lecture permits the exploration of a single concept and its relation to a particular subject in which the audience is concerned. Better yet is the formal course, which, by permitting multiple sessions over a span of weeks, allows the presentation of many complex and interrelated theoretical issues on which the paradigms in the various disciplines are built.

It is not only tradition that has influenced education in favor of the teacher/lecture mode in virtually all disciplines, especially at the postsecondary level, but it is the proven efficacy of this model, which over the decades and centuries has led students to new insights and new intellectual excitement. Since we view the ultimate purpose of bibliographic instruction as the transmission to students of the underlying intellectual and bibliographic structures that affect research in their specific fields, we are convinced that only the classroom mode will accomplish our objectives with the flexibility and freshness the subject deserves.

Notes

1. Marie P. Canfield, "Library Pathfinders," *Drexel Library Quarterly* 8 (July 1972): 287–300, Katherine Cipolla, "M.I.T.'s Point-of-Use Concept: A Five Year Update," *Journal of Academic Librarianship* 5 (January 1980): 326–328, and "Pathfinder in Bibliographic Instruction," *Bibliographic Instruction Handbook* (Chicago: Association of College and Research Libraries, American Library Association, 1979), pp. 61–66.
2. Larry Hardesty and Frances Gatz, "Application of Instructional Development to Mediated Library Instruction," *Drexel Library Quarterly* 16 (1981): 3–26; Thomas G. Kirk, "A Comparison of Two Methods of Library

Instruction for Students in Introductory Biology," *College and Research Libraries* 32 (November 1971): 465–474; and Judith Violette, "Library Instruction with Slides and Slide/Tapes," *Improving Instruction: How to Teach and How to Evaluate*, paper presented at the Eighth Annual Conference on Library Orientation for Academic Libraries, Library Orientation Series, no. 9 (Ann Arbor, Mich.: Pierian Press, 1979), pp. 83–87.

3. Phyllis Hughes and Arthur Flandreau, "Tutorial Library Instruction: The Freshman Program at Berea College," *Journal of Academic Librarianship* 6 (May 1980): 91–94.

4. Hannelore B. Rader, *Five-Year Library Outreach Orientation Program. Final Report*, ED 115 265 (Ypsilanti, Mich.: Eastern Michigan University Library, 1975).

Part II
Understanding the Research Process

In at least two respects bibliographic instruction is an anomaly. For one, at some unidentifiable point several decades ago, academic departments ceased to transmit basic library research methods to students as a standard part of the curriculum. This situation is especially ironic in that virtually all disciplines devote a certain amount of time and effort to instilling in students the dos and don'ts, and very often also the whys, of their own research methodology. It is unthinkable that beginning chemistry students would be allowed to perform their first experiment in the laboratory without a prior introduction to safety regulations, to the types of equipment and glassware available, and to the basic characteristics of the substances they will be using. A similar indoctrination takes place at an early stage in all sciences and social sciences, whether experimental or observational in nature. Typically a separate course in methodology is required of all majors, or at least of all graduate students in any given field—including, very frequently, the humanities disciplines, although their methods courses are not so much proscriptive as descriptive of various schools of thought.

Bibliographic instruction is also an anomaly in that it lacks a commonly held theoretical basis. Only recently have the tenets of learning theory been applied with rigor to the BI process. The more important lack, however, is the absence of a conceptual foundation for bibliographic instruction. The casual observer watching either an expert reference librarian or a senior scholar operate in a library is likely to conclude that magic or serendipity is at work, since the logical connectives between the research problem at hand and the volumes consulted are less than obvious. Asked to justify reasoning and behavior, librarians or scholars are seldom able to provide a satisfactory answer, claiming that they were just doing what the problem required. If they do attempt to justify their activities, the explanation may seem random and disjointed. Experts can rarely reconstruct their intellectual processes, and they tend to recall only the conclusion and one or two steps they took to arrive at it.

The importance of providing students with a conceptual basis for library research techniques cannot be overstated. Much has been said in the literature of education about cognitive learning, that is, about using the natural human thought process as the framework for teaching new ideas and new skills to students of any age. One of the particular arguments in favor of cognitive learning is that it draws on existing patterns of logic that students have developed to help them understand new subject matter. Furthermore, by concentrating on logical connectives and then filling out the picture with new information, students feel more comfortable because they can place what is being learned in a familiar framework.

Cognitive learning readily applies to bibliographic instruction. For example, even advanced students find grasping the scope of the *National Union Catalog* very difficult unless the task is related to a common need (to locate a book in another library) or parallel situation (news media reporting events from all over the world). In addition, cognitive learning is more transferable than rote memorization or other teaching principles, and transferability is a major object of any BI program. Specifically, there are four dimensions of transferability: across time—as the individual completes school, begins a career, and throughout life; across place—that is, from library to library; across disciplines; and across levels as the individual advances in knowledge and skills. These four transferabilities are the ultimate aim of any BI effort, and they can best be achieved through a program based on *concepts* rather than on the presentation of titles.

This section—Understanding the Research Process—is an attempt to clarify the conceptual framework for library research in various fields, a framework that is often second nature to the expert. We discuss in detail several key underlying concepts that help to explain the existence—and absence in some cases—of reference tools in certain areas. Also considered, in Chapter 4, is a scheme for breaking down a complex research question into its simple components so that these components can be dealt with in a logical fashion. Chapter 5 elaborates general search strategy, a common notion to people in bibliographic instruction, but one rarely set out in terms of the dynamics that exist among evolving disciplines, the information these disciplines generate, the formats in which information is communicated, and the means of control by which one can identify that communication. The characteristics, evolution, and search strategies of the large, most commonly taught discipline families—the humanities, historical sciences, and social sciences—are covered in Chapters 6 through 8, including a comparison of the major differences among them.

Search strategies for the large discipline of natural science and technology are not covered here. For information about the nature of the sciences, see the outstanding article by Topsy N. Smalley and Stephen H. Plum in *Theories of Bibliographic Education: Designs for Teaching* by Cerise Oberman and Katina Strauch (New York: Bowker, 1982).

This section—Understanding the Research Process—is the heart of this book, appropriate for and adaptable to virtually any situation, any set of objectives, or any BI mode.

4
Research
Problem Analysis

Independent surveys conducted by the Library Instruction
Round Table of the American Library Association and by the
Virginia Library Association concluded that one of the most
important skills that library instruction needs to convey is
the ability to ask a precise reference question. Librarians
from all types of libraries, who deal with all levels and categories of users, shared this opinion.[1] This chapter introduces
one method of explaining to students the skills required in
breaking down any complex research topic into its simple
components, then arranging those components in a logical
order and pairing each one with the most appropriate reference tool.

The approach discussed here has proved to be easily understood and immediately appreciated by students at both the
undergraduate and graduate levels. With modest adaptation, it
would apply to all levels and types of libraries insofar as it
resembles the scientific method of inquiry and provides an
easily adaptable framework in which to rearrange the many
parts of a typical research problem. It provides students with
perhaps the most important intellectual model for their continued research in any field. Once students have mastered the
individual steps involved in analyzing their research problems, they will be able to extrapolate techniques "up" as they
advance in their fields and "cross" into another discipline or
"over" to any general field of consumer inquiry.

Why Research Problem Analysis?

Any research librarian can testify that virtually all students and researchers come to the library without having sufficiently narrowed and defined their topics. As a result, they are soon frustrated either because they waste time trying to find information and materials without a clear understanding of the most efficient way to do so in that particular library, or else they state their question in a form that is too general for the librarian to answer without first initiating a lengthy reference interview. This is not to say that the ideal situation between user and librarian is to omit the reference interview altogether. Unless the reference librarian is both a polymath and a psychic, and hence has no need to discuss the problem at hand with the questioner, it will always be an important first step to conduct some form of case history in order to understand clearly the background and scope of the question asked. The research librarian needs to spend a few moments clarifying and pondering the user's need; otherwise the first response to the apparent question may miss the mark and provide information that is not needed or that is already known.[2] At the very least, the conscientious librarian needs to know at the outset exactly what steps the student or researcher has taken to that point and with what results, so as to avoid repetition and hence the waste of everyone's time by retracing the same steps. On the other hand, the librarian does not want to overlook a key tool by assuming that the user has already consulted it or, in the case of a particularly complex reference work, by assuming that the user who reports not finding any information has used the tool correctly.

So then, why is it important for users to conduct their own reference interview before speaking to the librarian? One reason is obvious to anyone who has ever worked at a busy reference desk. The completely raw reference question—most commonly proclaimed in a phrase such as "I have to write a paper on the effect of the Vietnam War on U.S. military policy, and I don't know where to start"—cannot be dealt with without first playing a game not unlike twenty questions, in which the librarian asks the user a series of highly specific questions in order to understand the real need underlying the initial statement.

It is not only younger students or neophytes to research who ask too-broad questions, but also veteran library users, faculty, and graduate students who have reached a certain level of sophistication within their discipline. The problem is that librarians are repeatedly faced with amorphous questions posed by users who are, in fact, throwing themselves on the mercy of the professionals. These users assume all too often that the individual on duty is an expert on their particular topic and, furthermore, that all necessary materials are present in the library and capable of being adequately consulted in a very short time (often within the hour or two the student has set aside for the research). The professional staff must then continue to repeat the lengthy process of question negotiation, knowing all along that with just a little prior reflection the user could have saved everyone much time and tedium.

During the lengthy discussion generated by an open-ended reference question, the user may consider the librarian stupid or inadequate and may be offended because the intent of the question is not instantly clear. This is particularly the case with experienced researchers and faculty members who do not realize that a question that is perfectly clear to them, and may be defined to themselves in their own terms, is still too vague to be handled immediately by the sources as they exist in the library.

Research problem analysis or question analysis slows down the process of topic definition that goes on in the research librarian's head. As the research librarian goes over this process in slow motion with students, they will come to understand their topics more clearly and to realize that much of the preliminary decision-making about how to proceed with the project can be done on their own and outside the library. Students will be better able to predict the scope and the time frame for their overall work and, to some extent, anticipate their end product.

The goal of teaching research problem analysis is not to make mini reference librarians out of library users. The goal is to make them more sophisticated library users, who can, insofar as possible, determine the appropriate steps for their own research and the approximate order in which to pursue those steps. Furthermore, research problem analysis can be grasped and applied by students of any educational level so that this aspect of library instruction theory can be successfully applied in primary and secondary schools as well as at the academic and advanced research levels. A presentation of the question analysis method can make an effective one-hour lecture.

Just as no researcher or technician enters the laboratory to begin an experiment without first having planned the steps involved and allotted an approximate amount of time to each one, so it is important for anyone whose laboratory is the library and its collections to complete preliminary planning before undertaking any research and before consulting the research librarian. By teaching students to perform their own basic reference interviews according to certain definite steps, librarians will achieve at least two goals: They will conserve everyone's time since the reference questions that follow a careful question analysis will be more precise and hence more readily answered than they would be otherwise, and they will heighten user self-confidence and intellectual self-consciousness as users learn to better control their topic and hence their research behavior.

The Nature of Research Topics

Eight separate but related steps to a thorough analysis of any research problem or topic are discussed in the following pages. These steps culminate in the construction of a search strategy, detailed in the following chapter. Before outlining the steps in question analysis, however, it is important to understand the distinction among research topics.

As in any area where human logic and language come into play, research questions can be expressed in one of three ways; they are by nature either simple, compound, or complex.

Simple research topics

A simple research question typically requires a single fact, a piece of information. For example, here is a simple question: When was Charles Dickens born? The answer requires specifying a single year—1812—which can be discovered from a nearly infinite number of sources. Dickens's birth date can be found in such biographical works as the *Dictionary of National Biography*, in encyclopedias, in almanacs, in literary handbooks, and even in most card catalogs.

As any librarian realizes, it is possible for two apparently equally reputable sources to give a conflicting answer to the same simple question. Resolving such conflicts by consulting

additional authorities is, of course, an important step in vali-
dating the entire research problem, but for our purposes here,
the point is not discrepancies in information, but that a
simple question requires a simple, usually unique answer.

Compound research topics

Compound research problems consist of two or more components of equal value. An example is: How old was Charles
Dickens when *David Copperfield* was published? This compound question has two coequal components, and the researcher could approach the question in any of several ways,
each one equally valid and efficient. For example, it is possible to consult any of a number of types of tools or specific
titles (such as those mentioned above for the simple question,
When was Charles Dickens born?) to obtain Dickens's birth
date and to identify from another source the year of publication of the novel *David Copperfield*. Having those two dates,
one could subtract and arrive at Dickens's age at the time the
book first appeared. It does not matter whether the birth date
or the publication date is established first; that is what is
meant by "coequal components" to a compound research
question.

An alternative approach, of course, is to consult a major
biographical study on Dickens, for example, the entry in the
Dictionary of National Biography or a major book-length biography of the novelist. Such a study would very likely give
the exact information wanted in one place. It might, however,
be more difficult to find the information in a monographic
work, especially one without an adequate index.

Still another way to solve the question would be to rely
exclusively on primary source material, for example, a diary
that Dickens might have kept during the year in question, and
in which he might have mentioned his age at the time of
publication. A contemporary secondary source, such as a review of the novel in one of the many Victorian literary journals, might also establish his age at that point. Obviously,
these two options using nineteenth-century materials are
more difficult and more time consuming than the first option, which is to break the topic into two simple components,
each of which can be answered readily by any number of
sources.

Here is an example of a more lengthy compound question

involving more than two components: How old was Charles Dickens when *David Copperfield* was published, and where was the novelist living, to whom was he married, and how many children did he have at that time? Again, the order of seeking the answers to each of the component simple questions is for the most part irrelevant. The actual research may show that the answer to one simple question leads directly to the answer of another, or that a source that answers one will also answer one or more other components. The logical issue here is that theoretically in a compound research problem, all parts of the topic have equal status and hence it is up to the researcher to decide for whatever reasons—convenience being in many instances the best one—the order in which to approach answering each of the components.

Complex research topics

Complex questions, like compound sentence structures, have two or more components (usually more) which are hierarchically organized in a logical sense; that is, simple component A must be answered before simple component B, and the two (A and B) must be answered before simple component C. For example, the research topic "What are the autobiographical elements in Charles Dickens's novel *David Copperfield?*" is a typical complex research problem. Although an infinite number of approaches to the overall question are possible, one might proceed by establishing, as was the case with the previous compound example, Dickens's birth year and the year of publication of *David Copperfield.* In this instance, however, one would then continue by, for example, reading biographical material on Dickens or trying to identify all early reviews of the novel in order to confirm the hypothesis that at least his contemporaries viewed the novel as highly biographical.

In real life beyond the elementary or middle school level, virtually all research problems fall into the complex category, and hence must be broken down into their simple components. These components must be ordered in a logical fashion before any other element of the question analysis can proceed. The common trap here is that complex research topics in any discipline are usually stated as simple English declarative or interrogative sentences. The Dickens example is a case in point. "What are the autobiographical elements in Charles Dickens's *David Copperfield?*" is a simple grammatical question. Underlying it, however, are many possible simple sub-questions that would relate to the overall topic.

Students at all levels tend to be misled by an apparently straightforward, easy-sounding topic, never taking the time before they enter the library to delve into its implications and to consider all the possible approaches indicated by the subject matter. An analogy might be the common experience of anyone attempting to acquire a new manual skill. To the amateur observer, driving a car, scuba diving, or gem cutting may seem like single activities that can be learned by concentrating on a single set of rules. In reality, however, each skill is made up of a large array of more discrete movements, which must be mastered and then followed in sequence to achieve desired results. The fallacy of treating a complex research topic as if it were readily reducible to one or two sources is common and results in librarians' having to probe deeply with the student to discover exactly what sorts of material and how much are wanted. Often the student's responses to the questions asked by the research librarian indicate that the student has not considered any of the aspects of question analysis (discussed below) and, furthermore, has never even realized that the topic is, in fact, complex and will require more thought and more work in the research area than the student anticipated.

Question Analysis

Eight intellectual steps are involved in a thorough analysis of any research problem. These steps together build a search strategy. The steps are:

1. Surveying the topic and clarifying unfamiliar terms.
2. Breaking the topic into its simple subtopics.
3. Determining appropriate formats of primary and secondary materials necessary to research the topic.
4. Estimating the quantity of material needed.
5. Specifying the quality of authority of material needed.
6. Budgeting the time available to do the research.
7. Listing the relevant disciplines concerned with the topic.
8. Indicating the categories or types of reference tools that will help to identify and locate the necessary materials.

Of these eight steps, all but the first can be done outside the library. Pointing this out to students will often amaze and please them, as they tend to envision every suggestion by a librarian to mean that they have to spend more time in the library. On the contrary, a thorough question analysis, which will in the long run save the student a great deal of time and frustration, can be adequately completed at home in many cases. Only if the student is unfamiliar with some of the terminology involved in the topic or needs some basic background information found in an encyclopedia is it necessary to spend time in the library as part of the analysis process. If neither a dictionary nor an encyclopedia is necessary for understanding the problem, the student should be able to complete all the other steps in the process alone, or if the student has trouble formulating any of the steps, it might be useful to brainstorm with a friend to get another opinion on various approaches to the topic.

The eight steps are discussed in detail below; however, the order can be somewhat flexible. All the steps should, however, be covered, whether the project is a five-page research report or a dissertation.

Surveying the topic
and clarifying the terms

This step can be omitted if the student or researcher is already sufficiently familiar with the background of the topic and the terminology (or jargon) it involves. Typically, however, the researcher will not be completely comfortable with at least some aspect of the subject. It thus becomes necessary to consult the appropriate secondary source material, such as an encyclopedia or handbook, for survey information and a specialized dictionary for the definition and connotation of terms involved.

Breaking the topic
into simple subtopics

At this point, intensive brainstorming, either alone or with friends, is needed. However simple sounding the research topic may be, it undoubtedly can be construed or viewed from a variety of angles. It is essential that the researcher fully comprehend the many avenues of possible inquiry so that the one or ones ultimately chosen are consciously selected over all the rest.

Among the many types of simple subquestions that may be derived from an overall topic are those concerning time frame, that is, the historical period under consideration, geographic location of the subject of the study, or demographic features if the project concerns specific groups within the population. Sometimes, as in the Charles Dickens example above, what is needed is to ask a number of open-ended questions. For example, in the case of the autobiographical elements in *David Copperfield*, exactly who were Dickens's closest associates, both friends and family, before the novel appeared? Are their characteristics reflected in any of the characters in the book? What events in Dickens's life are mirrored in the plot? These and many other questions could be asked, all relating to that topic.

Every research problem will, of course, dictate its own set of potential subquestions for exploration. A preliminary job of the thorough researcher is to articulate these possible approaches and then to choose among them those that best satisfy the hypothesis or intended thrust of the overall effort. Furthermore, the researcher, having chosen the simple subquestions on which to concentrate, must attempt to determine an appropriate sequence in which to tackle each subquestion. This is not always an easy matter and very often will evolve as the research proceeds. However, it is important to make at least a preliminary sorting of subtopics at the point of performing the research problem analysis in order to begin the process of research somewhere.

Determining appropriate formats

The third, and perhaps the most difficult, part of research problem analysis involves predicting the physical and metaphysical formats of the material needed. By physical format, we mean the "package" or format in which the necessary information is available, for example, book, newspaper, microform, audio or audiovisual aid, manuscript, document, or journal article. The list could obviously be extended and might well include computer-readable format. By metaphysical format, we mean the representational nature of the material sought, that is, how close in time it is to the phenomena it records. The more common way of expressing this idea is to distinguish between primary and secondary source materials. This concept seems extremely difficult for most people. That may be so because in school, students in the sciences and social sciences rely largely on textbooks. When they are exposed to experimentation and recording the results of their experiments, they typically do not need to go back in the literature of their field to other writers who have worked on a similar problem. As a result, they have only vague notions about the difference between the raw data collected in the field or in the laboratory and the commentary on similar data that may appear in a journal article or textbook.

Only at the graduate level, and only slowly then, does the distinction between primary and secondary sources become clear. In humanities the situation is somewhat different and may perhaps be explained by students in philosophy and literature, for example, perceiving their primary source materials, that is, their literary or philosophical texts, as the same physical format (bound book or journal article) as their secondary material, the criticism or the commentary. To make matters more obscure, both the primary and secondary texts in the humanities are obtained in an identical way, that is, in the library or at a bookstore. The humanities student has by and large no need to create or attempt to create a work of literature or to rub shoulders with someone who does that primary creation. The situation is somewhat better defined in the historical sciences in that the infinite variety of the human record and the infinite possibilities of reinterpreting it become apparent to students while they are yet undergraduates. Many institutions, however, do not require history majors to discover and evaluate primary sources on their own. Hence, while the history major's notion of what constitutes a primary source and a secondary source may be somewhat clearer than that same idea is to classmates specializing in other fields, it is still far from perfect.

The importance of understanding the probable physical formats of the materials to be collected in the course of the research problem cannot be overstated. Materials needed will to a large extent dictate the fact and finding tools (the reference works) that need to be consulted. Fact and finding tools (discussed in more detail later in this chapter) are terms we use to differentiate the broad classes of reference books: fact—contains the information (almanac); finding—leads to another source (index). Certain physical formats, for example, newspapers or microforms, are controlled bibliographically by certain tools or groups of tools, and not by others. Likewise, indexes and bibliographies address only primary source materials or only secondary source materials, and it is important to know what one is looking for before choosing the tools.

One way for the bibliographic instructor to attempt to convey the difference between primary and secondary source material is to discuss with students the kind of data on which they base their own life decisions. Using as a quick definition that a primary source is the closest reproducible and perceptible representation of some natural phenomenon, lead a class discussion in which students are asked how they have found out about some recent current event. This should elicit answers such as television broadcast, newspapers, weekly magazines, or perhaps word of mouth from a friend. All these, insofar as they may be regarded as the first reports of the event, may be called primary sources. Some students will point out from time to time that there are also "official accounts" of the same event, for example, the official transcript of a presidential news conference or statistics issued by the Congressional Budget Office with regard to the cost of living. These too are primary source materials.

To make the contrast with secondary materials, one could point out that the same newspaper that carried the account of the current event might also contain an editorial commenting on that event. This is secondary, within the same physical format but having an intent that is once removed from the first representation, and serves instead as a thoughtful commentary on the original.

Moving from current events to any discipline at random, students should quickly get the idea that it is not so much the "touchy-feely" aspect (pottery shard or crumbling diary) that determines whether something is primary or secondary, but rather its intangible closeness to whatever circumstance or happening is under consideration. To make sure that the idea has been clearly perceived, it is always good to ask students what is a primary source in the field of literature and see if they will notice that the primary source, for instance, a novel, and a secondary source, a book-length criticism of that novel, have the same physical shape, size, format, and cost, for that matter, and yet have two different intents with regard to the original novelist's conception. The distinction between primary and secondary literature is one on which advanced research, both in the library and outside, depends.

Certain secondary sources, however, are further removed

metaphysically from the phenomenon than other secondary sources. Librarians have been accustomed to regard bibliographies as a sort of tertiary source, one step removed from the secondary reactions and two steps removed from the original phenomenon and its representations. This, of course, can be a matter of controversy because some bibliographies list only primary materials, some only secondary, some a mixture, and some, the bibliographies of bibliography, bring together a disparate assortment of other lists. For all but the most erudite scholar, these distinctions are unnecessary, but the student should be able to grasp the concept of removal from the original event or creative act or assembled data and know that when someone refers to a tertiary source, it is the same as referring to a list of works that themselves respond to a primary source.

The next three steps in the question negotiation process center on the individual student or researcher rather than on the nature of the topic, but since the results of these steps have a definite effect on steps further down the line, it is important to consider them here.

Estimating quantity of material

Simply stated, this step in question analysis asks only the extent of the student's or researcher's final project, whether it is simple curiosity or a brief paper requiring only a handful of footnotes; whether it is a larger research undertaking, for example, an exhaustive research study for a business, a master's thesis, or doctoral dissertation; or whether it is intended as a scholarly journal article or monographic treatment of an entire subject. Students rarely have difficulty responding to this particular step in the analysis scheme, probably because assignments are often clearly stated in terms of an approximate number of items to be consulted for the finished product.

It never hurts to jot down at this preliminary stage the tentative mixture of materials in terms of quantity, that is, to anticipate that 5 to 10 books should perhaps be consulted, 10 to 20 journal articles, and 4 to 5 newspaper accounts. Obviously, the quantity issue goes in tandem with the formats discussed above since the quantity of material of a primary or secondary nature will vary from topic to topic, and a paper requiring all secondary sources in whatever physical formats may be just as long and take just as much research time as the paper of a similar length requiring all primary sources only.

Specifying quality of material

By quality of material, we mean the authority of its origins, whether primary or secondary. Is material from the popular press sufficient? Does it need to be a scholarly account? A mixture of both? Are certain writers so paramount in the field that their work must be read and cited, or is the topic so new and so interdisciplinary that there are only a few writers and the student will be doing well to identify them?

The issue of quality gets back to one of the basic tenets taught in all reference courses, that is, given two reference works that are identical in scope and of a similar date, one may be preferred over the other on the basis of the authority of its authors or perhaps on the basis of the reputation of a publisher or the institution that provided a base for the development of the work. Quality also comes into play in any form of library instruction when students are urged to realize that the catalog in most libraries, whether on cards or online, is not a qualitative tool, but is merely a form of bibliography listing the materials in that particular collection on a particular campus. Therefore, in specifying the quality of the material desired for a particular project, the student cannot rely merely on the subject headings in the card catalog or in an unannotated bibliography, but must go instead to some more authoritative source such as the bibliographic essay, an annotated bibliography or index, or a known scholar in the field. (As with all other steps in the question analysis sequence, the quality issue will be discussed in other places in this book.)

Budgeting time available

Even more than understanding the quantity of material required for a certain project, most undergraduates are all too aware of the time they have available for research. Librarians as well as teaching faculty are forever reminded that students procrastinate and leave not only the writing of their papers until the last moment, but the research on which the writing depends until the next to the final hour. The reference librarian is often confronted with a panic-stricken student clinging to a topic that is poorly understood, with assignment guidelines that have not been thoroughly thought through, and a deadline the next morning. The most appropriate tools in such a case are dictated as much by time constraints as by the topic, often more so. Since most of us have at one time or another waited until the last moment to complete research on a topic, this is a dilemma with which we can sympathize, if not condone.

Assuming, however, in the best of all possible worlds, that an infinite amount of time is available for research, it is still important for the student or researcher to determine at an early stage exactly how much time may be necessary for each segment of the work at hand. A good reason for this is the necessity of requesting materials via interlibrary loan, which can delay the research up to several weeks. Knowing in advance that the necessary materials are at other institutions permits the researcher to make interlibrary loan requests at the beginning of the project so that they are likely to be received before the work is complete.

It is important not to confuse the determination of time available for research with the time element, which may often be a subquestion of the overall research topic. That is, it is possible to specify research regarding the events that occurred in one month in 1798, but also to have an entire fourteen weeks in which to do this research. These are two different chronological considerations and should not be confused.

Listing disciplines involved

In more restricted undergraduate assignments, this step in the research question analysis might be omitted. It is appropriate at this point for the student or researcher to brainstorm either alone or with someone about exactly what fields or disciplines would logically be interested in or have had something to say about the topic. In the last few decades, virtually every topic has been explored or elements of it have been considered by scholars who are technically in other fields. Moreover, most topics have an interdisciplinary nature and should be examined from the point of view of the two or more fields they most concern. Even in disciplines as seemingly cut and dry as literature, it is always fruitful to consider whether auxilliary disciplines, such as history or sociology or linguistics, may have a bearing on the topic or on some of the identified subquestions of the topic. If exploring other whole disciplines seems inappropriate, it is still worthwhile speculating whether a given subfield of the parent discipline may have an insight to offer. Public policy is a well-developed subfield of political science and may very well be appropriate if the research problem concerns local government.

The obvious importance of determining in advance the relevant related disciplines is to make sure that when a search strategy is constructed for the research problem, the appropriate types of tools and the specific titles of each type that will be most useful are designed into the strategy.

Indicating types of tools

This eighth step is the culmination of the research problem analysis prior to assembling a tentative search strategy. The significance of this step cannot be underrated since, as with any human endeavor, intellectual or physical, creativity and progress stem from insights about existing concepts and tools and from their novel juxtaposition.

A researcher who is aware of the inherent nature of the type of research tools in a given discipline is able to transfer that knowledge and those expectations about a paradigm of tools to a different discipline as well as to a different institution. Students too, whether at the secondary or college level, have an acquaintance, whether or not they realize it, with the central characteristics of various families of reference tools (encyclopedias, dictionaries, almanacs, indexes). High school students and undergraduates should be able to identify the families of tools by name, given their previously ascertained research needs and the features of a given group of reference works. They should also be able to predict the probability that if a type of tool, X, exists in one discipline, a similar tool, whether or not it is called the same thing, may exist in discipline Y. For the most part it is not essential for high school students and for freshmen and sophomores in college, before they have chosen a major, to know too many specific titles, and it is much more important for them to recognize and be able to explain the distinctive characteristics of each type of tool.

To make the realization and the learning easier, it is useful to divide reference works into two large categories, what we previously labeled fact tools and finding tools. Fact tools are those reference works that are consulted, usually briefly, with a specific simple, factual question in mind, the purpose of which is to yield a fairly discrete answer to such a specific question. Types of tools in this category include language dictionaries and dictionaries of special terms in a given discipline; handbooks and companions; statistical compendiums; gazetteers; directories of all sorts including biographical directories such as the *Who's Who* group; almanacs and books of miscellaneous information; yearbooks and chronologies; concise histories of whole countries; quotation, synonym, and abbreviation books; and the many specialized works or sets that compile or synthesize important material in a given field, for example, the masterplot series or treaties in force.

Most students/patrons are sufficiently familiar with one or more specific examples of fact tool categories, but they can with guidance derive the unique characteristics of each group of tools. For example, one could elicit ideas from a class that attempts to define a type of fact or finding tool and put the combined responses on a blackboard where all can see them. Since search strategies are based on groups of tools rather than on specific titles, it is imperative that students have a clear conception of exactly which fact tools achieve which results and the extent of probable overlap between types of tools. For example, an almanac will often give the same information as a history or a handbook. Or an abbreviation might appear both in a language dictionary and in a specialized dictionary of abbreviations. Rather than have students attempt to memorize the characteristics of each group, suggest that they examine sample titles within groups with which they may be less familiar, for example, gazetteers, returning to discuss with one another their perception of the utility and basic features of all tools of that type.

Finding tools do not give information directly, as do fact tools, but they lead the student/researcher to the information contained in another format. For example, a bibliography, an index, and a checklist are all intermediary devices that should assist the researcher in identifying and, in some cases, in actually locating necessary material. No doubt the most familiar of all finding tools, and the one most students will overlook when asked to name varieties of tools, is the library's own catalog, which is simply a finding tool with numerous approaches leading to the material in the library's own collection.

A rather difficult situation arises with regard to the distinction between indexes and bibliographies. Librarians realize

that the terms are often used synonymously both by publishers and by scholars, but students will want to know the
difference between the two. Perhaps the best, although not
perfect, way to explain this distinction is to say that bibliographies are lists of material that exists no matter where it may
be located, whereas an index is concerned with a finite universe of materials and everything listed in an index will lead
to one member of that finite universe. Most students will
recall the function of the index in the back of a textbook, for
instance, and realize that the page numbers given there refer
to the textbook in hand and not to any other item. The same
can be said for a periodical index in which the group of periodicals analyzed is clearly listed in the front of each volume
so that students will never be surprised by the inclusion of a
citation to a journal that has not been specified already. An
analogy might be the difference between making a grocery list
(that would be like a bibliography) and making a chart of the
food located in every aisle of a particular grocery store (that
would be like an index). This distinction may seem like a fine
point to some students, and if they are not curious about it, it
might be better left to a later time in the instruction. It is,
however, an important concept just because indexes and bibliographies are so essential, along with library catalogs, in virtually every search strategy.

Obviously there are other groups of tools besides the fact
tools and finding tools discussed so far (see Table 4-1). Most
students think of encyclopedias when they think of a reference work. Encyclopedias are by nature hybrids, surveying
the existing knowledge on a topic, and hence serving as a
secondary source, but containing bibliographic citations and

Table 4-1 Fact and Finding Reference Tools

Fact Tools	Hybrids	Finding Tools
Handbooks (Literary characters, opera, plot summaries, TV show characters)	Encyclopedias Histories	Bibliographies (citations, essays)
Biographical dictionaries		Indexes
Atlases		Abstracts
Gazetteers		Annual reviews
Concordances		Bibliography of
Dictionaries		bibliographies
Almanacs		Catalogs
Directories		

references to other related material; hence they also serve as finding tools.

Similar to the obvious encyclopedias, the general ones in English and foreign languages, and specialized encyclopedias for the various disciplines and discipline families, are the universal or monumental historical sets for given countries, for instance, the Cambridge Histories of whatever country or time period. An argument can be made that abstracts, such as *Psychological Abstracts*, are also hybrids, which both summarize a longer item and give a full reference to it. By extension the same could be said of any annotated bibliography or bibliographic essay insofar as it describes the material as well as points to the complete form of the item. (One student claimed that a gazetteer should be counted as a hybrid since it not only gave brief factual information about any place on the surface of the earth, but also gave latitude and longitude, and hence was a finding tool in a geographical sense!)

Many tools that seem to be exclusively "fact" or exclusively "finding" in nature can serve the other purpose, and in that sense are hybrids. A good example is the *New York Times Index*, which, although primarily used to identify the date, page, and column of a particular item in the newspaper, also serves, through its summary, as a synthesis of the material carried in the paper, and all librarians have had occasion to find a factual answer directly in the index without needing to go to the microfilm of the *New York Times*.

Postanalysis Strategy

Where do we go from here? Having completed a thorough research problem analysis on a topic, the next step and the one that must precede any effective utilization of the various types of reference tools just discussed, is the construction of an overall tentative search strategy for the problem. Constructing such a search strategy in the larger context of the research process as a whole is the topic of Chapter 5, which discusses the general shape of a search strategy, followed by Chapters 6 to 8, concerning modifications on that shape, dictated by the various discipline groups—the humanities, the historical sciences, and the social sciences.

At this point it is useful to reflect on the utility of teaching students at every level the basic steps in the research problem analysis scheme. All but the most elementary research topic has within it numerous subcomponents that must be identified and ordered before the reasoning and the research can proceed. Research expertise at any level lies in carefully isolating those simpler components and in matching each component with the type of tool or tools that will most directly and adequately respond to it. Since the procedure for analyzing a topic is so similar, on one hand, to the scientific method and, on the other hand, so applicable to day-to-day human reasoning about any complex need, it is easy to instruct students in these eight basic steps and have them readily understand the purpose and utility of sitting down before beginning their library research to ascertain the answers at each stage of the analysis. Much time will be saved by the user/patron who has taken the few minutes in advance to negotiate the topic and predict insofar as possible the physical and metaphysical formats and the types of tools and possible disciplines that are involved, because the librarian will be able to shorten the reference interview and begin suggesting specific titles within each type of tool almost immediately.

In a larger bibliographic instruction program, one involving multiple contacts with the same students, the question analysis segment makes a very nice beginning to a course or series of lectures. Since bibliographic theory is much more important than the specific knowledge of X number of reference works, a good introduction to such theory is a consideration of the concepts that underlie the research problem itself and that are the reason students need the tools in the first place. Feeling comfortable analyzing their own research topic will immediately stimulate user/patron interest in the search strategy and subsequent steps to be outlined in this book. By presenting users with a new and more efficient way of thinking about their research tasks, we are preparing them to transfer the same abilities to other projects, other disciplines, and other libraries. Research problem analysis is the foundation on which all other bibliographic theory must rest, because all the tools that now exist and that will exist in the future were devised to respond to the needs of actual research. Users must understand the origin and nature of their own needs so that they can then select the appropriate bibliographic tool to handle each discrete "job" of a larger complex task.

Notes

1. Results given at the Eighth Annual Conference on Library Orientation for Academic Libraries, Ypsilanti, Michigan, May 1981, and not yet published.
2. James Benson, "The Hidden Reference Question: Where Are the . . . ," *Southeastern Librarian* 29 (Summer 1979): 90–92.

5
Search Strategy
in the
Research Process

Search strategy—or research strategy as it might better be called—is the organization of the various types of fact-finding and hybrid tools in a logical, efficient order to solve a given research problem. Once the tools have been ordered according to type, it is relatively simple to determine the most appropriate title or specific tool of each type to be consulted at each point.

In the construction and execution of the search strategy the training of the reference librarian becomes invaluable. Library users too can become acquainted with the chief characteristics of the most important reference tools of each type, both those of a general nature and those that control certain disciplines or discipline groups. The major thrust of library instruction since the mid-1960s has been to expose users to a vast array of reference titles, typically arranging them in search strategy order and hoping that users will be able to reduce the examples to their common elements and thus be able to extrapolate other search strategies and predict the existence of alternative titles if those they were taught are not available or do not work. The existence of general guides to reference works, Sheehy and Walford, as well as the more specialized annotated guides to particular disciplines and discipline groups, are a major benefit in the search for the right title for a particular need. The student must, however, be able to appreciate what type of tool is involved because most guides are arranged in that fashion.

The Reference Librarian's Strategy

A certain intellectual process goes on in the reference librarian's head following the completion of the reference interview, the question negotiation, and before the search strategy is suggested to the user. This does not imply that all or even any users should be taught to think or function exactly as experienced reference librarians would. The objective for the user is rather to be able to deal with any research problem on its own terms and to be able to carry on the more routine parts of the search strategy by consulting background and obvious finding tools, which results in a more focused research problem. Reference librarians need not fear that extensive library instruction will so prepare users that the need for experienced reference librarians in libraries will decrease; the increased ability of users to perform their own research question analysis and to begin to formulate and execute their own search strategies will mean that reference librarians will be able to spend more time with these same users at more advanced stages in their research. All parties concerned will then be more challenged and more gratified as they work together toward a common goal.

How does the reference librarian formulate the search strategy? Taking into account the steps of the question analysis sequence (Chapter 4) that are user specific (quantity of material needed, quality or authority of material needed, and time available to complete the research), together with the apparent scope of the problem, the veteran reference librarian will make certain mental leaps that sometimes baffle the user in the course of constructing the first search strategy. For example, a fairly common, straightforward, yet complex question is deciphering a journal article citation. Given only the initials of the apparent journal, a date, and an author's name, the librarian may conclude that what is needed first is a handbook-type fact tool, which will decode the acronym, followed by either a serials directory or perhaps the *Union List of Serials* or *New Serial Titles* to indicate the precise entry.

If the librarian noticed that the author's name was unusual, the librarian might suggest that the most appropriate search strategy would begin with an index to journal articles in the field in question, hoping that once the list of entries for the author within that year were found, the rest of the citation could be verified.

This is an equally valid approach under the circumstances. Still another approach might be to go back to the text to where the footnote is appended and see if it contains any clues as to the rest of the citation or whether the context might indicate that this is not a journal article but a paper read at a conference, and hence the acronym that needs deciphering is not a journal title at all, but an acronym for a society.

Last, the librarian together with the user may guess the title in question from another source or previous experience, but the user may claim that the journal is not held in the library. If the librarian suspects that the user has had difficulty with the filing rules in the card catalog, it may be appropriate to assist the individual with the catalog. If the serials record is online, the librarian may turn to the terminal to ascertain whether or not the journal is held.

The point here is that there are many approaches to even the most common and apparently simple user problem and that one goal of theoretically based library instruction is to make users aware of the various alternatives so that if one search strategy formulation does not work, they can acknowledge the existence of another approach. There is rarely a single correct diagnosis to a user's research problem, and there is almost never a single correct prescription to "cure" the complaint. With these thoughts in mind, we will describe the most basic form of search strategy and suggest how it can be expanded with the complexity of a research topic.

Basic Search Strategy Model

The basic search strategy model relies on finding tools to collect primary and secondary material on a topic. More elaborate search strategies, involving the entire array of fact tools and the various tertiary tools such as guides to the literature and bibliographies of bibliography are discussed later. At this point, this basic model will explain the various elements involved in constructing a search strategy and will serve as an example that might be adopted for a class presentation.

Since there is some ambiguity in the literature regarding

the term "search strategy,"[1] let us define it narrowly as the ordered arrangement of types of finding tools appropriate for the collection of material on a particular analyzed topic. An amplified search strategy would be expanded to include the various fact tools and hybrids that complement the basic search strategy outline and that advance the research by providing specific detailed information along the way.

The largest concept subsuming the amplified and the basic search strategies would be termed the research process, which occurs from the point at which a topic is begun through the question analysis stage, the planning of a search strategy, and a complete execution of it. By extension, the research process can also encompass the researcher's own synthesis and reporting of the findings. Throughout this book, we use the term "search strategy" or "amplified search strategy" when referring to the ordering of types of tools or, in some cases, to the ordering of specific tools.

The time factor

What makes the construction of the basic search strategy involving finding tools much more challenging than a routine recipe is the importance of chronology, of the time factor to the overall topic. The reference librarian will instinctively, often without recognizing it, draw a conclusion about a search strategy based solely on the time frame indicated by the topic and knowledge of the relative currency of the types of tools and the specific titles available. The best way to illustrate this principle is to take a current events topic that is for the most part free of attachment to any particular discipline and so can serve as a general model. For instance, if the research topic involves specific information on a political assassination that occurred within the last month or so, the only information available—whether primary, that is, the first news reports of the incident, or secondary, the commentary about the incident and its impact—will be found in newspapers, news magazines, and news broadcasts and in the various online data and wire services. One gains access to these materials only by browsing or performing an online search, for example, of the New York Times Information Bank.

If the particular assassination occurred, say, more than two months ago, some additional options will be found in the *Readers' Guide,* and the various newspaper printed indexes should have already appeared to document the event and reaction to it. Almost at once a two-step search strategy becomes apparent—use of a periodical index and then the card catalog (or finding aid such as a union list) to locate periodicals in a given library. (Since we now live in an era of "instant books," one or more commercial publishers may have commissioned a lengthy report of a major international incident and rushed it into print soon after the event. Assuming that a library were to acquire such a work soon after its appearance and catalog it immediately, it would then be possible to use the appropriate subject heading in a card or online catalog and be led, even at this early stage, to book-length material on the topic. This is still a relatively rare occurrence, but it should not be forgotten as publishing technology advances.)

If the analyzed topic regarding the political assassination indicates among the various subcomponents that a historical dimension to the problem of modern political assassinations is wanted by the student/patron, then the basic search strategy can expand to begin now with a hybrid tool, that is, with an encyclopedia followed by yearbooks or almanacs that will give chronological or contextual accounts of previous recent assassinations, then the periodical index and the card catalog as before. Again assuming the particular event has occurred within the last few weeks, there is not likely to be any relevant bibliography on it. However, there is undoubtedly an existing "ready-made" bibliography on the topic of political assassinations or, more specifically, political assassinations in X country. Depending on the extent of historical information that is wanted, a bibliography might be logically inserted after the encyclopedia and before the periodical index. Remember, bibliographies and periodical indexes are available in several formats—the familiar printed version, online indexes, online catalogs, and the card catalog itself with its traditional approaches to any given title.

The fourth time consideration that is possible with a current events topic would occur a year or so after the original event, when both reactive journal articles and reflective books have appeared on the subject. Here we have the complete basic strategy—encyclopedia, yearbooks, almanacs, bibliography, periodical indexes, card catalog (to discover which journals and books are held by the library), and last, as is always the case in any complete search process, browsing the most recent as yet uncontrolled materials.

Presented with the basic search strategy formula, most users will say, "Ho-hum, what's new about this?" and claim they have been using encyclopedias, bibliographies, periodical indexes, and card catalogs and have been browsing their entire lifetime. They may not realize, however, that when a topic includes time as a critical factor, such as a current event, the utility of the various tools is based directly on the time frame and on the lapse between the phenomenon studied (the primary source or event) and the commentary it elicits. This explains why it is impossible to find books as early as people might expect on an incident that occurred or a theory that was first published within the last few months. Without a continual conscious recognition of the time factor as an overlay in every aspect of the research process, users become frustrated or angry that the material they need is "not in the library" or even suspicious that librarians are intentionally hiding needed information. This is ironic because people generally seem to have a fairly good sense about time as it affects other activities, such as the amount of time it usually takes before this year's high-style fashions can be found in the local department store. For some reason, perhaps because an aura of magic remains about information generally and how libraries operate in particular, people all too frequently assume that if something has happened, the library has it or can find it without delay, when in fact the format that will contain the necessary information has not yet appeared.

Particularly relevant to this subject as it involves a high school, public, or small academic library is that the collection itself has boundaries, so that the mere existence of material on the topic is not an assurance that it is available at that particular moment. Many factors must be taken into account, everything from the scope of the collection to the budget, delays in ordering material, any backlogs in cataloging, and circulation of material. Users need to be apprised of such factors so that they do not rely solely on a library that cannot meet their needs, but know that they can ask for assistance in locating the material and in obtaining it elsewhere if it already exists. The availability of online searching and document delivery is especially critical for basic search strategies involving current materials, since such systems as the *Magazine Index* and the *NewsSearch* database can provide very recent bibliographic information online or in offline prints, which may satisfy the user until more material is available.

This, then, is one good way of conceptualizing a basic search strategy within the larger research process. Students can be taught the basic principles of organizing finding tools for a current events topic in a single session, keeping in mind the relative rate with which the various tools appear. It would be well to reinforce such a presentation with an actual individualized assignment, each student being given a different current events topic to think through in terms of the types of finding tools that are likely to be useful. It would be even better to ask students also to do a search with specific tools to prove the point, but that may be more than time allows. An online demonstration of a current events database, such as the New York Times Information Bank, might be appropriate and should certainly be an attention-getting complement to such a presentation, but the time, expense, and potential frustration of students who may want searches and then discover they have to pay for them may be a contraindication. In any event, the rudiments of a basic search strategy need to be fully and completely understood before the user can comprehend the amplified strategy in a particular discipline. A basic model for an amplified search strategy connected with a hypothetical discipline is the next topic.

Scholarly Communication and Bibliographic Structure

The relationship between how researchers perceive and the resulting publishing patterns has a significant impact on the chain connecting the scholar, the scholar's work, the publication of that work, and how other scholars identify that work bibliographically. But whereas scholars are primarily concerned with satisfying their own particular research needs, librarians are more apt to trace the broad outlines of research procedure. In recent years instruction librarians have been especially eager to understand the chain of how ideas get into the literature so that they can explain it to others and defuse the myth that all library work is serendipitous.[2]

The underlying principle in the theory that follows is that if one understands the nature of a discipline, its age, and its stage of development, one can predict the reference sources (bibliographic structure) that will be available in that field. With knowledge of the nature of a discipline and its parallel bibliographic structure, one can more easily construct an effective search strategy for information in that discipline.

Michael Keresztesi[3] believes that one important dimension of any discipline involves time, that is, the historical development from its inception of any given field of knowledge. When, where, and why did the discipline emerge? How quickly did it develop? How did it subdivide subsequently into still other disciplines? This historical dimension provides the time frame, which in turn has a critical bearing on the material that will be available at any given point, and consequently on the fact, finding, and hybrid tools that will exist in the discipline. He believes that a direct relationship exists between the quality and publishing formats of a discipline and the reference tools. His description of the bibliographical nature of a discipline concerns the quantity of primary and secondary source material it generates, any peculiarities that exist in the material, and their origin and importance. It includes how new knowledge is assembled and communicated within the field, and between the field and society at large, and finally what reference tools exist that allow those outside the field to have access to the primary data (the knowledge generated) and all the other spin-offs that occur in the field. Together with the historical overlay, this bibliographic conceptualization of the contours of a discipline provides the best model we have yet found for understanding and predicting the research characteristics in a field. It is also the best model we have found for teaching the research characteristics and ultimately the bibliographic expertise that pertain to a discipline.

Some people may object that this model is too complicated for the average user or even for the bright undergraduate. On the contrary, we believe that by providing students a framework that both describes the generation of knowledge in a field and simultaneously allows them to anticipate the probable bibliographic control of that knowledge, we are providing an invaluable key they can use throughout their lives to understand the role of information in society.[4] Time constraints of a BI program or single presentation and difference in the background or intellectual level of a given audience will, of course, mean that the Keresztesi model will have to be pared down or embellished to meet the needs of users.

Growth of a Discipline

In Keresztesi's thinking, the historical and bibliographic contours of any discipline are intimately linked. How do new disciplines arise? Essentially, in the twentieth century a discipline can originate in three ways: from the combination of two previously existing fields as is common in the social and physical sciences, for example, bioengineering or psycholinguistics; from an existing field, such as the medical specialties that were originally part of general medicine, for example, nephrology and neurology (a process known as "twigging"); or from the needs and pressures of society, for example, women's studies, black studies, or future studies. In any case, the birth and growth of a discipline can be outlined in four stages—pioneering, elaboration, proliferation, and establishment.

Stage one: pioneering

In the pioneering stage, a single great thinker puts forward a hypothesis, performs an experiment, makes a discovery, or otherwise issues an intellectual manifesto that is unique and recognized by others as a significant contribution to human thought. Alternatively, and more commonly in the twentieth century, there are a small group of pioneers, typically academics, located at institutions throughout the United States and in foreign countries who have traditional teaching and research responsibilities in an established field, but whose research interests or theoretical inclinations have led them separately to new insights. These people, the early pioneers, are likely to discover one another's existence in a more or less casual or haphazard way, often accidentally at a major conference they may attend in their established field by means of an idea posited in a paper someone gives or by means of casual talk about research interests that occurs outside the formal meetings. These pioneering individuals discover that others have also thought about or may be pursuing the same new train of thought and research.

Another possibility is that someone exploring a new dimension contacts a known expert in the closest possible field, to consult with that person about whether the new approach has any "future." The exchange of references and ideas and the forwarding of preprints in the so-called invisible college (the nonpublished communication network that exists both in academe and in the research world inhabited by government and industrial researchers) will often lead one person working alone in a new area to discover others who are involved in the same investigations. Very often the new approach will be regarded as suspicious by the traditionalists in existing well-established fields. They may either dismiss the new work as irrelevant or denounce it as threatening (a phenomenon that can be witnessed in the reaction of scientists and humanists to the field of ethnobiology). This means that the ideas may not be explored fully in traditional ways such as journal articles or conference proceedings. Typically, avant-garde thinkers communicate among themselves; they share and criticize ideas and data over the telephone or by mail in a fairly hermetically sealed group before attempting to extend the findings to a larger, undoubtedly more critical if not skeptical, audience.

Research at the pioneering stage is financed in traditional ways. Research proposals for outside funding support, are written for work that is of an established nature. If a pioneer pursues a new idea, it is with financing intended for a known, accepted purpose. Where no outside funding is available, the pioneers spend their own time and money on the equipment and travel necessary to pursue the new ideas.

In some new disciplines at the pioneering stages, there may also be an attempt to convert others to the new idea. This may occur at a later point in the development of a new discipline if the pioneer risks being considered a maverick, which could lead to a denial of tenure or funding. In the pioneering stage some academics may try out their ideas on "unsuspecting" students by suggesting the new hypothesis or the new research methods and findings in lectures that are part of the traditional, established course. This is important because the only record other than the lecturer's own notes may be the notebooks of the students who have heard the lecture.

Stage two: elaboration

In the twentieth century, elaboration follows closely on the pioneering stage in all but the most top secret research. The characteristics of the elaboration stage are an increase in the number of people engaging in or supporting the new discipline. This spread will be noticed most geographically, as the pioneers and their early adherents feel a need to organize themselves, at least to the extent of some sort of list, if not also a new organization, so that they can identify one another and be in closer contact. Also in the elaboration stage, those involved in the field will hold meetings either on their own or announced as part of a larger gathering, perhaps again within one of the parent disciplines.

The quantity, and one hopes the quality, of contributions to the field will grow geometrically so that both new source material, new primary data, and the beginnings of secondary interpretation of that data will begin to spread. Terminology and methodology will become established by practice if not yet by codification. Also at the elaboration stage, the early founders and thinkers will somehow be identified and recognized by those who have more recently entered the discussion.

In terms of funding, it is possible that a more innovative granting agency may provide small amounts of money for research specifically on the topic to be covered. Also, more adventurous academic institutions may permit a one-time course in the field so that the early thinking and practice will be transmitted in a more organized fashion to students.

Stage three: proliferation

At this stage, not only do the practitioners in the discipline find that they have many, many colleagues around the world (which means, of course, that the people no longer know one another personally), but formal organizations of a national/international scope will be founded. The output of data and interpretation will become enormous and will be available in many languages. There will be concern with methodology and formal training for the discipline.

Also at the proliferation stage, the discipline may start to combine with another to "twig" into subfields, which then will repeat the cycle. International foundations and institutes and research centers will become involved in providing a home for research. Existing knowledge in the discipline will be synthesized, organized, and incorporated with knowledge from related fields. Undergraduate majors and perhaps masters programs may be established. Methodology becomes codified, and professional training is sanctioned so that a specific degree or credentials will mean that those who receive it have had a certain core of training and experience.

Stage four: establishment

By the establishment stage the discipline has achieved full academic respectability. In most cases this will mean that it exists as an academic department in its own right in at least some institutions, that it has generated doctoral candidates and a fully developed curriculum for the training of people in the field, and that it has a completed network of research centers and research projects. Furthermore, the fully established discipline will be stratified, naturally divided between theoretical and applied work, perhaps, or between different schools of thought that are compatible but have not broken off and formed their own embryonic field. Federal government and private agencies will be eager to fund continued research in established disciplines and will want to stimulate creativity among practitioners. The subject matter will, of course, become more complex and will diffuse and influence other fields, sometimes combining with them to form yet another new specialty.

A final and perhaps more trivial characteristic of the established, fully developed discipline is that certain institutions may create an honorary endowed chair in the field so that the pioneers, or at any rate their immediate followers, will be "canonized" as leaders in what would now be recognized as an important field of knowledge.

Discipline growth and bibliographic structure

Taking the Keresztesi model for the development of any discipline, one can continue through the four stages of growth to chart the communication that occurs at each stage, the way that communication is captured, and then the way that communication is controlled in the bibliographic sense. This progression (see Table 5-1) can be pointed out to library users so they can better predict what format of materials to look for given the development of the disciplines in which they want to do research. For example, at the pioneering stage when only a few individuals are involved, one has informal meetings, correspondence, possibly some pamphlets, isolated lectures or parts of lectures, news stories and interviews in some cases, the very first journal articles, perhaps a newsletter, and, in the case of funded research, a section in an annual report that might outline the new discoveries. Each of these methods or manifestations of communication yields a specific sort of primary source document. Informal meetings at conferences may result in minutes, in later notes of the participants to themselves, or in memoirs in which participants recall their first discussion with another pioneer.

Letters of correspondence, provided they are saved at both ends, are primary source documents. Pamphlets, if they are printed and distributed, are primary source material. The manifestation of a lecture is the notes of either the lecturer or the audience. (This always makes a good argument for students' preserving all their lecture notes; the notes may in fact be primary source material for an embryonic discipline!) News stories and interviews are captured in newspapers, in journals, or on tapes if the interview is broadcast on radio or television. The first articles, of course, appear in journals, but the developing discipline will not yet have its own formal journal. If a newsletter is started by the pioneers for their own information, a backfile of these will prove invaluable to anyone trying to recapture the early communication among them. Annual reports to funding agencies, whether government or private, may contain data or new ideas that will eventually evolve into a new field of inquiry.

At the pioneering stage, the minutes, letters, pamphlets, lecture notes, newspaper articles, and broadcast tapes are all relatively ephemeral; if they are to be controlled, they should be in an archives, which can be located only by communicating with the likely repository, checking directories to archives and special collections, or using such tools as the *National Union Catalog of Manuscript Collections*.

Preserving such early primary source material is a critical problem for any discipline. First, the pioneers themselves must have some sense of the importance of their early work so that they preserve all sorts of material relating to their early thinking and that of their colleagues and place the material with an institution that will care for it, control it, and make it available to generations of scholars to follow. Second, it is a difficulty for and a responsibility of libraries and archives to remain aware of new developments in any and all fields and to take the initiative to contact the pioneers and offer to house those materials that will later have a great bearing on the field.

The less ephemeral forms of communication—the early journal articles, the newsletters, and the annual reports—might or might not be controlled by existing indexes and bibliographies under, of course, traditional subject headings, which are more than likely inadequate to the new situation. In many respects it is lamentable that communication in the twentieth century takes place so frequently over the telephone or by teleconferencing and that no product of the transaction is preserved. Much creativity and many insights about the development of a field and its future shape are forever lost because face-to-face conversations are not preserved.

At the elaboration stage, all the methods of communication and source materials and corresponding control tools exist, as in the pioneering stage, but to these are added a first formal organization, which will have as its source material some kind of membership roster, if not also bylaws. The first courses taught in the field will have for their spin-offs a collection of essays, which the students will use in lieu of a textbook. A first scholarly journal may yield collections of data and bring together the work of all the pioneers who published in it over time. Articles will appear in textbooks in related fields to introduce students to the existence of the new discipline and its ramifications for other work. As mentioned earlier, the pioneers may also generate their memoirs, or autobiographies or biographies of them may appear; these are other source materials. (See Table 5-1 for an overview of discipline growth.)

Control tools, in addition to archives and existing periodical indexes, might be bibliographic essays in a journal discussing the wealth of material that has appeared in the new discipline, possibly a glossary or thesaurus of jargon terms for the new field, and reviews in existing journals of the intellectual content or impact of the adolescent discipline.

At the proliferation stage, again everything that precedes will continue, but when an international organization is founded, an international roster of people will be involved. There will be additional journals, textbooks, whole monographs, proceedings of conferences in the field, and annual reports of projects that have been specially funded. The bibliographic structure may include a guide to the field, handbooks and/or methodologies, an early history of the discipline, encyclopedia articles discussing the field, and special bibliographies, indexes, classification schedules, and subject headings.

Finally, an annual review of research in the field is likely to appear.

At the establishment stage, manifestations of communication may be course catalogs that describe the curriculum assigned to the degree in the field. Publishers may establish monographic or textbook series that cater to those in the discipline. Source material will also be in the form of dissertations and master's theses, government reports, and government documents. All these items can be controlled with such tools as a separate encyclopedia, a separate bibliography of dissertations in the field, a directory of specialists or consultants, and possibly a list of specialized journals and collections.

Use of parallel communication and bibliographic structure

The above discussion concerning the development of a discipline from its inception to maturity and the corresponding manifestations in the "literature" may seem of value only as a curiosity. On the contrary, this scheme is essential to bibliographic instruction theory and practice. Once students and researchers fully understand the general contours of the development of a discipline they will be able to predict accurately the sort of fact and finding tools likely to exist at any stage in the growth of the field. For example, knowing that a field is at the elaboration stage, one can with some assurance assume the existence of a glossary of terms, but not any completed dissertations or an annual review of the research. The reverse is also true. Knowing that an international directory and an encyclopedia article exist in the field, one can say with assurance that the field is at least at the proliferation, if not at the establishment, stage and plan the amplified search strategy accordingly. If the discipline is too immature to have its own complete bibliographic structure, one can look to neighboring disciplines for information, for example, to find biographical information on one of the pioneers at a point before a separate biographical directory exists for the field.

To some extent new developments in an existing field will not break off and form a separate discipline. However, these developments can also be regarded according to the paradigm, and, in fact, society will often speak in these categories. An overview of BI growth as a subdiscipline is shown in Table 5-2.

Table 5-1 Growth of a Discipline

Stages and Activities	Methods of Communication	Source Material	Control Tools
Pioneering			
Single great thinker or small group with similar "maverick" interest	Informal meetings	Minutes	Assuming primary materials have been preserved, they can be identified via directories to archives and special collections
Data/idea generation	Correspondence	Letters	
Propaganda	Pamphlets	Pamphlets	Standard (existing) indexes, bibliographies, and subject headings
Financing by traditional means	Lectures	Notes	
	News stories and interviews	Clippings and tapes	
	First articles	Articles with data, articles with interpretation	
	Newsletters	Newsletter backfile	
	Sections of annual reports	Report collection	
Elaboration			
More followers	First organization	Member roster	Reviewing medium in journal
More contributions	First courses	Collections of essays	Bibliographic essay
New terminology	First journal	Collection of data	Glossary or thesaurus
Founder(s) recognized	Articles in textbooks	Memoirs/biography/ autobiography	

Proliferation			
Worldwide spread of interest	International organization	International directory	Guide
Undergraduate major	More journals	Proceedings	Handbook
Methodology established	Whole textbooks	Annual report of funded projects	History
Professional training organized	Monographs		*Who's Who*
Conferences			Encyclopedia articles
Twigging begins			Special bibliographies, indexes, classification, subject headings
Outside funding			Annual review of research
Establishment			
Academic departments set up	Course catalogs	Dissertations	Dissertation bibliography
Doctorates awarded	Publisher's series	Government reports and documents	Separate encyclopedia
Professional standards			Directory of consultants
Research institutionalized			List of special journals and collections
Federal research grants			
Specialized publishers			
Endowed chair			

Table 5-2 Growth of Bibliographic Instruction as a Subdiscipline

Activities	Manifestations
Stage: Pioneering (1967–1971)	
Small group of mainly reference librarians become convinced of the need to instruct users formally about library tools and their efficient use	Correspondence
	Handouts and notes resulting from BI programs
	Local news stories and interviews
Informal gatherings at ALA or regional library meetings where ideas and experiences are shared and enthusiasm is generated	Reports in library literature
	Early journal articles
	Section of library annual report or of report to BI funding agency
First BI programs started	Published proceedings
Continuing contact among pioneers	Minutes from committee meetings
Brief mention of topic in library science lectures	
National clearinghouse (LOEX) established with grant funds	
First LOEX conference	
ALA Committee on Instruction in the Use of Libraries founded	
Stage: Elaboration (1971–1977)	
ACRL BI Task Force becomes a section	Description of units in *ALA Handbook of Organization*
Library Instruction Round Table formed in ALA	Newsletters and minutes from BI groups
First courses taught in library schools	BI guidelines and model statement of objectives developed and published
More internal and external funding of special BI projects	Reading lists, syllabi, and notes from courses
More librarians involved locally and nationally	More articles published with certain journals emphasizing BI
Numerous workshops and conferences on BI	Annual bibliography published in *Reference Services Review*
Papers given at discipline association meetings	Proceedings volumes continue to appear
Professional positions require BI ability	Vacancy announcements in journals
Terminology refined	Glossary of BI terms in *Bibliographic Instruction Handbook*

Table 5-2 (cont.)

Activities	Manifestations
Stage: Proliferation (1977–)	
Broader exchange of ideas	Column of opinion on BI issues
International groups start	appears in *Journal of Academic*
to form and international	*Librarianship*
conferences are held	Books and manuals begin
Methodology develops	to appear
State of the art compiled	Proceedings of international
Courses are reviewed for	conference published
inclusion in regular library	Encyclopedia articles appear
science curriculum	on BI
	Book-length retrospective
	bibliographies and textbooks
	are published
	Whole journal issue of *Library*
	Trends is devoted to overview
	of BI
Stage: Establishment (1977–)	
Dissertations appear on BI	List of dissertations
Attempts made to standardize	compiled by ACRL BI Section
BI	Research Committee
Think tank considers the	BI Section working on standards
future of the movement	for statistics and staff
	development training in BI
	Think tank conclusions
	summarized in *C&RL News*

This chapter discusses the principal dynamics in creating simple search strategy, one involving finding tools only, and amplifies that strategy to include the varieties of fact tools by considering the natural progression of any discipline as it develops over time. We believe that this perspective is critical to users at all levels and in all disciplines to give them the framework in which to understand their own research problems and the confidence to predict the appropriate fact, finding, and hybrid tools to meet their needs. Not incidentally, it is critical that all reference librarians come to an understanding of these principles as well, since they have a major influence on the selection of reference works to solve a particular analyzed research problem. Veteran reference librarians may well have developed through experience the feel for the progression of a discipline, but seeing it laid out in stages should help them to grasp the situation more quickly and more clearly, just as seeing Michael Keresztesi's outline helped us to do so some years ago.

Notes

1. Sharon J. Rogers, "Research Strategies: Bibliographic Instruction for Undergraduates," *Library Trends* 29 (Summer 1980): 69–70.

2. Thelma Freides, *Literature and Bibliography of the Social Sciences* (Los Angeles: Melville, 1973), pp. 5–18; Andrew Pope, "Bradford's Law and the Periodical Literature of Information Science," *ASIS Journal* 26: (July–August 1975): 207–213; B. C. Brookes, "Bradford's Law and the Bibliography of Science," *Nature* 224 (December 6, 1969): 953–956.

3. We are enormously indebted in this section to Michael Keresztesi of the Division of Library Science at Wayne State University and previously instructor in the School of Library Science at the University of Michigan. It is Keresztesi's basic conception of the universe of knowledge and the stream of scholarly communication on which our own models rest and from which we have developed virtually all of the theoretical portion of our work. An introduction to Keresztesi's thought appears in *Directions for the Decade: Library Instruction in the 1980s*, ed. by Carolyn A. Kirkendall, proceedings of the Tenth Annual Conference on Library Orientation for Academic Libraries, Library Orientation Series, No. 12 (Ann Arbor, Mich.: Pierian Press, 1981), pp. 41–49.

4. Elizabeth Frick, "Information Structure and Bibliographic Instruction," *Journal of Academic Librarianship* 1 (September 1975): 12–14, and Topsy N. Smalley, "Bibliographic Instruction in Academic Libraries: Questioning Some Assumptions," *Journal of Academic Librarianship* 3 (November 1977): 280–283.

6
The Research Process in the Humanities

Academic tradition divides the so-called humanities into three groups: disciplines such as literature and philosophy, the practitioners of which react to and interact with primary sources generated by others (written humanities); pursuits that themselves yield aesthetically pleasing primary sources in whatever medium (fine or creative arts); and activities that realize and interpret (performing arts). In addition, some hold that the historical sciences, insofar as they organize and reflect human endeavor, should also be counted among the humanities.

This chapter dicusses the characteristics and resulting bibliographic manifestations common only to the written humanities disciplines. Our reasoning is that the fine or creative arts depend less on person-to-person communication and structured research than they do on talent, inspiration, perseverance, and opportunity—all fragile assets, the successful combination of which is notoriously unpredictable. The performing arts, on the other hand, require physical and intellectual skills of great precision and sensitivity in order to translate the playwright's, composer's, or choreographer's ideas into aural and spatial reality. Each act or performance is unique, and although it can be recorded, studied, and even categorized, it is temporal and can never be reproduced. As a consequence, neither the fine arts, the creative arts, nor the performing arts have complete communication structures and the corresponding sets of fact and finding tools that would capture those structures in a reliable fashion. Search strategy can, of course, be devised for topics in the arts, but for the most part research must rely on the sources and logic of other discipline groups, most notably the written humanities.

Nature of the Humanities

The humanities are distinguished as the oldest group of recorded human experience, on the one hand, and as noncumulative endeavors on the other. These two distinctions reinforce each other since everyone who specializes in the humanities must go back to primary sources (the "wellsprings of civilization") and experience them uniquely. Thus, millennia of human thought must be read and responded to by each individual in every subsequent generation. In the humanities there is no substitute as in the other discipline groups for this mind-to-mind contact of author with reader across the printed page. No synopses and no literary histories, however thorough, can ever take the place of an enlightened interaction between the text and the student of it.

Another distinguishing feature of the humanities is that—at least in the twentieth-century Western world—there is no set curriculum that all those intending to specialize in the humanities must follow in a specific sequence. As a result, although one may with some degree of confidence assume that an English major is acquainted with certain "canonical" works ranging from those of Geoffrey Chaucer to those of John Cheever and that a graduate student will be even more knowledgeable, to predict exactly what any given person may have read at a particular point in his or her education is impossible. From the BI point of view, this makes selecting common allusions or examples something of a challenge, which can only be overcome in the course-related or course-integrated modes where it is possible to learn from a faculty member or syllabus exactly what students are reading at that point and so relate the instruction to those interests.

The written humanities as a group include literature in all its national guises, comparative literature, the study of language as it relates to human expression, philosophy, theology and religion, and the critical and therefore secondary responses to the fine or creative arts. This final category consists of music history, musicology, and art history, for example. Obviously, the humanities disciplines have characteristics of the historical sciences on the one hand and of the social sciences on the other. In this chapter, we focus on the features that the humanities disciplines have in common with one another and that have a bearing on their bibliographic structure and the research process of students and scholars in those fields.

Historically, secondary sources in the humanities are related both to philology and to Western philosophy. Linguistics, classics, English and American literature, and the various modern foreign language departments in our colleges and universities are all descendants of nineteenth-century philology, which emphasized a close study of the primary text. The various literature areas in particular are by now full-grown fields, exhibiting all the features of a mature discipline and the corresponding bibliographic tools to control primary and secondary sources—to the satisfaction of scholars, if not of reference librarians. Linguistics is somewhat newer as a separate field of study and is in the process of twigging, as fields such as semiotics, phonology, and psycholinguistics split off. Philosophy, together with its cousins theology and religion, is centuries old and has remained vital and vibrant throughout that time. As has linguistics, the fields of philosophy, theology, and religion have yielded new disciplines over the years and doubtless will continue to do so. Music, art history, and related disciplines share almost identical characteristics with literature as regards the needs and communication patterns of scholars who are producing secondary sources.

The research patterns of scholars in the humanities are more-or-less stable since specialists in the various subfields are expected to receive their training in one of the standard academic departments. Hence they are exposed to the entire range of primary and secondary source material and to the rigors and traditions that have developed over centuries. However avant-garde their own work, they are likely to follow the research and communication behaviors that distinguish the parent disciplines.

Scholar Research Behavior

Scholars in the humanities almost always work alone, both in the sense that they perform their research by themselves—or with the help of a student assistant—and in the sense that they believe themselves engaged in a unique project. Starting from what they see as a special perception about one or more primary sources, humanities researchers deal either exclusively with the sources themselves or with the secondary literature that has accreted around them over the years. Humanities research takes place for the most part in libraries and archives and in the private studies of individual scholars. It is often essential for the scholar to visit research repositories known or thought to contain rare source material that must be examined in person.[1]

For the most part, humanities scholars undertake their research with little outside funding, either from their institutions or from foundations or government agencies. Such grants as Fulbright Fellowships are scarce, and most scholars receive any given award but once in their careers. As a result, in an attempt to conserve personal resources, a person is likely to save up research for several projects to get the most out of a single trip. Often, too, when funding is available for travel to permit consultation of necessary materials, support is minimal. Living expenses and direct research costs (for example, photocopying) may have to be borne by the individual.

Humanities scholars seldom if ever share their findings with colleagues before the final publication of an article or monograph. Such secretive behavior is partly a function of the private nature of the research in the first place and partly of the presumed uniqueness of a given project and the scholar's fear of having an idea "appropriated" by someone else in the field. Reticence is less common if the work involves a textbook, an anthology, a standard edition, or a reference tool; in these cases much correspondence and collaboration are required. If a major funded project involves several humanities scholars, the sponsoring institution or agency will have a right to expect regular progress reports and will probably also describe the effort in detail in a newsletter or fact sheet.

Scholar Communication Patterns

Publishing in the humanities is fairly clearcut; most research appears as either a journal article or a monograph in book format. The importance of other forms of communication—for example, preprints, reprints, or proceedings—is negligible compared with their significance for other discipline groups. Reprints, that is, extra printed copies of an entire article that the author received from a journal publisher, are common in the humanities and frequently exchanged as favors among colleagues. Reprints do not, however, constitute a major communication link among scholars since journal issues invariably appear before reprints are available; hence the reprint is no "news." The exchange of reprints is more a social phenomenon than a method of intellectual communication in the humanities.

Several points should be made about publishing in scholarly journals in the humanities. For one thing, numerous journals are appropriate for any given article a researcher may wish to submit. Consequently, it is not always clear to others working in the same area where relevant articles might turn up. This makes regular browsing of current issues more important than it may be in other disciplines and also means that there is no substitute for monitoring the major bibliographies and periodical indexes. Since multiple submission of the same article to several journals is taboo, months can pass before a contribution is accepted if one or more publications reject it initially. The most prestigious journals are refereed—that is, all submissions are sent, often with the authors' names withheld to ensure impartiality, to scholars in the field for their recommendation on which articles should be published—which only increases editors' response time, and in any event the feeling is that publication of research findings is not pressing.

Another salient characteristic of journal article publication in the written humanities is that scholars traditionally regard at least the major European languages as common knowledge, and hence they will publish articles in any number of languages on any given topic. It is not unusual to find an article about Baruch Spinoza written in French and published in an Italian philosophy journal. That same issue might very well carry other articles on the philosopher in English, in German, perhaps even in Japanese. Occasionally but not frequently, an article will be preceded by an English-language abstract, but seldom is a humanities journal translated in entirety into English, and in these rare instances the issue will appear in translation years after the original. It is much more common for a major scholarly journal routinely to publish articles in any of several Western European languages. This may not present a problem to those trained in the rigorous continental tradition, but it is certainly a difficulty for all but the most brilliant and eclectic American scholars trained since World

War II. The language competency requirement for the Ph.D. in virtually all universities in the United States can be fulfilled with one or two reading courses in a foreign language, or in some instances by taking an exam or successfully passing graduate level courses in a language. This does not, of course, mean that the student is comfortable enough, especially years later, with a foreign language to do any in-depth research or reading in it. Furthermore, many humanities departments will substitute an ancient language—Greek, Latin, or Anglo-Saxon—for a modern foreign one, and although the classical influence can be applauded, it does not contribute to contemporary communication among scholars and will not do so unless articles are published in the older tongues. (The closest we have come to a return to the classics is the amusing reversion to Latin some years ago by the *Internationale Bibliographie der Zeitschriftenliteratur* and *Internationale Bibliographie der Rezensionen* indexes for spine titles!)

Journals in the humanities generally are published quarterly or less frequently; many claiming quarterly publication appear months after the cover date on each issue. In some cases double or triple issues or a complete scrapping and reworking of the numbering scheme occurs in an effort to catch up. The truth is, of course, that other than being an aggravation to the scholars whose articles appear late, a minor nuisance to personal subscribers, and a major headache to serials librarians, who continually claim things that are on their own unique and unpredictable schedule, there is no great urgency about 99 percent of the work published in the humanities.

Whether a particular article in a humanities journal appears this month or next, this year or next, has no earth-shaking consequences for those who will read it and be influenced by it. By and large the course of the discipline is not changed significantly when one article appears "out of sequence" with another. This goes back to the principle that scholars in the humanities work in private and do not engage in the kind of intense incubation of an idea or validity testing that researchers in the social sciences and sciences rely on. It is not at all uncommon in the humanities to find letters to the editor or even entire major articles of confrontation or refutation to an earlier publication as long as two or three years following the initial article. The same, of course, is true of the book-reviewing cycles in the humanities. As a result, and especially because scholarly works typically go out of print quickly, waiting for reviews in the more prestigious journals is often an exercise in futility. By the time the review, however judicious or laudatory, does appear, the book may be unobtainable.

Exceptions to the quarterly or less frequent publication of scholarly journals in the humanities are the various "literary reviews," such as *Atlantic Monthly, Saturday Review,* and *The New Yorker.* These more popular publications bridge the gap between the scholarly, esoteric journals on the one hand and the humanities as presented in newspapers, weekly news magazines, and the media generally on the other. Such "middle-brow" periodicals are addressed to the educated, but not to the specialized, public, and help both to form taste and to reflect it. Furthermore, humanities scholars who "make a name" for themselves and who have a certain flair in their thinking and prose for making current intellectual movements accessible to the educated public are frequent contributors to these periodicals, using them as forums for their thought-in-progress. Reviews of contemporary art, literature, and music appear quickly in these highly regarded publications.

Still another feature of journals in the humanities is that their orientation will likely be around (in the case of literature) a given period, genre, or author, or (in the case of philosophy) a specific school of thought or national movement. Sometimes a journal's focus will even combine period and genre or nationality and discipline, for instance, *Modern Fiction Studies* and the *Journal of English Linguistics.*

Most journals today are sponsored by either specialized societies—particularly the case of single-author newsletters so well documented by Margaret C. Patterson in her bibliography[2]—or else by academic departments in colleges and universities. Relatively few humanities journals are issued by major commercial publishers or by university presses. The reason is obvious: Scholarly journals in the humanities do not make a profit, at least not at the current subscription rates, which tend barely to cover the costs of materials, printing, and mailing, and certainly in no sense recompense authors and editors, who almost never receive any remuneration for their efforts.

One might think that because scholarly journals are relatively inexpensive, they would receive wide distribution; ironically, however, comparatively low salaries often prevent scholars from subscribing to more than one or two journals other than those they receive automatically as part of memberships in professional societies. Because profits are so marginal, finding bookstores, let alone general newsstands, that will carry scholarly journals is difficult. Only those who live in major cities or university towns are able to buy issues of scholarly journals off a rack. Furthermore, although this is an era of copyright consciousness, it is usually easy to obtain permission without charge or with a nominal fee to reprint portions of articles from scholarly journals in the humanities. The problem, however, is that obtaining such permission may be very time consuming, because one is generally dealing with an editor who has many other academic chores besides answering correspondence.

Most societies in the humanities have as one of their major objects and activities the publication of one or more scholarly journals, which are carefully—and these days often anonymously—juried. A large part of the annual dues to the organization goes to support the journal, which very likely will have an in-house editor at the association's headquarters. As is true of journals sponsored by academic departments, however, those that are published by societies do not pay contributors—other than by sending them several reprints or extra issues for distribution to colleagues (and sometimes they will even request a small payment for these). Because of the jury system, the acceptance process is excruciatingly slow, or so it seems to younger scholars for whom a tenure decision may hang on the outcome.

A twentieth-century phenomenon is the little magazines. These publications carry fresh primary source material that would have no other outlet in our society: the plays, poetry, short stories, and serialized novels that are not picked up by commercial or small publishers and that are not popular enough to be included in the large circulation periodicals. Little magazines are for primary sources in the humanities what scholarly journals are for secondary. (Of course, that distinction is not always clear-cut since some scholarly journals also publish poetry and interviews and print newly discovered documents.) Little magazines are, however, a major communication link in the humanities, especially in literature, offering material that would otherwise go unpublished. Like the scholarly journals, most little magazines are not profit-making and are published as an act of love on the part of the editors without hope of compensation beyond breaking even. Another similarity is that little magazines often do not keep to a set schedule, but they appear whenever sufficient material warrants the release of the next issue. Also, like scholarly serials, little magazines are often hard to obtain unless one subscribes; so scholars must depend on libraries to receive these titles.

The history of scholarly publication in the humanities is closely tied in the last century to the history of Victorian periodicals, a subject so intricate, so complex, and so important that separate societies exist for its study.[3]

Other forms of public communication among scholars in the humanities include letters-to-the-editor, which appear in perhaps half the scholarly journals, and extended in-print controversies among specialists debating a point of view or refuting an earlier commentator's position. Such discussions can go on for years and have been institutionalized in such publications as *Notes and Queries* and *American Notes and Queries*. Similar communication occurs in the *New York Times Book Review*; these inquiries always follow the formula: "For a book about X, I am seeking Y kinds of information. Please respond to ——."

An extremely useful function of many scholarly journals, but not of the little magazines, is the regular or occasional publication of annotated bibliographies or bibliographic essays on highly specific topics. *Bulletin of Bibliography* is the extreme—and extremely good—case of a serial wholly devoted to publishing bibliographies on highly specialized topics, preponderantly in the humanities. Some journals, such as *Studies in English Literature, 1500–1900,* have institutionalized this feature so that each quarterly issue carries a bibliography focused on a different period. Other journals will devote a single issue to a given author or topic and will include a bibliography as one article in that particular issue. Generally, researchers who compile such bibliographies are extremely thorough, and they clearly set out their principles and scope in an introductory note. Many times these bibliographies are more up-to-date and more inclusive than those on the same topic in the major literary bibliographies such as the *MLA International Bibliography* or the *Year's Work in English Studies.* The importance of *Bibliographic Index* in identifying bibliographies appearing in journals cannot be overemphasized.

Proceedings of association conferences in the humanities are generally not separately published as they are typically in the social sciences and sciences. Instead, an interested editor of a specialized journal may offer to publish the proceedings of a short conference or of a few select sessions within a conference. Or, a publisher, probably a university press, will agree to publish the proceedings much as publishers may volunteer to do a collection of articles in honor of a notable scholar. If neither of these avenues for eventual publication materializes, those making presentations at a conference must submit their papers, just as they would an article, to an appropriate journal and then wait the agonizing months to receive a decision on acceptance.

In general, attendance at conferences is not intellectually critical to specialists in the humanities, especially if they have established their own private network of correspondence with the few other individuals in the world who are working on the same area, and if they make an effort to keep current with the dozen or so relevant journals or little magazines that' carry work in their area. Conferences, of course, serve not only a social and employment function, but also a broader professional one of establishing contacts among specialists. Regional and topical conferences often bring together the most eminent researchers in a field, who would not be likely to attend the more diffuse conferences of professional associations. Foreign scholars are also more likely to be present at such highly specialized gatherings to share their insights and approaches.

Monographs and book publications in the humanities have some prominent characteristics. First, few textbooks appear in any of the humanities other than those addressed to the secondary or beginning college level. On the other hand, there are numerous anthologies, either of material that previously appeared in scholarly journals or was presented at conferences. Anthologies of specially contributed articles are frequently compiled in honor of a great thinker in a field or, less often, to commemorate an event, such as the founding of an academic department at a university. These volumes, called *Festschriften*, mélanges, or homage volumes, can be a rich source of information on a particular author or topic.

Monographic series are extremely prevalent in the humanities, especially in Germany where every university and every *philosophische Fakultät* will issue one or more series of volumes, often numbering into the hundreds. In the United States and Great Britain, numbered monographic series are much less common, but scholars in the humanities are publishing monographic treatments on absolutely every subject, and these are being published not only by university presses, but by the larger and more enlightened commercial publishers as well. This is not to say that many, or even any, scholarly works in the humanities are best-sellers these days or that any publisher expects to do more than break even, but some publishers are still willing to undertake the careful editing and fine printing of monographs in the humanities, and in doing so they provide scholars with yet another communication link.

Various dissertation series also appear, several from publishers in Europe as well as the quasi publication provided by University Microfilms International for the majority of United States Ph.D. dissertations. Of course, those most interested in a topic are generally other Ph.D. candidates working in the same area; for when a work has true and lasting merit, it is usually published eventually in an updated and revised version by one of the standard university or commercial publishers.

The time lag in the publication of books in the humanities is not much greater than that in the social sciences or the sciences, at least if one counts time from the submission of the manuscript and its acceptance to the appearance of the final volume. The constraints of the editing and production of any book are uniform across discipline groups; so rarely does a book appear sooner than six months after acceptance. (Publishers who do not have the manuscript typeset or input into a computer, but require the author to submit camera-ready copy for reproduction, can work on a much tighter schedule and will have lower costs.)

Finances and the Profession

Much has been written and many tears shed bemoaning society's apparent low valuation of scholars in the humanities as evidenced by their salary and by their relatively low status among professionals. Much ado has also been made about the extremely bad job market for new Ph.D.s in the United States in any of the humanities fields and of the scarcity of alternative careers that would adequately both use their extensive skills and prove aesthetically and intellectually challenging. Research support is also meager in the humanities, whether from academic institutions, private foundations, or public agencies. Furthermore, the duration of most grant support is short in this field, usually no more than an academic year and usually without renewal. Amounts generally supplement a regular salary rather than substitute for it; so humanities scholars must continually worry about personal finances even as they acknowledge the congratulations of colleagues for having received a prestigious award.

Fellowships and apprenticeships, another aspect of the humanities, have a bearing on bibliographic structure. Aside from the custom of appointing graduate students as teaching or research assistants, few "sidekick" opportunities are available in the humanities. An exception would be the few major projects such as the *Middle English Dictionary* at the University of Michigan, which employs numerous postdoctoral scholars, or the *Wellesley Index to Victorian Periodicals*, which has the same sort of staffing.

One result of the absence of apprenticeships is that when students finish their dissertations, they are expected to "go it alone" ever after. The mentor-protégé relationship ceases all too frequently on the day of the oral defense and—in certain sad cases—it is replaced by competition between the erstwhile graduate students and their former advisers. Often, all the fledgling can hope for is support from younger colleagues in a similar situation. Unfortunately, this go-it-alone tendency in the written humanities only serves to reinforce each person's own research limitations. The consequence is faculty inability to sense students' near total ignorance of library research methods. The "old boy" intellectual network once fostered by the academy has been transformed in our time into largely social and political ties among humanities scholars, who have only the vaguest notions about the bibliographic structure of their fields.

Generation of Sources

Figure 6-1 is a model of the generation of sources in the humanities. The problems that affect these dynamics concern transmission of the written word across time and cultures: editing and printing history of any text, translation, and performance. Each successive individual in this model necessarily interacts, even if unconsciously, with all previous sources and individuals as well as with the original phenomenon; in

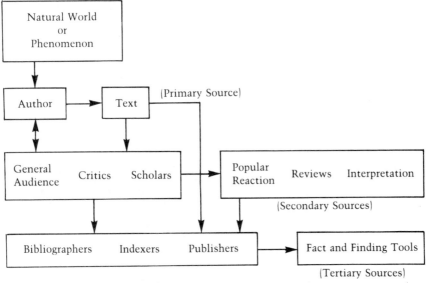

Figure 6-1. Generation of sources in the written humanities: a basic model.

other words, the model is continually accretive as each person is "caught up" by the primary source.

In Table 6-1, a basic diagram that is deceptively simple, we assume that a primary source is already in hand and that the research topic has been chosen if not yet fully defined. We have used this table as an all-purpose handout in BI lectures for humanities courses. Adapted in that way, it is helpful to print it lengthwise on two sides of a sheet of paper, leaving approximately one-third of each page blank to the right, for students to jot down the specific titles they consult for each type of tool named. Such a chart can become a helpful addition to a research diary, indicating exactly what steps were taken in developing a project.

Given the critical importance of communication via journal articles in the humanities, step III and step IV A and B (Table 6-1) should be elaborated so that students come to recognize the premier role of finding tools for their research.

An understanding of the shape of the humanities and of the basic research process for their study is essential to anyone majoring in the area. Nothing is at all difficult about the discipline contours sketched here, but nonmajors taking humanities courses may not want to deal with the entire scheme, and only concentrate on the search strategy itself. In

Table 6-1 Library Research: Basic Strategy for the Humanities

In Order To	Refer To
I. Find out what reference works exist relating to your general topic	Guide Card catalog under appropriate subject heading(s) as found in *Library of Congress Subject Headings* Librarian
II. Survey factual background of topic	Fact tools: A. Basic reference works: encyclopedias, handbooks/companions, special dictionaries, biographical sets/directories B. Monographs: literary histories, biographies, "classics" of scholarship
III. Identify existing ("ready-made") bibliographies and survey research background	Guide, as in Step I Bibliography of bibliographies Bibliographic essays (reviews of research) Items in Steps I and II
IV. Compile your own bibliography (always noting exact source of each citation)	Finding tools: A. Bibliographies: general, completed; general, ongoing; specialized, completed; specialized, ongoing B. Indexes: periodical, current; periodical, retrospective; newspaper; specialized; citation C. Card catalog, under subject D. National and special library catalogs E. Book trade bibliographies F. Dissertation lists G. Browse current journals
V. Locate materials	Card catalog, by main entry Union catalogs and lists Interlibrary loan, if necessary

VI. Read, take notes, evaluate sources, formulate new subtopics or questions to pursue; repeat relevant steps above for each subtopic; develop your own arguments and outline.

VII. Consider other types of material and research tools: manuscripts, archival material, microforms, government documents, maps, phonorecords, reviews, citation indexes, statistics, oral history, and so on.

VIII. Consider related disciplines: art, education, film, folklore, history, journalism, linguistics, and so on.

any case, each point in this chapter can be expanded or embellished to meet the needs of more advanced students.

Notes

1. An especially fascinating assortment of stories about research "hunts" in literature has been published by Richard D. Altick, *The Scholar Adventurers* (New York: Macmillan, 1950).

2. Margaret C. Patterson, *Author Newsletters and Journals: An International Annotated Bibliography of Serial Publications Concerned with the Life and Works of Individual Authors,* American Literature, English Literature, and World Literatures in English, vol. 19 (Detroit: Gale Research, 1979).

3. The Research Society for Victorian Periodicals (RSVP), founded in 1969; headquarters at Southern Illinois University, Carbondale, Ill.

7
The Research
Process in History

The disciplines that have been discussed thus far, that is, disciplines that fall under the humanities, and those in the following chapter on social science exhibit somewhat similar general characteristics. History, on the other hand, seems to be a hybrid somewhere between the humanities and the social sciences. This is evident not only in the primary sources that exist for the study of history, but in the variety of secondary literature produced by historians and in the reference works generated to define, control, and identify the secondary literature. The discipline models that apply to humanities and the social sciences work well when discussing history, but it demands its own unique approach when building a conceptual model for bibliographic instruction.

One dominant characteristic of history as a discipline is the debate over whether it is a humanity or a social science. Writers such as Bert F. Hoselitz[1] stress the humanities origins and the esthetic evaluation of written history as literature. Hoselitz traces the changes that occurred during the nineteenth century and the European influence that began to make history more scientific. John Higham analyzes the impact of specialization on the intellectual life of Europe and America and describes the unique evolution of the professions in this country as they were influenced by democracy. Historical writing as a province of the "gentleman scholar" was particularly affected.[2] A 1969 state-of-the-art survey of history by the Behavorial and Social Sciences Survey History Panel recognizes that even today some historians use the humanities approach and some use the methodology of the social sciences,[3] and each side tends to be aligned with certain subfields of history. Some even consider history as art or as science.[4]

Although the debate over the nature of history would not necessarily be the center of a history-oriented BI lecture, an understanding of the evolution of history as a discipline, and of the various viewpoints that exist toward the use of primary material of history or even what constitutes primary material, will help the BI librarian to focus the lecture for the audience. Even within a small history department, faculty may have widely diverging viewpoints as to the nature of historical research. As a result, a successful BI lecture on primary material for one course may be a disaster for another.

Another characteristic of history, which helps to shape the conceptual model, is the age of the discipline itself, beginning with the writings of the Greek historians and stretching through time up to the current events of today as shown on television. The literature is old and vast and is the result of a number of methological schools of thought and approaches. Like the text of an original Greek poem that has been redescribed and reevaluated over the centuries by critic after critic, so the documentary evidence of years of civilization is sifted and resifted by each new generation of history scholars. The dichotomy of old history being reevaluated, while at the same time current history is being generated, means that the canvas of time over which any scholar or student must scan is equal to the written history of civilization itself. In this sense, history is a humanity and reflects the model of literature or fine arts, which begins with a work of art and generates a new school of criticism with each generation.

History is characterized by active participation in and output by both amateur and professional historians. During the nineteenth century, when specialization in the academic world led to the new disciplines of anthropology, psychology, and sociology, history, as an established discipline practiced by scholars, was also affected. History, however, proved to be unique. As a core of academic professional historians evolved, a large number of active amateur historians continued to exist. They wrote and published alongside their academic counterparts. The dichotomy exists to the present day. What other nonliterary discipline has a Pulitzer Prize? Biography, regional history, and history of the American Civil War all find ready markets in the United States and are reviewed in such magazines as *Saturday Review, Time,* and the *New York Review of Books.*

The dichotomy has also produced a wide range of local, state, and regional historical societies, which may be public or semipublic, as well as private groups and clubs whose emphasis is a particular region, period, or ethnic group, such as the former Mississippi Valley Historical Society, First Families of Virginia, and the State Historical Society of Michigan.[5] The number and variety of these institutions is characterized by a directory to state and local historical societies,[6] directories to ethnic societies, and even more specialized directories such as those concerning museums of historical significance in Michigan. Few other disciplines, except perhaps the theater, can match the enthusiasm and wide range of interest in a subject.

The professionalization of history at the end of the nineteenth century was marked by two developments: fragmentation and subspecialization within the field of history, and standardization of the methodological approach through the introduction of more scientific methods. Until the mid-nineteenth century, the emphasis in history had been on the broad view of military, diplomatic, or political matters, generally approached by country or period. Specialization by historians and the standardization of methodological approaches meant that other areas were now explored, including economic history, cultural history, intellectual history, and, more recently, the history of ethnic groups. The national or international emphasis of the nineteenth century became local and regional with the writing of county and state histories and histories of the Midwest, South, or western frontier.

The application of social science methods has meant that the emphasis on primary material, that is, letters, diaries, manuscripts, newspapers, or other written evidence that remains extant, which has always been important to history, has been expanded. Now included are photographs, oral accounts, material culture evidence such as furniture, clothing, and tools, crime statistics, account books of businesses, membership lists of various societies, and so on. All are clues to the political leanings, cultural emphasis, or sociological context in which major political or diplomatic events occurred.

Not only have the types of primary evidence examined by historians expanded over the years, but the availability/access and format of such evidence had shifted. During the nineteenth century, state and local historical societies reprinted primary documents in monograph series or other publications, making the "written" primary evidence available to scholars at large. Today, the trend continues with the reprinting of various diaries, bills, codes, and state papers, but the format is now microfilm. Access is thus restricted by both the cost of purchasing an entire set and the need to purchase special equipment for viewing and reproduction. An even more recent trend is the data input into computers for manipulation, for example, statistics and the census record; a database also permits multiple access points to a large body of information, for example, architectural surveys.[7] Ironically, the technology that allows manipulation of data far beyond that which can be handled by one person also requires both technical expertise and large sums of money. Thus, access to information never before available to historians is coupled with the restrictions of economics and specialized training.

The emphasis by historians on gathering and examining primary data and relevant secondary literature has two important spin-offs. First is the need to locate and look at primary documents, which has always led to a concern with bibliographical apparatus. Production of bibliographies in the field of history dates from the eighteenth and nineteenth centuries and continues today with unabated fervor. Second, the emphasis on original research means that the historian must review the facts and put them in context. Group research with one person responsible for a portion of it or reliance on several graduate research assistants to do a historian's work is not a general practice.[8]

Although the field of history and its several subspecialties exhibit the unique characteristics just outlined, other disciplines have historical aspects and, therefore, can be conceptualized by BI librarians in the same way as the field of history: the historical aspects of anthropology, archaeology, and geography, as well as the history of science, the history of medicine, the history of art and architecture. All have a time span, all rely heavily on the evaluation of primary documents, and researchers in these fields exhibit great interest in the production of bibliography.

Literature and Reference Works of History

As with the other disciplines described in this book, a direct relationship exists between the content of history and the formats of both the secondary and tertiary (reference books) literature. The standardization of methodology led to attempts to codify or unify the approach to history. This was done in two ways. One was the production of very large multivolume sets of history such as the *New Cambridge Modern History* (Cambridge, Mass.: University Press, 1957–). A second way was to have a UNESCO-sponsored international congress of historians each decade to review the progress and methodology of historians. Each effort has slowed in recent years. The fragmentation of history, particularly in the 1970s, into social history, ethnic histories, women's studies, and urban history, has made it difficult to have one unified approach to a span of history. For the same reason, there is not an encyclopedia of history or a single agreed-upon summation of history or methodology. There are many books of historiography, such as *The Modern Researcher* by Jacques Barzun and Henry F. Graff (New York: Harcourt, 1970); *A Guide to Historical Method*, edited by Robert Jones Shafer (Homewood, Ill.: Dorsey Press, 1974); and *Understanding History: A Primer of Historical Method* by Louis Reichenthal Goltschalt (New York: Knopf, 1950). The closest conceptualization of a methodology is in the *International Encyclopedia of Social Sciences*, which includes the social science aspects of history. The emphasis in publication of secondary literature continues to be monographs or monographic sets for larger topics and journal articles for exploration of smaller facets of history.

There is no dictionary of historical terminology, although the facts and events of history can be found in handbooks such as the *Oxford Companion to American History*, *Oxford Companion to Canadian History and Literature*, and the *Encyclopedia of the American Revolution*, as well as various dictionaries of political science. Despite its name, the *Dictionary of American History* is also a handbook, being a record of various events, laws, dates, battles, and people. In addition to handbooks that record the facts, chronologies abound in the field of history, such as *Chronology of the Expanding*

World, 1492–1762 by Neville Williams (New York: McKay, 1969) and *The Encyclopedia of American Facts and Dates,* 6th ed. by Gorton Carruth (New York: Crowell, 1972). Handbooks and chronologies establish facts and dates that are important in the substantive narration of history.

As already mentioned, directories are common, directories of state and regional historical societies, directories for regions, and directories of ethnic groups, particularly those that emphasize historical holdings.

In terms of finding tools, bibliographies abound. Bibliographies of historical sources both primary and secondary are found in the nineteenth century and continue in abundance into the twentieth century. The bibliographies of bibliography for world history are evidence of the number of bibliographies and the interest in bibliography. Examples are *Bibliographies in American History: Guide to Materials for Research* by Henry P. Beers (New York: Wilson, 1942) and *Historical Bibliographies: A Systematic and Annotated Guide* by Edith M. Coulter (Berkeley: University of California Press, 1935). There are also selected bibliographies, such as the *Harvard Guide to American History* (Cambridge, Mass.: Harvard University Press, 1974), and comprehensive, retrospective bibliographies that reflect the subfields of history. Retrospective bibliographies may concentrate on a state or a region, on a single country or time period, or on a topic (social, intellectual, cultural, ethnic). There are bibliographies of only primary materials or secondary materials, for example, *American Diaries in Manuscript, 1580–1954: A Descriptive Bibliography* by William Matthews (Athens: University of Georgia Press, 1974) and *The Truman and Eisenhower Years 1945–1960* by Margaret L. Stapleton (Metuchen, N.J.: Scarecrow, 1973), as well as bibliographies that lead to both, for example, *A Guide to the Principal Sources for Early American History (1600–1800) in the City of New York,* 2d. ed. rev. by Evarts Boutell Greene and Richard B. Morris (New York: Columbia University Press, 1953).

Indexes in history have until recently tended to be spotty and slow in production. Large multivolume retrospective indexes do exist, such as Bibliothèque Nationale, Dépt. des Imprimés, *Catalogue de l'histoire de France* (Paris: Didot, 1855–95), but ongoing current indexes are difficult to find until the twentieth century. With the advent of *Historical Abstracts* (Santa Barbara, Calif.: Clio Press 1955–) its companion *America: History and Life* (Santa Barbara: Clio Press,

1964–), and *Recently Published Articles* (New York: American Historical Assn., 1976–), coverage is now quite timely of international, national, and regional and local history.

The field of history, however, is marked by the absence of an ongoing annual review. A survey of the scholar research behavior conducted in 1967 by Dagmar Horna Perman showed that historians preferred to scan lists of articles or books rather than relying on someone else's evaluation of a year's publications or on abstracts of an article's content.[9]

Primary source material for history is as varied as the areas of history itself. Students of history need to understand the variety and variability, which includes the following: manuscripts, including letters, diaries, travel accounts, and maps; archives, including archives of companies, religious groups, institutes, institutions, and various government agencies (national, local, regional, and territorial); printed materials such as newspapers, old periodicals, almanacs, portraits in books, biographies and autobiographies, historical series, maps, government documents (international, federal, territorial, state, and local) songs, and literature.

Nonprint primary sources include oral history, photographs, artwork, and film, as well as artifacts such as spoons, knives, dresses, and quilts found in museums. Primary sources can be found in various formats: print, nonprint, microfilm (which could include newspapers, archives, state records, manuscripts, government documents, and census records), and computer databases.

A Model for Students

When constructing a concept model for the field of history—whether to explain to college seniors the resources available for studying the Federal Period, to stress to high school seniors the viewpoints that must be understood when evaluating various newspaper accounts of current events, or to describe family history sources to a local genealogical club—several important characteristics about the field of history should be emphasized: (1) the time span involved, (2) the age of the subspecialty, and (3) the nature and number of primary sources.

One way to talk "theoretically" about the problems inherent in library research in history is to pose topics that illustrate the dimensions of history as a discipline, such as the following:

1. What was the Confederate army's strategy at the Battle of Bull Run?
2. Compare the circumstances surrounding the Kennedy-Khrushchev talks of the 1960s and the Sadat-Begin talks of the late 1970s.
3. What was the role of Mexican-Americans in local society when New Mexico attained statehood?

The first question above illustrates the time span involved; that is, secondary material about the Battle of Bull Run would appear from just after the Civil War to the present. The American Civil War has long been a popular topic from political, military, economic, and social points of view. Specialized books, chronologies, handbooks, and bibliographies on it are available. A researcher will face the problem of selecting and choosing from both popular and scholarly material. Secondary material will be accessible from approaches as broad as the United States—History, to the Civil War, to the Confederacy, to material that might be available in the Virginia historical journals or in biographical materials on generals who led the campaigns. The problem is one of selection and approach before tackling the mass of information available.

The second question—on the Kennedy-Khrushchev, Sadat-Begin talks—illustrates the dichotomy of time with older material existing in both popular and scholarly books and journals under basic, general headings, such as U.S. Diplomatic Relations, versus the more current event segment, which may contain popular items (newspapers, news magazines) but little scholarly material. One can discuss the method of approaching current materials as primary materials.

The third question, on Mexican-Americans, illustrates the difficulty inherent in dealing with a topic that is old, but that has recently regained scholarly attention. It would be almost impossible to find material directly under the heading Chicanos or Mexican-Americans or the various terms that might be used locally in New Mexico. The existing primary and secondary material must be reevaluated with this particular aspect of history in mind. Similar problems in access to information were found a number of years ago when interest increased in women's studies and black history.

Another approach, which emphasizes the characteristics of history as a discipline, is to explore the wide range of primary documents. The following list illustrates how, using a fairly straightforward topic such as question 3 above, one can see at a glance the disciplines that might be explored with this topic, the availability of secondary sources, and the vast number of primary sources available for original research.

Disciplines	*Secondary Sources*
History	Encyclopedias
Anthropology	Histories
Sociology	Books
Political Science	Anthologies
Law	Journals
Religion	Conference proceedings
Fine Arts	
Music	
Literature	

Primary Sources

Manuscripts: diaries, letters, travel accounts, maps

Archives: railroads, ranches, churches, government (national, local, territorial, foreign, state, judicial, executive, legislative, military)

Printed: newspapers, periodicals, biographies, autobiographies, maps, broadsides, almanacs, statistics, travel accounts, literature

Nonprinted: Oral history, photographs, film, artwork, music

Museums: artifacts

Formats: print, nonprint, manuscript, microform, computer database

One approach used at the University of Michigan with both upper-level honors students and graduate students is to have the class generate the list of sources that might be available for a particular question and then to group them on the board in clusters. The lecturer can then identify primary sources within the library, discuss problems in identifying the various formats, and describe the use of primary material, such as manuscripts or statistical compilations.

Notes

1. Bert F. Hoselitz, *A Reader's Guide to the Social Sciences* (New York: Free Press, 1959), pp. 26–69.

2. John Higham, "The Matrix of Specialization," *Organization of Knowledge in Modern America, 1860–1920*, ed. by Alexandra Oleson and John Voss (Baltimore: Johns Hopkins University Press, 1979), p. 2.

3. David S. Landes and Charles Tilly, eds., *History As a Social Science* (Englewood Cliffs, N.J.: Prentice Hall, 1971), pp. 5–21.

4. Henry H. Stuart Hughes, *History as Art and as Science: Twin Vistas on the Past* (New York: Harper & Row, 1964).

5. Hoselitz, *Reader's Guide*, pp. 57–59.

6. *Directory of Historical Societies and Agencies in the U.S. and Canada* (Madison, Wis.: American Association for State and Local History, 1956–).

7. The rapid growth of databases utilized by historians was discussed by Judith S. Rowe in "Primary Data for Historical Research: New Machine-Readable Resources," Reference and Adult Services Division Program, American Library Association Annual Conference, San Francisco, July 1981.

8. Landes and Tilly, *History As a Social Science*, pp. 19–20.

9. Dagmar Horna Perman, ed., *Bibliography and the Historian*, The Conference at Belmont of the Joint Committee on Bibliographic Services to History (Santa Barbara, Calif.: Clio Press, 1967), p. 18.

8
The Research
Process in the
Social Sciences

This chapter concentrates on the social science of psychology because its characteristics and tools closely reflect the "ideal" social science structure and also because librarians are frequently called on to present BI lectures to psychology students, who are expected to identify relevant literature to support their experimental designs. We consider in detail the discipline of psychology as representative of all the social sciences, discussing its nature and development, including communication patterns of its scholars and the bibliographic paradigm that controls the literature they generate. A full research plan for psychology is described, with an outline of the actual lecture one can give on the topic. We also compare these aspects of psychology research with corresponding elements in the other major social science disciplines: anthropology, economics, political science, and sociology.

The Nature of Psychological
Literature

Psychology is a relatively young discipline, having developed out of the disciplines of philosophy and medicine in the late nineteenth century. It is experimental and observational in nature and depends heavily on current information. Researchers tend to know other scholars working on similar issues and they communicate personally with one another by telephone, letter, or preprints (mimeographed reports distributed before possible publication).

Although this type of informal communication is indeed current, it rarely finds it way into libraries and has virtually no bibliographic control. Proceedings of psychology conferences do, however, reach libraries and are somewhat controlled. The "invisible college" (network or clique) of scholars is instrumental in inviting its members to present their latest work at meetings. Bibliographic control of conference proceedings is divided among several sources; the proceedings typically take two years to purchase and catalog, and if a particular proceeding is not owned by the library, it can be difficult to obtain.

Journal articles form the bulk of psychological literature. Although articles are somewhat dated (one to two years old) by the time they are published, they are still among the most current forms of such literature and are readily available in the library or through interlibrary loan.

Differences between primary and secondary material are not an issue in psychology as they can be in the humanities. Psychologists work with reports of empirical research and research reviews, rather than with an original manuscript and its various editions and literary criticism over the years. Primary data are not as important as current secondary material. Most of the literature is a series of empirical research with experimental results reported in journal articles. Some argue, therefore, that journal articles in the field of psychology *are* primary documents.

Indexing and abstracting sources are well developed in psychology and provide good bibliographic control for journal literature with a reasonable time lag. In addition to *Psychological Abstracts*, there are such titles as *Sociological Abstracts* and *Child Development Abstracts*, with little overlap between them. Many of the indexes and abstracts are available online.

Books in psychology are most frequently collections of readings, articles, and technical reports for use in undergraduate courses. Some psychology books report full descriptions of studies; others expand on an idea or theory. The process of writing and publishing a book is longer than the process of journal publishing, which means that the information in books is older than that in journals. Another consideration is that, generally, books are not refereed as rigorously as journal articles, and, therefore, the quality may not predictably be as fine. On the other hand, there are differences in the screening process for book publishing since books are developed, scrutinized, researched, and edited by book editors, and journal articles are refereed.

Review articles are prevalent in psychology. Scholars find it useful to survey the status of knowledge in a particular area and summarize the chain of research up to the present. Special serials are devoted to publishing review articles, such as the *Psychological Bulletin* and *Annual Review of Psychology*, as well as journal titles that begin *Advances in . . .*, *Review of . . .*, and *Progress in . . . .*

Background information and historical perspective are less relevant in the field of psychology than they are, for example, in the humanities. Since emphasis is on current research, there is less need to compile retrospective bibliographies of articles and books. Emphasis is on bibliographic control of living authors and current research, with little interest in older or deceased authors. Less effort, then, is made to compile an exhaustive bibliography of an author's work and reactions to it. The focus is on the ideas rather than on the personality, unless an author has developed a new school of thought or theory, for example, Jean Piaget and developmental psychology, or B. F. Skinner and John Broadus Watson and behaviorism. Therefore, the prevalent bibliography in psychology is the review article. Most research in psychology focuses on subject or concept. One seldom enters the literature of psychology with an author's name.

Perhaps because journals are essential to psychology, several directories provide useful information about scope and submission policies (for example, Markle's *Author's Guide to Journals in Psychology, Psychiatry & Social Work* (New York: Haworth Press, 1977). The other type of directory in this field is biographical and includes both the irregularly issued *Directory* of the American Psychological Association and its more frequent *Membership Register.*

Handbooks that survey a subfield of psychology may be updated every 10 to 15 years. An example is the *Handbook of Social Psychology* (ed. by Gardner Lindzey, Reading, Mass., Addison-Wesley, 1968). Handbooks provide far greater detail and more specific information than does the encyclopedia, although the subject coverage is much more narrow. Histories in psychology are rare, again because the most current thought is the most useful to psychologists. There are also reference books specific to unique aspects of psychology, such as those that describe psychological tests and lead the researcher to articles about them. An example is *Mental Measurements Yearbook*, ed. by Oscar K. Buros (Highland Park, N.J., Gryphon, 1938–).

Psychology Research Plan

Ideas in the literature develop from a specific journal article, to inclusion in an anthology, to a review of the literature on the topic, to mention in a textbook, to eventual inclusion in an encyclopedia of social sciences or psychology; or in other words, from very specific and detailed sources to increasingly general ones. The search method, however, reverses that process, beginning with the general and moving increasingly to the specific, as the researcher learns more about the topic and further defines the research question. The librarian who understands these principles can thus offer researchers a systematic approach to the library and its resources.

Following in this section is a description of a one-hour presentation designed for upperclass and graduate students or faculty. It assumes that the individuals have tried to do research before, that they may have encountered an index (no doubt, *Psychological Abstracts*), and that they have miscellaneous observations about the library for which the librarian can offer a structure.

The presentation begins by discussing the students' probable experiences in the past, assuming that they have had no formal training in search strategy at any level and that this, indeed, is all right. This approach encourages a relaxed atmosphere for learning. Next, previous research is considered by explaining three ways in which research might have been done, pointing out the pros and cons of each:

1. Locating one article.

2. Talking to an expert.

3. Using bibliographic tools.

The first method is to locate one article on a topic, read it, check references given in the bibliography, search for and read those articles, again searching out references in the bibliographies, and so on. The advantage of this method is that all the materials focus directly on the problem in question. However, the citations only go backward in time, and if there is more than one viewpoint or perspective, the alternative approaches may be missed because they have been omitted from the references in the chain of articles read.

The second method is to talk to an expert in the field (for example, a professor) who can suggest a specific study on the topic. Experts may direct the student to studies not found any other way because the subject is too recent to have been indexed or cataloged in a library, or it is the type of material for which there is poor or no bibliographic control. Either of these two conditions offers a challenge in locating the material in a library. If references are to society publications or to proceedings, they may not be in the library because it is difficult to learn of the existence of such materials. Talking to experts in the field can be less than systematic if it is the only method used because it relies on an individual's immersion in a subject and a thorough familiarity with all the literature on the topic. Many items that the expert does not regularly monitor may have been missed. And, as reference librarians know, citations from memory tend to be somewhat "scrambled" and can be off by several years.

The third method is the use of bibliographic tools in the library, such as periodical indexes, abstracts, and bibliographies. These materials do not give information about a topic directly, but lead the researcher to the source where information can be found. Bibliographic tools are systematic, they do not rely on an individual's memory, and it is possible to retrieve and survey material expressing a variety of viewpoints, perspectives, and alternative approaches to an issue. There is also the potential for tracing the influence of an important concept forward in time by using the network of citations in the *Social Sciences Citation Index* and *Science Citation Index*, both of which cover psychological journals.

Generally, a combination of all three methods is recommended. It is helpful to examine a bibliography at the end of an article and follow up additional references that may be pertinent. Again, one can obtain valuable references in conversation with experts, but bibliographic tools provide a systematic approach and help avoid tunnel vision.

Students should be encouraged to keep a research diary for major papers, an economical and time-saving device. The research diary allows students to keep track of steps that have been taken for the project. For example, has the card catalog been checked, which indexes have been consulted, which years and what subject headings? By tracking these details, earlier volumes can easily be checked, and students will know what to recheck if a new subject heading is discovered. The diary also allows students to remember where they are in their research if they are diverted from the project for several weeks; it will enable them to retrace their steps quickly without having to redo the work. It also allows students to do research in a piecemeal fashion and between classes. The idea is that steps taken can be remembered and not needlessly repeated.

At the beginning of research, when the topic is not yet clearly defined, it is useful to work back and forth between compiling references and reading material on the subject. After reading a few articles, the direction of the research narrows and focuses, and thereafter the amount of time necessary for research may be reduced. When the topic is well defined, students can more easily identify relevant references. If students try to collect all references before reading any material, a great deal of time can be spent on writing down irrelevant references.

After discussing previous research methods and the value of keeping a research diary, the lecturer must outline the actual steps in a search strategy in psychology. As each step is discussed, write the key word for each action or type of tool on the blackboard, as shown in the following list.

Steps in psychology research

1. Define topic: encyclopedias and amount of material available

2. Annual reviews

3. Bibliographies

4. Indexes and abstracts

5. Card catalog

6. Other formats

7. Other disciplines

8. Citation indexing

9. Browse

10. Book reviews and biography

Each of these steps is discussed in detail in the following pages.

Step 1: define topic. The recommended search strategy begins with defining the topic. There are at least two ways to do this. The first is to read an overview article in an encyclopedia. Some scholarly encyclopedias include psychology, but only one is devoted solely to the subject, the *International Encyclopedia of Psychiatry, Psychology, Psychoanalysis and Neurology*, ed. by Benjamin B. Wolman (New York, Van Nostrand Reinhold, 1977, 12 vols.). The encyclopedia is the place to start if one has no ideas about a topic at all or if little is known about a specific area. This can be especially true if a researcher is doing work on an interdisciplinary topic or on a subject that is outside the researcher's field of expertise.

A second way to define the topic is on the basis of how much material is available and how difficult it might be to access it. One suggestion is to look at a recent volume of the most relevant journal index, in this case *Psychological Abstracts*, and determine how easy or difficult it will be to find information. Is there a subject heading on the topic? If yes, are there so many articles on that topic in one year that further refinement is necessary? For example, *children* will have several pages of references in one volume. If there are no subject headings, material on that topic will be buried in subject headings that are broader and less specific (for example, *personality traits* instead of *anger; group behavior* instead of *small group interaction*). If students are working on dissertations, they may be delighted not to find a subject heading on their particular topic because it clearly points to a new area of research. However, most undergraduates prefer to find existing material and subject headings and do not care whether a topic is unique. It should be pointed out to students that it is their option to decide in advance if they have enough interest in an obscure topic to spend time ferreting out the few relevant articles on it.

Step 2: annual reviews. Having chosen the potential topic, the next logical step is to look for a review article of it, which will give a summary of the chain of research. Review articles indicate what has been accomplished to date, which studies were replicated, and what are fruitful future directions of research. Finding a review article early in the process saves much time.

Step 3: bibliographies. Bibliographies are the third step in the search strategy, and another labor-saving device. They take advantage of someone else, the compiler, having already combed the literature and gathered references on a given topic, usually in a variety of formats. Often the literature for several years will be cumulated in one list. Both review articles and bibliographies can be identified by means of the *Bibliographic Index.*

Step 4: indexes and abstracts. The fourth step is to consult indexes and abstracts. It is helpful to point out that indexes lead researchers to journal articles; abstracts do the same, but in addition provide short descriptions of the articles so that the researcher has a better idea of the importance of particular material. Functionally, indexes and abstracts lead the researcher to the same type of material. Because of the nature of this discipline, psychology researchers spend the bulk of their time on this step in the library.

As already noted, current information is vital to psychology. Journal articles and conference papers are where new ideas first appear and enter the chain of literature that will contribute to the growth of the discipline. At this point, the BI instructor should discuss indexes to conference proceedings. The discussion for the instructor will, of course, depend on how available conference proceedings are within the library where the instruction takes place.

Step 5: card catalog. Having introduced access to conference proceedings, refer students to the card catalog as the place to check to see if the library lists the conferences identified. Deferring the catalog to this point is helpful because indexes and abstracts are a far better place to search in psychology. Some problems in using the card catalog include, in most cases, LC subject headings that are too broad for the specific research topic. Subject headings may not exist at all if the subject or idea is new. Subject catalogers at the Library of Congress have to consider and weigh the timeliness and/or worthiness of creating a subject heading.

If BI students will be working in a large research library, it should be pointed out that the card catalog is a very unselective list of what the library owns. One inch of cards equals one hundred books, so researchers are left to flip through cards and check for known authors or publishers, or check publication dates. Another drawback to the card catalog in some instances is that it does not include all the material within the library. Possible exclusions are government documents, journal articles, statistics, dissertations, maps, newspapers, holdings of branch libraries, and microforms. Thus, if the student goes only to the card catalog, much literature will remain untapped.

The biggest drawback of the card catalog for psychology is that it leads people primarily to books, and books are typically less relevant in this field for the following reasons: (1) the material is usually more dated than that found in journals, (2) books are usually not refereed, and (3) books in the social sciences tend to be collections of readings that may also have appeared earlier as journal articles. Therefore, it is very important to consult the indexes and abstracts for psychological topics *before* using the card catalog.

Step 6: other formats. Thus far in the search strategy, the researcher will have gathered mostly books, journal articles, and conference proceedings. The student should be encouraged to think about what other types of materials, other formats, might be appropriate for and add credence to a particular research area. Suggest some possibilities that might be relevant for the group, for example: (1) statistics on divorce rates in the United States during the last century, (2) public opinion polls to determine possible changes in attitudes about premarital sex during a period of time, (3) maps to show changing population distribution or changing political boundaries, (4) newspaper accounts of a specific event, such as the eruption of Mount St. Helens in the state of Washington, (5) personal diaries or oral histories of individuals who experienced an event, such as surviving the eruption of Mount St. Helens, (6) dissertations, (7) government documents, such as congressional hearings and committee prints on pending legislation or government reports of research grants. Offer several examples to stimulate thinking about other possibilities for research. Instead of launching into a discussion of where to find all these items, ask students to determine what sort of material would add substance to their papers. Then they can check with a reference librarian about how to find that material.

Step 7: other disciplines. Next, students should consider what disciplines other than psychology would have an interest in conducting research in a specific area. The student will want to gather information from a variety of viewpoints. An example can reinforce this idea for the student: Material on the topic "Experiences of Black Women in Business" could be found in the literature of women's studies, black studies, business, sociology, and law, as well as psychology.

Step 8: citation indexing. At this point, citation indexing can be covered, assuming the students did not begin the research with relevant citations. Citation indexing is the means of tracing a known publication's influence *forward* in time in order to discover more recent treatments or revisions of a topic. If several appropriate citations have been found, either from the students' own searching or from their talking with an expert in the field, they could use the citation volumes of the index at an earlier stage. (As noted earlier, *Social Sciences Citation Index* and *Science Citation Index* cover psychological journals.)

Step 9: browse. Browsing is the ninth step, and students are usually pleased and relieved to learn that this is a very acceptable, useful, and legitimate action in library research. They can be encouraged to look left and right, as well as up and down on the shelf when going into the stacks. It is also important for students to realize that there is a significant lag between the time that journals are published and when they are indexed. Browsing can help bridge this gap.

There are ways of browsing intelligently. The first way is to notice, when going through the indexes and abstracts, whether certain journals tend to reappear. If they do, suggest browsing the last year or so of unbound issues to see if another article on the topic has appeared. Second, discuss the use of *Current Contents* in the context of browsing in psychology and related disciplines. *Current Contents,* published by the Institute for Scientific Information, is a series of journals in various fields. It contains reproductions of the tables of contents from selected journals. As such, it is an easy way of browsing a large number of relevant journals. A third useful method for directing browsing efforts is word-of-mouth from professors and colleagues about which journals are most likely to publish in a specific area. And four, scan a journal directory with a subject approach for likely journal titles to browse, for example, Markle's *Author's Guide to Journals in Psychology, Psychiatry & Social Work.*

Step 10: book reviews and biography. As discussed earlier in this chapter, monographs and, therefore, book reviews are less important to psychology than they might be to other fields. Consider looking for reviews if an important book may have stimulated scholarly reaction. If the researcher would like to learn about the background, education, and experience of key authors, it may be helpful to consult a biography.

To reinforce the concepts to be learned by the BI student, review the list of steps in psychology research earlier in this chapter. They represent key points in the search strategy. These steps can help the student keep track of the flow of the search strategy, as can a discussion of specific titles that would be useful at each step. Give the class a handout listing the tools discussed (with blank spaces after each entry so that students can take notes). Distributing the handouts at this point accomplishes two things. First, the students will not be distracted during the earlier theoretical portion of the lecture. Second, students can concentrate on what is said about specific titles without having to scramble to copy down complete references and call numbers.

One may want to make modifications in emphasizing the reasoning behind the search strategy to suit the particular level of the class or the size of the library where the research takes place. For example, if the library is small, it may be only an exercise in futility to cover conference proceeding sources because the library is not likely to have the published proceedings anyway. Likewise, if the library is unlikely to have most of the journals indexed in the indexes and abstracts, the student may get frustrated using them at all.

Even believing that indexes are more useful in psychology research than is the card catalog, modifications in the search strategy may have to be made to fit specific classes or libraries. One might also eliminate the concept of citation indexing for underclass students (freshmen and sophomores) if this is a "one-shot" lecture. (The instructor is doing well to have students absorb the search strategy, let alone citation indexing.)

This search strategy in psychology is a suggested guideline for a logical approach to the library that will prevent students from going back and forth over their own steps. The point is to make researchers aware of what the various elements are in a systematic search within the library and what is a logical order for those elements.[1]

This search strategy may not work, however, for all topics. Some topics are obviously too new to be included in an encyclopedia or in a review article. Students should think about their topic: How new is it? In what stage of development is it and, therefore, what types of publications can they expect to find? What sort of reference tools might exist to provide bibliographic control of the existing literature that has already developed?

The particular stage of development of the topic will influence where the student begins the search strategy. If students understand how information is generated, what sort of bibliographic tools exist, and what they can anticipate, they can efficiently work in the library, using reference sources that will lead them to the kind of information they want. Comprehending the nature of a search strategy can make students feel comfortable about possibly ignoring sources they now realize will be unproductive.

Comparing Other Social Science Disciplines

The search strategy process for psychology can be applied to other social science disciplines as well, even though they vary a great deal in the prevalence and quality of each type of reference tool discussed in this chapter. For example, multivolume encyclopedias are devoted to the fields of psychology and education; this is not so in sociology, anthropology, and political science. In the course of instruction for one of these latter disciplines, it can be useful to review the whole scheme of search strategy and then, when discussing specific tools, point out that a particular tool may not exist for the field you are discussing. Consider alternative tools for that stage of the research. In this case, for example, suggest as an alternative tool the *International Encyclopedia of the Social Sciences*, explaining its strengths and weaknesses. Annual reviews are relatively easy to find in psychology, education, anthropology, and sociology, but they are almost impossible for political science, economics, and geography. In all cases, cover the one major journal in the field that is likely to carry review articles (for example, *Psychological Bulletin* for psychology, *Geographical Review* for geography, and so on) as a good place to browse.

Students should be aware, in going through journal indexes, that these journals carry review articles and so should check references in these sources first. Such sources as the *Literature and Bibliography of the Social Sciences*, by Thelma Freides, and *Sources of Information in the Social Sciences: A Guide to the Literature*, by Carl M. White and associates, and other guides to the literature identify journals carrying review articles.

Bibliographies are rare in psychology but prevalent in anthropology. This may be because currency of information is so vital to psychology and bibliographies of more dated material are not as useful in research. Indexes in the field of psychology are current, accurate, and comprehensive; indexing in sociology is not nearly as meticulous, current, or comprehensive. Economic journal indexes tend to have a four- to five-year time lag. Political science is not indexed as completely or currently as is psychology, but the field's indexes show increased improvement concerning American topics with the advent of the index *United States Political Science Documents* (USPSD).

Books tend not to be well indexed in psychology. They are more important in the fields of anthropology, political science, and sociology, and they are listed in the *International Bibliography of Social and Cultural Anthropology*, the *International Bibliography of Political Science*, the *International Bibliography of Sociology*, and for economics, the *International Bibliography of Economics*. As ongoing bibliographies controlling the literature in these fields, these international bibliographies can be considered as "indexes" to relevant books and articles. Perhaps one- to two-thirds of the references in social sciences are to monographs versus 10 percent in science. Some social sciences, such as political science and economics, are more heavily oriented toward computer or nonprint materials, and researchers in these fields may not be interested in learning traditional library search strategy, but rather want to know how they can get fact books (statistical handbooks, census data, and the like) in order to obtain data for the computer. From these they calculate historical trends and future projections.

Using this basic search strategy in psychology, adaptations can be made to fit the particularity of each social science discipline. This basic lecture or presentation can also be adapted to the sciences since currency of information is so vital in that area as well.

Generally, it is important to bear in mind the special structure and needs of a specific discipline, its development, what sorts of tools have been generated, how the information is used by scholars in the field, and what types of materials will, therefore, be of most interest to them. Keep in mind also that a teacher cannot convey everything in one lecture—so the idea is to focus on what is most important.

Major Differences among Discipline Groups

The social science discipline family, just as history and the humanities, has its own "genetic" profile, and each discipline within a family has its own paradigm, which will reflect the family characteristics to an extent but will also be idiosyncratic. It would be impossible to discuss in detail the distinguishing features of even the established fields of study, let alone those just beginning to develop, but let us concentrate here on those facets that should be stressed in concept-based library instruction. They are:

Importance of primary sources.

Speed of dissemination of new ideas.

Extent of collaboration.

Citation indexing.

Financial backing.

Interest in nontraditional materials.

The first major difference among discipline groups concerns the importance of primary sources and whether they are published or derived by observation or experiment. In the humanities, primary source material, in manuscript or printed, is usually but not always housed in libraries or archives. In history it is more common to have primary information not yet collected and published; so the historian must find, retrieve, and classify material for the first time before starting to interpret it. In the social sciences, primary material may already have been published, but the most avant-garde work in any discipline will have only recently appeared, probably having been presented as a paper at a conference or just published in a major journal.

The second characteristic that differentiates among discipline families is the speed at which both primary and secondary sources are disseminated. As one would predict, those in the humanities and historical fields are extremely slow, and in some cases haphazard, about promulgating their research. Rarely is it critical for one scholar to learn immediately the findings of another, who may well be located in a foreign country. Eventually the news gets out, and eventually others interested in the topic will come across the results through the use of bibliographies or by browsing, if not by word of mouth. In the social sciences, research conclusions must become known quickly since other projects require that information as part of their own research. A significant delay between the time an experiment is concluded and the time its results are issued is also regarded somewhat skeptically by members of the social science (and scientific) communities, who want their literature to reflect only the latest technology and schools of thought, not work that is two or more years old and hence passé.

The extent of collaboration is a distinctive feature among discipline groups. In the humanities and historical sciences, there is virtually no major collaboration either in the performance or the publication of research. Seldom are articles or monographs coauthored. In the social sciences, the opposite is true; multiple authorship is the rule rather than the exception, and many people contribute to a single research effort.

Citation indexing—the means of tracing a known publication's influence *forward* in time in order to discover more recent treatments or revisions of a topic—is relatively unimportant in the humanities and historical sciences, although traditionally scholars in these areas go to great lengths to trace ideas *backward* in time to authenticate their own work. Conversely, citation indexes and their use are quite critical in the social sciences. One can conclude that the more intent a discipline is on present research, the more it depends on citation indexing to pinpoint the few relevant previous thinkers who have dealt with a given research problem.

Financial backing varies immensely among discipline families. The major associations and societies in the humanities and historical sciences are "poor cousins" compared with the relatively affluent organizations to which social scientists and scientists belong. As a result of this difference and the wide gap in relative foundation and government grants, the humanities/historical sciences can rarely support the level and speed of bibliographic control that the social sciences/ sciences can command. (An important exception is the Modern Language Association, which, with the help of computerization, has achieved a remarkable nine-month turnaround for the *MLA International Bibliography* in recent years and which has received significant foundation funding to improve the taxonomy of the *Bibliography* and to add a rotated, faceted index beginning with the 1981 volume.)

The various social sciences reflect very different degrees of bibliographic control, ranging from the outstanding *Psychological Abstracts* to the extremely difficult and frustrating *Sociological Abstracts* to the tiny but useful *Abstracts in Anthropology*. The price of a commercially produced finding tool or journal is set to generate profits for the publisher, who assumes major expenses to ensure thoroughness, accuracy, and timeliness. Unfortunately, research libraries are caught in the financial squeeze as subscription costs of scientific series climb at an astonishing rate. One long-range benefit of advanced, conceptually oriented BI should be heightened user awareness, especially among scientific researchers, of their intellectual and economic impact on libraries. In any case, the relationship between money and the speed of dissemination of communication within a discipline is direct and undeniable.

A sixth comparison among discipline families can be made on the basis of practitioner interest in nontraditional materials, that is, in forms of communication other than journal articles and monographs. Other than cinematic films and audio recordings, humanities scholars and students have little use for anything but the published book or article. Historians, searching for primary material, are willing to consider any sources, regardless of format, that may give them a view of their period or topic. Social scientists tend to be very data oriented, but seem not to care how data is presented as long as it is accurate and appropriate to their needs. Audiovisual records of experiments or experimental results are becoming more and more common in these fields.

Each discipline family has its own distinctive characteristics, which are reflected in the tendencies of individual family members. It is, therefore, impossible to formulate a single search strategy and expect it to transfer without modification even to another discipline within the same family. A search strategy created for an economics topic will not work for anthropology, and vice versa. Tools that exist for one discipline may, for perfectly good reasons, not exist at all—or exist in an outdated form—for another. Similarly, the order in which various fact and finding tools are consulted will change radically depending on the discipline involved. Consequently, an important step in question analysis is to predict exactly which disciplines may have been concerned with a topic so that appropriate search strategies can be devised for each one and so that faulty research assumptions can be avoided. Dissertations can and should be written on the characteristics and dynamics of every established field; an excellent example of what needs to be considered is Thelma Freides's book, *Literature and Bibliography of the Social Sciences* (Los Angeles: Melville, 1973) and the interesting series of occasional articles on scholarly journals in various disciplines, which appeared in the *Times Higher Education Supplement* beginning in November 1979.

Never pass up the opportunity to learn about the intellectual nature of a discipline and the research logic and behavior of its practitioners. Reading plus discussion with scholars about their thought processes, research needs, and communication patterns afford the best justification for a conceptual approach to BI. These people think in terms of problems and means to their solution, not in terms of specific reference books; so to expose library users—some of whom will likely become researchers in the future—to the most realistic conditions, we should stress ideas and probable sources rather than precise tools for limited purposes.

Note

1. Anne K. Beaubien, *Psychology: Selected Basic Reference Works*, 2nd ed. rev. (Ann Arbor, MI: University of Michigan Library, 1980). This is an annotated guide to psychology reference sources arranged in search strategy order. The author uses the guide in her BI course for psychology students to reinforce search strategy and type-of-tool concepts and to supplement her discussion of specific titles.

Part III
Presenting
the Research
Process

Of the several modes of bibliographic instruction, only the live lecture mode, or some hybrid mode involving the live lecture in part, can convey the intricacies of the concepts we have presented in the previous chapters. Since research and the research process are complex and theoretically vague, depending on a clear explanation of the nature of a given discipline and parallel bibliographic structure, it is essential that any attempt to present the concepts occur in the traditional classroom setting, either with a one-hour single lecture or better yet a series of such lectures, that is, the BI course. The following chapters will concentrate on the specifics of live presentations, specifically the one-hour lecture and the BI course.

9
Planning a Single Lecture

The single live lecture is by far the most prevalent form, or mode, of bibliographic instruction in an academic setting. No doubt this is due to the age-old prevalence of the lecture in education generally as the traditional method of group instruction. Even in an era marked by widespread availability of audiovisual technology and strongly influenced by the availability of computer-assisted instruction for virtually every field, the lecture remains, together with the textbook, the principal, predominant means of communicating information and knowledge uniformly to groups of students.

The single live presentation, although perhaps not quite so frequent in the nonacademic library, is nonetheless an undertaking common to all areas of librarianship, including school, public, and special settings. Anyone who trains staff or "introduces" users to the scope of a collection or teaches a class as part of a bibliographic instruction program will find the approaches and practical steps outlined in this chapter most useful. In fact, ease in designing and delivering an effective single lecture is one of the most important skills needed for any public service library professional.

Our definition of the single lecture is a unique encounter between the teacher and a group of any size where there is no guarantee of a personal followup or evaluation of what has been taught or learned. Many BI librarians refer to the single live presentation as a 1-hour lecture, and, in fact, in many instances it is intended to take a 50- to 60-minute class period. On other occasions, however, the available time is either shorter or longer; so it is more accurate to speak of the "one-shot" lecture, which does not imply a particular length of contact with the audience. In this chapter we generally refer to the single lecture as the "one-shot." This lecture, under whatever name, includes any length of presentation that is planned in advance and the object of which is to instruct students in the tools and techniques of library research.

We can enlarge on the basic definition of the one-shot lecture by examining some other characteristics. First, the single or one-shot lecture does not imply that the librarian giving the presentation must do so alone and without any additional "visual" support. No matter how well structured the content, how personable and pleasant the delivery, or how animated the "performance" or movement of the librarian, the lecture format does not preclude mixing other appropriate modes in what is basically a live presentation. Some of the most effective lectures include audiovisual aids (transparencies or a videotape) or other classroom teaching techniques (group discussion or guided exercises) that are carefully incorporated into the lecture. It is improbable that an art historian would lecture without using the slide projector, or that a musicologist would make an important theoretical point without playing selected examples to reinforce it, or that a database searcher could effectively convey the instant, personal, interactive nature of online searching by verbal description alone. Sometimes the most effective means of illustrating a theory is to stop the lecture and give a brief, live demonstration involving other librarians or members of the audience. Research on learning and teaching has also shown that interspersing activities, even during a short lecture, can have a profound and positive effect on how students learn.

The one-shot forms the basic unit in any course or curriculum. It encompasses the full range of teaching skills: outlining learning objectives, planning content, ordering content, choosing presentation techniques that will enhance learning and permit maximum interaction of the audience with the material, streamlining preparation, successful delivery, and awareness of immediate classroom feedback. Skills needed for a successful single presentation can be utilized in almost any setting to cover a wide variety of topics for any age audience for a short or long period of time. Once librarians have mastered these skills, they can easily transfer and repeat them to form an entire course.

Advantages/Disadvantages

The primary advantage of the one-shot lecture is that it is versatile and flexible, and hence the likelihood is greater of being able to provide relevant instruction to any given group at a time and depth (degree of detail) appropriate to the people involved. This relevance in turn will increase the motivation of students to learn the material. The flexibility means that after the initial time-consuming preparation, subsequent presentations of the same basic information to another group or to a similar group can be devised in a shorter amount of time. Examples either of specific titles or of topics that are appropriate for a given reference procedure can be varied to keep them current and to arouse student interest with little or no advanced work. The principles of conceptually based, one-time presentations can be transferred to lectures for other audiences. For instance, if the librarian has been successful in planning a single presentation around the idea of question analysis as outlined in Chapter 4, he or she can use that model in presentations intended for a chemistry, social science, literature, or fine arts audience, in each case varying the examples and perhaps also the complexity of the discussion.

The personal interaction between the librarian and the library user, which the face-to-face lecture permits, is of immense benefit. The instructor is able to observe during the presentation whether students are understanding the material and, most important, whether they are able to make the logical connections between the theory and its application for their own research needs. The librarian has a priceless opportunity in the one-shot lecture to sense immediately whether students have understood the concept being presented and, if there is any ambiguity, to correct it immediately before going on to another topic.

It is possible in the one-shot to cover too much material, in too great a degree of complexity, in too short a time (common shortcomings of audiovisual productions or other "canned" modes). The skillful instructor will sense when students have become overloaded with material and will backtrack to reexplain a point, or will ask questions to ascertain understanding, or insert some form of quiz or exercise to reinforce the information. All these techniques are, of course, highly recommended for any effective group presentation, but they cannot be practiced unless the instructor is sensitive to the response of the group as well as being skilled in the various means of learning reinforcement.

The public relations value of the one-shot lecture cannot be overstated, both in terms of the visibility of the professional librarian within the user community and in terms of the library's willingness as an institution to cater to the specific needs of its clientele. The library should be able to provide on demand cogent, interesting, perhaps even entertaining lectures that highlight the library's resources and the processes to exploit it. This is one way to convince an academic community that the library is not only a service institution, but is also an important teaching unit in terms of basic research concepts and information-seeking skills needed by users for projects or research in any discipline or any topic. The library's ability and willingness to support the front-line academic process in the mode (that is, the lecture) with which most academics are themselves most comfortable cannot fail to win confidence in the library's many other services.

Of all the BI modes, the face-to-face ones most easily permit instruction in the concept formation and problem-solving needed for research problem analysis, type of tool identification, search strategy, and the many other underlying paradigms that support the research process. Since every individual has different intellectual strengths, has had different experiences, and approaches concepts and their application in a unique fashion, it is important to present theoretical topics in a way that best permits the individual to learn by asking questions or indicating the need for reexplanation or reinforcement of what has been presented.

Other advantages of the one-shot are that it permits various kinds of visuals or hands-on experience as a complement to the oral presentation. It is also relatively easy to make handouts to accompany or reinforce the lecture. In terms of the space required, the classroom setting can be within a library or, if that is not possible for a large group of students, in a campus auditorium.

On the minus side, the one-shot lecture has, in most instances, a finite audience, that is, only so many people can be reached at one time. Scheduling is difficult because the time of the librarian (juggling preparation time, scheduled desk time, and other commitments), the audience, and the space must be coordinated. The amount of preparation time needed by a librarian for a single presentation is high, ranging from 10 to 15 hours from the time the session is scheduled to the time of actual presentation. The preparation time may be halved for a representation of the same material with minor modifications before a different group, but no matter how many times a core lecture is reused, at least a half day is involved in careful reformating or modification. Similarly, any other aids—audiovisual, for example, handouts, or annotated bibliographies—require additional time, money, staffing, equipment, or expense.

Other disadvantages include the necessity for the librarian to possess or to learn group communication and teaching skills, the need for faculty cooperation if the instruction is to be course-related or course-integrated, and if not, at least faculty encouragement so that publicity, and if possible endorsement, of the library's instruction efforts reach the students through the classroom.

A last and, in many people's view, most critical disadvantage is the difficulty of valid objective evaluation of one-shot lectures. It is virtually impossible to use even a few minutes of the limited presentation time to elicit student evaluation. Even if the attempt is made, students will be giving only initial subjective reactions, and there is no proof that they will retain what they have seen and heard during the lecture. Evaluation after the lecture is likely to be unsatisfactory because of a low return rate and/or because students will not take the evaluation attempt seriously unless it is somehow tied to a course grade or other incentive that they know about in the first place.

Planning the One-Shot Lecture

The following factors must be taken into account at the time arrangements are made for a one-shot lecture: size of the audience, level of the audience, subject background or common experience individuals in the group may share, whether the group is involved at the time in a subject-specific class, and if so whether a specific assignment is attached to it with a library research component. To have a feeling for what students may already know is crucial. Are they comfortable getting around within the library, with library policies, and with the array of services that are provided? Have students had any previous library instruction in whatever mode? Has the classroom faculty member made any attempt to initiate students into the bibliography of their field? How much time will be available for instruction: a single 50- or 60-minute class period, two class periods end to end, parts of two class periods, an entire evening? Where will the lecture take place? What equipment is available—blackboard, overhead projector and screen, power outlets? Is there an elevator to transport books to and from the teaching site?

Each of these factors, while fairly straightforward and mundane, can have an impact. Some librarians have devised a checklist of these points, which serves as a reminder to cover each aspect in the planning stage and as a record of the instruction for statistical purposes. Such a list means that requests for instruction can be taken at a central contact point and then passed on to those who are doing the instruction.

After all these factors have been considered, it is time to draft the objectives for the one-shot presentation. (See Chapter 2 on setting objectives.) If the library has an ongoing multi-faceted library instruction program, it will already have a general objective. For an individual one-shot lecture, one must write two or three terminal objectives, and as many enabling, highly specific behavioral objectives as are warranted by the material to be covered. If no general objective has been stated for the library's instructional efforts, it is difficult to write terminal and enabling objectives for a particular lecture.

The drafting of objectives should focus the attention and energy of the librarian early in the preparation and should also serve as the basis for whatever form of evaluation, if any, is attempted. By writing an objective, even for a very short lecture, one can easily later incorporate the lecture into a longer curriculum or course. The important thing is to get the objective written down without also spending an inordinate amount of time drafting it or fussing over it.

Organizing the One-Shot: Nine Options

A high percentage of all one-shot lectures are organized by a title approach—the titles being arranged in some logical order, whether by type of tool, search strategy, relative usefulness of the tool for the student's purposes, chronologically, alphabetically by author, or numerous other ways. Popular as it is, in most cases the title approach is less meaningful to students than a conceptually oriented structure for the limited time available. In the following pages, we discuss nine different options for organizing a one-shot lecture:

Orientation/instruction.

Title-only.

Single concept or skill.

Type-of-tool concept.

Question analysis.

Search strategy.

Information structure/discipline growth.

Format.

Mix-and-match.

Included with the explanations of the options are some ways of actually using them in the classroom. These various principles of organization should be considered both for applicability in a particular situation and because they may be more easily transferred to subsequent presentations in the long run than the title-oriented traditional methods. Furthermore, in trying out each of these approaches, we found that students are typically so intrigued by the underlying concepts that they start making their own connections to their disciplines even before the lecture is over.

Orientation/instruction option

Although the librarian may be primarily interested in instruction rather than orientation (the aspects of navigation around a specific facility), very often a librarian is asked to conduct a special tour of the reference collection or possibly of the card catalog and appropriate reference works and indexes for a specific class of students. In that case, it is appropriate to consider to what extent a tour can incorporate both locational and instructional objectives. When fulfilling such a request, remember that students may resent the notion of yet another tour, feeling they are already familiar with the building and its services. On the other hand, the faculty member who is asking for a class tour may really intend for the librarian to show the students certain, possibly highly specialized, fact and finding tools for a specific discipline or topic. Unaware that the librarian could do this in the classroom situation, the faculty member asks for a tour. So, in the initial contact the librarian might explain that it is possible to do a classroom lecture, but if the faculty member would still appreciate the tour, the librarian could attempt to do both either at the same time or one following the other. At this point the assignment becomes difficult, since the arrangement of every building and reference collection, not to mention variations in the content of reference collections, is unique. The attempt to walk even a reasonably sized group of students through one or more rooms in the library without unduly disturbing other readers, at the same time trying to explain the importance of and use of key tools, can be one of the greatest challenges facing any instruction librarian.

It is important to sit down and try to discover if any route through, into, or around the reference collection makes sense in terms of the tools to be presented. Typically, the librarian will discover that even if the architecture does not bar such a tour, the classification system does; even a perfectly arranged reference room may have encyclopedias at one end and handbooks for the same field at another. It may be possible to arrange centralized seating for the group in the room so that midway in the tour students can sit down and examine the most important tools near the shelves where the tools are housed.

Adding the card catalog can also be a complication in the tour structure, since it may be important to explain the Library of Congress or other system of subject headings, say something about the filing rules, notable inclusions and omissions in one's local catalog, exactly what information one needs to copy down in order to find materials in the stacks, and how to translate that copied information into a floor designation. This is a lot of detailed information to cover, and when students are standing for long periods of time, they may not be taking notes or may be paying only partial attention to what is being said.

Another factor becoming more and more prevalent, and which works two ways, is the appearance of an online terminal in the reference or catalog areas. On the one hand, students will be fascinated with the new technology and wish a demonstration; so the instructor should be ready with a relevant topic to be searched online. On the other hand, students may forget everything that has been said about the use of the card catalog, assuming, unfortunately, that all material is now available online. An explanatory handout distributed at the end of the tour may prove especially useful for filling in those important details that students have suppressed. A map or floor plan of the areas through which the tour has passed, with notations marking the important points in the subject field, might also be a helpful aid to such a one-shot.

If the teacher who has coordinated this group approves and is willing to assign an exercise following the tour, you might consider giving students a short list of questions on the major tools discussed; this is an important reinforcing technique that will get them back to the appropriate shelves to discover for themselves the importance of the material there.

Title-only option

As we said earlier, this is by far the most common structure for the one-hour presentation. Whatever arrangement is used, the objective is to present a certain selected group of titles to the students in the hope that they will find these works useful for their own research. Among the most common ways of organizing a title-based lecture is to arrange the titles alphabetically by author or main entry; alphabetically by title; in call number order (which, of course, will also usually be by type of tool in a disguised fashion more or less); by publisher, for example, G. K. Hall catalogs or Wilson indexes (this may end up being by type of tool, but unless that is specified, students will not understand why publishers should be a principle of arrangement); by date of publication if that is an important factor in the discipline; or by recommended order of use. (Lecturing about tools in search strategy order, but not telling students what that order means or why they want to know about it, will not prove effective in the long run; students will not be able to transfer a concept that is not fully understood.)

Of all the approaches discussed here, the authors are least in favor of the title-based option unless there is some justification in the situation for adopting it. We would not throw away this most traditional structure just because it is common and traditional, but we do not see anything intrinsically effective in presenting students with a long, or even a very short, lecture stressing the characteristics of titles, but not

also describing their universal characteristics as representative of a type of tool that the student will find in other fields.
Most librarians can vouch from their library school reference
courses that the title-based approach does not adapt well to
real-life research situations, so why teach that way?

Faculty members are most likely to assume that the title
approach is the only way to make a presentation, and they
may list for the librarian the titles that absolutely must be
covered, seeming not to care in what order or with what justification the presentation is made. It is often both politic and
wise to consider the other options presented here, which will
serve as a framework on which to hang the title that the
faculty member has in mind, so that the presentation will be
coherent in the sense of the logical progression from one title
to the other, stressing characteristics rather than peculiarities
of the various items presented. What makes the whole one-
shot hang together is that the titles are arrayed around an
underlying theme.

Single concept or skill option

Perhaps the most manageable structure around which to build
a one-shot lecture is to concentrate on the presentation and
elaboration of a single idea or a single research skill; for example, building a lecture around the concept of a periodical
index and/or bibliographic databases, the varieties of maps
and atlases and their relationship to gazetteers, or the procedures involved in locating items referred to at the end of an
encyclopedia article. One of the pluses of the single concept
or skill option is that it is appropriate for any audience no
matter what background, age or educational level of the individuals, or subject field. Of course, the concept or skill selected will vary with the characteristics of the group, but
there will always be some particular relevant research theory
or procedure from which the audience could benefit.

A particularly interesting angle on this option occurs in
certain fields, notably in archaeology, history, and music,
where a lecture could be devoted to the concept of primary
source material and a few of the most common ways of identifying, locating, and obtaining it. Similarly, an effective lecture could concentrate on a single central research tool of
great complexity, for example, the *Social Science Citation
Index* or the *Science Citation Index*, joining the difficult con-

cept involved with a careful presentation of its many uses. Explaining the principles, purpose, and use of the following tools would probably fill an entire lecture period: the *MLA International Bibliography*, the *Bulletin Signalétique*, *IBZ* indexes, or the *Monthly Catalog of Government Publications*. Every librarian can no doubt name other equally complex or confusing, yet crucially important, titles that would lend themselves to a single presentation.

Bibliographic databases—for example, those made available through vendors such as DIALOG and Systems Development Corporation—are a particularly good topic for the single concept one-shot. One can begin by briefly explaining how secondary literature grows in most scientific and social science disciplines, together with its parallel bibliographic structure. It is easy, then, to show exactly what portion of the literature bibliographic databases control.

At this point in the lecture, you may insert an "indexing game" in which participants are given a photocopy of a one-page article and asked to index it (see below for a full description). After the capabilities of indexes are discussed, you can point out that although printed indexes are limited (by economics) to only a few access points, the database version usually offers far more (access by date and by the words appearing in the abstract, and so on). The indexing game (shown below) sets up a full discussion of databases because the audience will have participated in defining what indexes, and therefore databases, are and can do.

Give participants a photocopy of a one-page article, perhaps from Time *magazine, and ask them to index it. Pretend that you are creating a new index and, through this article, you will start to establish how the index will be organized. Elicit possible ways to index the article (access points) from the audience and put the responses on a blackboard or transparency. As each suggestion is offered, explain what generic type of indexing the term represents.*

For example, if someone suggests that a word from the title could be used for indexing, explain that that particular type of subject indexing is called keyword *indexing, and point out the strengths and weaknesses of it. The advantages are that one can find information about very new ideas or jargon terms for which there are no subject headings. This can also be helpful for topics that are too specialized to have a subject* heading (such as brainstorming or queing). Keyword indexes also tend to be more current than those that require the intellectual process of assigning subject headings or a classification scheme. Since it is not necessary to employ a person to do the indexing, this type is relatively inexpensive. One does not need to know the first word in the title to find the article, and if the title is good, specific things can be found easily. The disadvantages include the necessity of entering every possible synonym for a concept (for example, employment, job, occupation, work, and specific occupations such as dentistry). If all synonyms are not covered, there will not be total recall, and, if those words do not happen to appear in the titles of articles, the material is lost. Keywords waste space in an index, and they do not have a hierarchy of terms; since intellectual decisions have not been made to group certain terms together (such as birds versus pigeons and robins). If the article has a "cute" title, you can explain how useless a keyword index would be in that case.

Some indexes use a keyword supplemental index, which means that they enhance the basic keyword index with additional words when the words in the titles do not adequately reflect the subject matter of the article (as America: History and Life since 1974). Catchword subject indexing was used in such nineteenth-century indexes as Poole's Index; it was an early form of keyword index, but it is more challenging to use than the computer-produced indexes of today because only one word of the title was taken as the catchword; therefore researchers have only one chance to find the article in the index. This is compounded by needing to know how an idea may have been expressed a century ago (for example, women in the labor force is found under "Working Girls"). Catchword indexing will only have to be pointed out if the group would probably ever have use for the nineteenth-century indexes that employ it.

If there is a controlled vocabulary for subject headings, there is a list somewhere of the terms that are used, and terms that are not used are cross-referenced to the terms that are used. Sometimes this list is separately published and available in the library (for example, Thesaurus of Psychological Index Terms and Thesaurus of ERIC Descriptors), and these can be helpful in translating the inquirer's natural language into the terminology of the index. If one of the participants suggests a corporate or personal name as a subject heading, you can point out that often such terms are acceptable in an index but that there is probably not a list of all the possible proper names. It would be impossible to generate a personal or corporate name thesaurus. If several subject headings are suggested by the group, you as teacher can lead a discussion on the number of terms that would actually be selected and used in the various types of indexes in question. You may also be able to help users make reasonable choices for subject headings depending on the nature of the index, for example, history as a term in a historical index is not a particularly useful heading, if it could be found at all.

The level of specificity for a geographic location will vary depending on the type of index. In some cases it would be possible to look up a town or a stream; in others, a state or a province is the logical level to explore, and for still others, one would do well to search by country. If students create any subdivided subject headings, you can suggest the most likely order of the subdivision given the index (such as Cartography—Michigan vs. Michigan—Cartography). Once author indexes are suggested, point out that authors may be in a separate index or interfiled with the subjects, and then ask which the students think would be most useful. The more general journal indexes tend to integrate headings; discipline indexes separate the author and subject approaches. It is more common to know authors in discipline research.

Titles are often a way to index articles—people are most familiar with this concept through the card catalogs of libraries. However, some indexes also provide a title approach, such as Readers' Guide and the more specialized current-awareness journals such as Current Contents.

Corporate affiliation of the author and citation indexing are both available through the indexes produced by the Institute of Scientific Information (publisher of the Science Citation Index). Classification schemes are utilized by indexes such as Biological Abstracts and International Bibliography of the Social Sciences. Our contention is that ongoing bibliographies can be thought of as the same type of tool as a journal index since their function is much the same—to provide bibliographic control of literature on an ongoing basis. Few people will suggest a classification scheme as a possible access point.

A list of possible access points to indexes, which can be put *on the blackboard or transparency as the group comes up with various approaches, is shown below.*

1. *Subject: controlled vocabulary, keyword, catchword.*
2. *Author.*
3. *Title.*
4. *Journal title.*
5. *Corporate affiliation of author.*
6. *Citation indexing.*
7. *Classification scheme.*
8. *Abstract (words in).*
9. *Date: historical period, date article published.*

For 8 and 9, better access is provided in the online version than in the printed index.

The above exercise can be a successful interactive session with the information about the advantages and disadvantages of each type of indexing naturally interspersed throughout the discussion. After the indexing game, you can hand out several volumes of each index you want to present to a class and ask the students to describe the features of that particular index. This sort of activity lays a good foundation, enabling individuals to work with any index they encounter—whether it was covered in class or not—and quickly understand how to use it and what it can and cannot do. It also makes possible covering a great many indexes in a short period of time.

Sometimes a request for a one-shot comes from a faculty member who wants students to learn how to exploit to full advantage the library's own card catalog and/or online catalog or the various important book catalogs that identify and locate materials. The degree of computerization of your library's bibliographic records will determine how you structure such a presentation. If you concentrate wholly or in large part on the traditional card catalog, you should cover at least the following six important matters during the presentation.

1. Clarification of exactly what is represented in the card catalog, which is that cards indicate books or journals owned by the institution, but do not include fine analyses down to the journal article or book chapter (unless, of course, your institution's catalog has a different scope) level.

2. A careful explanation of exclusions such as microformats, government documents, maps.

3. A brief explanation of the information to be found on a card within the catalog, including such peculiarities as indention and changing punctuation practices (which do not in any case reflect the dictates of any established bibliographic style manual, so that catalog entries must always be "translated" into Turabian, MLA, or another style).

4. Discussion of the Library of Congress or other system of subject headings as these relate to tracings, with emphasis on how to go from a concept to the appropriate terminology.

5. A brief description of the purpose of the call number, that is, why an alpha-numeric or wholly numeric symbol is used to arrange materials with like intellectual content in the stacks and how this differs from the subject/word approach to that intellectual content.

6. A brief overview of the most important and problematic filing rules in the local card catalog.

Covering this much material in an hour or less can be a challenge, especially if students ask many questions. Ideally, there should be at least one and one-half hours to cover these six aspects of the card catalog sufficiently, if not in any great depth, and also to allow for at least one class exercise. We recommend dealing with filing rules by giving every person a randomly mixed but identical packet of 20–30 entries to arrange, followed by a discussion of filing rules as applied to these cards. Here again handouts are in order to give samples and cut down on student distraction by taking notes.

If the greater part of an institution's collection is included in an online catalog, some of the six points listed above can be de-emphasized or eliminated, especially a discussion of filing rules, which are irrelevant if using an online catalog. If your library has public use terminals, you might substitute the searching protocols.

If the one-shot lecture dealing with catalogs is to be extended to the concept and use of catalogs of other libraries, you might discuss the *National Union Catalog* in detail and, if time permits, mention other national catalogs or the more specific G. K. Hall book catalogs. Students are often astonished to learn that there is a readily accessible way to discover the holdings of other libraries and are fascinated by this topic (as they will be also by the location information to be found in the record appearing on an OCLC, RLIN, WLN, or other network cataloging terminal). The natural connection between the library's home catalog and the way to use it to discover the holdings of other libraries can easily lead to covering both topics in the same session, provided it is long enough. If emphasis is placed on a subject approach to the catalog, it might also be good to cover the Library of Congress's subject book catalogs before discussing the *National Union Catalog* so that students realize that at least since 1950 a subject approach will lead to titles held elsewhere.

There is a great deal of debate among BI librarians at institutions of all kinds about whether to include in any given lecture the nuts-and-bolts information of how to find a book in the stacks. Frequently students express their delight at the information conveyed in a lecture, but then say "How do I find a book in the stacks?" In planning the lecture you must decide whether you will take the time to talk through the process of converting a call number to a stack location and actually retrieving material from the stacks, whether you will ignore the issue altogether, or whether you will give students an after-class exercise to test their own ability. This is particularly a problem with freshmen or transfer students new to an institution, who need a blow-by-blow description of how they find material in your library.

If you decide to devote an entire one-hour lecture to the theory and manipulation of your institution's catalog and if you decide to omit a discussion of how materials are actually found in the stacks, you might consider including a stack directory, along with the rest of your handouts, and a map or maps of floor locations. This will allow students to work from the concepts you have presented to actual discovery of materials they need on the shelves. Many students, especially those new to the institution, may not have as yet needed to retrieve items; so you cannot assume any previous experience about the layout or any idiosyncracies of your stacks.

Some readers may wonder how to fill the typical 50-minute class period if it is devoted to a seemingly simple single concept. For example, the concept of an encyclopedia can be readily explained to most audiences. Then what? Following are some suggestions to reinforce and amplify the idea:

1. Move from the concept of an encyclopedia to the procedures for tracking down in one's own library the specific items cited at the end of an encyclopedia article, including how to tell if the item is a book or journal article, how to locate each in the card catalog, and how to find the items in the bibliography.

2. Move from a discussion of the concept to its place in the bibliographic structure or communication channels of a particular discipline, assuming the audience is drawn from students concentrating in a particular field.

3. Move from the concept to general encyclopedias as examples of that concept and then a handful of specific discipline-oriented encyclopedias to show the manifestation of the concept in particular fields.

4. Move from the concept directly to specific encyclopedias within a discipline familiar to the audience, for example, the various encyclopedias in art.

If the concept to be covered is important for the audience, you should have no difficulty in using it as a centerpiece for an entire lecture that will be as broad or as narrow, as simple or as sophisticated, as your audience's presumed needs warrant.

Two related concepts may also be covered in tandem during the course of a one-shot lecture, for example, the concept of a periodical index together with the concept of a newspaper index. Or, a lecture might introduce users both to the library's serials records, to find out what volumes and issues are owned, and to the institution's microform collection, to make users aware that many series may be available also in or only in microform.

To some extent concentrating on a single or dual concept or skill combination is only a variation on the previous option—presenting a group of titles in some reasonable order. The crucial difference is that concepts or skills are focused and are certainly more transferrable to other disciplines, libraries, and skill levels than are what may seem to the student a miscellaneous assortment of reference titles. By concentrating on an organizing principle and its ramifications for research, the point is readily conveyed that there *are* organizing principles of research and that having a clear grasp of them—or, in the case of skills, being comfortable executing them—will have immediate rewards for each individual in the audience. An analogy might be that a person interested in knowing more about baseball will find spending an hour learning the basic rules of the game so that significant plays can be recognized more productive than spending an hour watching film clips of famous plays and attempting to derive the rules of the game from isolated examples. In bibliographic instruction, deduction is not always superior to induction as a learning principle, but given a limited contact with an audience, concentrating on one or two ideas and their effects is more likely to meet the objective of transferability than is an attempt to expose the audience to many details.

Many teachers in all fields affirm that given a choice between stressing ideas and principles and stressing specific examples, they prefer to concentrate on stressing ideas and principles, relying on the student's native intelligence to classify and project details as they are encountered once the appropriate concepts have been mastered.

Since bibliographic instruction relies so heavily on the concepts of information structure and transfer, it seems only logical that specific titles should take a back seat to general theory whenever the two cannot both be accommodated. Relying on students' ability to synthesize common notions from an array of particular events assumes that the students have been exposed to those events. Students' library experience is so narrow, haphazard, and anxiety ridden that most will not have encountered enough instances of any given type of research to be able to synthesize from them. It is therefore far better to present the principles in their most logical, most historical light and let the students' intelligence work from those principles on their subsequent experience, using the analytic approach rather than the synthetic.

Type-of-tool concept option

Rather than structure a one-shot lecture on a single tool or skill, one can concentrate on student understanding of the various generic types of fact, finding, and hybrid reference tools and their generalized characteristics. (See the discussion of type-of-tool recognition in Chapter 4.) This approach draws on students' prior experience, however varied or limited, and expands until an entire model has been presented and students are made aware of the great variety of reference tools they can expect in a fully mature discipline.

In contrast to what was said earlier about deduction being superior to induction as a teaching methodology, this particular option can rely on induction, based on students' prior encounters with libraries generally and reference tools in particular. Asking questions to elicit response and trigger memory is particularly effective. It is essential to have a blackboard or transparency to display all student suggestions as the interaction and lecture progress. Students in all disciplines and from all levels will find this a useful and thought-provoking way to learn about the variety of materials that exist in the reference field.

This option is split into the following three different approaches based on the apparent sophistication of the audience:

1. A general discussion of what the tools do.

2. A subject specific approach.

3. Specific titles.

In the first approach, you discuss the concept of each type of tool in the abstract in terms of what it does in the research process. For example, an encyclopedia article (in our terminology, one of the hybrid tools) both summarizes existing information on a topic and, by means of the references at the end of an article, leads the reader to additional information. An index, on the other hand, leads to journal articles and possibly to other kinds of submonographic material, such as individual contributions at a conference or to a collection of essays. A catalog leads to the finite contents of a library—usually by author, title, and subject.

A good way to reinforce the abstract concepts of the various tools is to ask students toward the end of the presentation which types of tools would be appropriate to find information on, for example, a current events topic. There is typically not enough time to elaborate on search strategy, that is, the most effective order of consulting the various types of tools, or on the bibliographic structure of disciplines in general in a one-shot lecture (unless the one-shot is, in fact, several hours long). The real advantage to working from student experience and using the discussion format to elicit their current understanding of what a given tool will do is that they are participating and recollecting their own previous encounters with all sorts of materials. When it comes to leading the group toward the types of tools they may not have brought up on their own, for example, gazetteers or quotation books or that old favorite, Masterplots, it is best to give a brief definition and ask if they have ever used or perhaps needed such a thing. At some point in the lecture you should sort all the types of tools that have been considered into their large categories and to present these systematically, distinguishing among fact tools, finding tools, and the hybrids, much as these are discussed in Chapter 4.

The second approach can be used to convey the concept of types of reference tools with a subject-specific audience, taking a topic in their field of interest, ideally one paralleling a current assignment, and discussing the various types of reference tools that would be involved in investigating the topic. Presumably the librarian, selecting a topic and considering the types of tools that lend themselves to its investigation, would do so in search strategy order. Given a limited amount of time, it probably would not be good to stress the strategy so much in this instance as the types of tools involved and exactly how they would attack the whole problem. This is a conceptual approach also in that as each type of tool is discussed again, one would consider exactly what sorts of information the researcher could expect or predict from each type.

A critical difference between this and the first approach is that by working from an actual topic to the types of tools involved, one would also be discussing why these particular types of tools and not others are important, whereas in the first approach, the entire array of possible tools (within reason, of course) is laid out and classified into the fact-finding-hybrid scheme. The other side of this difference is that if the topic chosen is too specialized or too narrow, it may not permit the exposition of various types of tools that would be desirable with that audience. For example, if the assignment is "find as many comments as possible on *The Great Gatsby*," the types of tools involved would be limited to various book-review indexes, bibliographies of twentieth-century American literary criticism, and, possibly, citation indexes, in this case, the *Arts and Humanities Citation Index*. These are all finding tools and do not represent the other types of tools prevalent in the study of literature—handbooks, biographical directories, literary gazetteers, and so forth. Hence, a broader topic is better, for example, social criticism in *The Great Gatsby* as it reflects F. Scott Fitzgerald's own life. This broader topic lends itself to a discussion of the full array of fact, finding, and hybrid tools for literature. If students contribute from their own experience to the discussion, capturing responses on a transparency or blackboard so that everyone in the audience can benefit from all contributions is especially profitable.

A third way to approach the type-of-tool lecture is to begin by eliciting from the audience generic types of reference tools and their characteristics. Then, as in both previous approaches, the librarian would group those mentioned into their larger families: fact, finding, and hybrid. What would then distinguish this approach is that for a subject-specific audience, a few specific titles (no more than three) of each type in their field can be introduced and explained in terms of the characteristics already defined for each type. For example, this part of the lecture might go from the concept of an index to periodical literature to a mention of the *Social Sciences Index* and *Psychological Abstracts* as specific examples of that concept. Here it is more important to discuss how these two indexes differ and yet share the common nature of an index as previously discussed than it is to show how each one "works" or is used. Again, it would be important to stress why and when an index in the student's special field is used—in other words, to derive subtly the notion of search strategy without launching into a separate lecture on that subject unless there is sufficient time to do so. The point is to go from characteristics to category, which would indicate that the students have grasped the objectives of the lecture.

An interesting reinforcement using this approach might be to bring to the lecture various examples of the different types of tools to be discussed, possibly having the volumes hidden by plain paper jackets. The students would be asked to examine each volume quickly, presumably not knowing its title, to see if they are able to categorize a specific item as to its reference nature, deciding what is in fact an index, a handbook, a biographical directory, and so forth. A variation on this is to make a transparency of annotations from Sheehy's *Guide to Reference Books*, but without the bibliographic information for each annotation, and see whether students, from reading the annotation, can correctly decide whether a book is a fact or a finding tool.

Question analysis option

Research problem analysis (Chapter 4) can also be reduced in scale to a one-shot presentation. Only two components of such a presentation are really important, and depending on the librarian's assessment of the group's sophistication and needs, these could be presented in either of two possible orders. First, categorize all research problems as simple, compound, or complex; then describe the eight steps outlined in Chapter 4 that the thorough researcher must consider before actually working through a complex research topic. For this presentation, choose a topic in the audience's field of specialization or area of interest. For a public library, one might discuss genealogy; for a garden club, resources on plants. For an elementary school, a current events topic would be appropriate. If the discussion comes first and the actual analysis second, analysis serves to reinforce discussion and gives users a handle by which to remember the various steps.

If, conversely, the lecture begins with a typical complex question and users are asked to brainstorm (this again assumes the use of a blackboard or transparency) about how they would approach the problem, it is critical to leave sufficient time to take the many varied and miscellaneously organized responses and put them back in a meaningful order so that users conclude the session with an idea of the most efficient approach to research question analysis. This second method may capture student's attention better than the first, since they participate at the very beginning of the lecture. On the other hand, students may become disinterested by what may appear to them an inconsequential exercise. It will be up to the librarian in consultation with the faculty member who may have requested such a one-shot to determine whether the "chicken" or the "egg" should come first.

Search strategy option

Chapters 5 through 8 discuss in detail the concept of search strategy in the research process in general and for various discipline groups. Like question analysis, search strategy can serve as the framework for a most effective one-shot for any group. We prefer this option when one has only a single opportunity to meet with a given group of people. The advantages are that it is based on natural human logic, relates to users' past frustrating experiences in attempting to do library research, and can be transferred to virtually any discipline or topic with only minor modifications. In short, it is the best all-purpose structure for a single lecture.

When planning an actual presentation, it is best to approach search strategy by first discussing the concept in the abstract, without regard to a particular topic (although comments might well be directed at search strategy in a particular discipline). We cover the logical steps the researcher must perform after having previously analyzed the topic. To begin discussion, it is often useful to ask students about their past methods of doing research (refer to the sample in Chapter 8). Typically, students will volunteer that in the past they have worked from references at the end of an encyclopedia article or from footnotes in a textbook or other known or recommended sources. Others will likely suggest using the card catalog or chatting with a knowledgeable expert and relying on that person's memory and judgment as to what are the most important concepts or works on the topic. Someone may also admit to having browsed the stacks for material on a topic without any qualitative recommendation for a given title. Last among probable responses is typically the use of periodical or newspaper indexes.

Write all reactions on the board as stated, without so much as a hint of censure or wince of dismay, which would completely foil the intent of the lecture. Then comment positively on the strengths of the various research methods that audience members have suggested and only remark on the negative aspects as drawbacks in the research process. For example, the drawback of consulting an expert is that the individual may not be completely aware of the latest developments in a field or may not fully remember the author, title, or year of an important publication, or else may neglect to mention an important thinker with whom he or she differs.

Following the discussion of search strategy in the abstract, the second half of the lecture should be a repetition of search strategy with mention of key titles for the discipline at each stage. The advantage of this is that users are exposed twice in the same session to an efficient sequence of steps, which, after all, is the defining characteristic of search strategy. The point is not to distract users with specific titles, but to impress them with the notion of an ordered approach to research using appropriate illustrations. In mentioning specific tools, it is thus not crucial to discuss the relative importance of each work and what it will yield in terms of furthering the overall research process. When repeating the search strategy with specific titles, all students should have in front of them the basic bibliographic information, call number, and location in the library of each item being mentioned so that they are not scrambling to jot down citations. If the time available is only a 45- or 50-minute class period, the search strategy option is ideal because it covers many concepts in a logical order, repeats those concepts, yet does not overwhelm users with bibliographic details. Furthermore, users will very likely be impressed if not excited with the knowledge that there is a straightforward way to go about library research just as there is an established way to go about primary research in any established discipline. (It may not be a bad idea to make that comment, pointing out to people that they expect to learn the protocol of research in the chemistry lab or observational technique prior to archaeological study or control setups in an experimental discipline, so why not also expect to learn about the best, most effective way to go about library research?)

The only difficulty with this option occurs in the historical disciplines where identifying and locating primary source material is paramount. As seen in Chapter 7, the problems of getting at primary source material and conceptualizing how it differs from secondary sources are extremely complex, and it is well to concentrate either on the variety of primary source materials in those fields or on search strategy for secondary source material, making clear to the audience what is being attempted. It may be possible, if time permits, to cover search strategies for primary and secondary materials, but unless users are very sophisticated, they may confuse the two. If time allows an in-class exercise as part of the session, the librarian might give students a complex research topic followed by a bogus and incorrect type-of-tool search strategy (not one with specific titles, unless everyone can be presumed to know the titles being mentioned) and ask them to rearrange the steps and give their reasoning.

Information structure/
discipline growth option

This method of structuring the one-shot is based on the discussions in Chapter 5 (for the most general case) and in Chapters 6 through 8 (for adaptations to various discipline groups). Here also are a number of possible approaches, the most straightforward being to take the actual discipline with which the students are involved and discuss in general terms its history and bibliographic development to the present. In most cases you can find a succinct discussion of the discipline in the *Encyclopaedia Britannica,* or in such guides as White's *Sources of Information in the Social Sciences,* or—a frequently overlooked source—the *International Encyclopedia of Higher Education.* Within the time constraints of the one-shot, there is seldom any need for a detailed discussion about all the intellectual drifts and connections in a discipline; it is more important to target one or more of the original pioneers and to discuss how their thoughts and communication with one another were captured and passed on to others, and how, in turn, the discipline has matured and fractioned into other specialties or whole new fields.

For a more general or mixed audience, including users from different subject backgrounds, it might be best to concentrate on one of the newer disciplines such as film studies, ethnic studies, or women's studies to show how quickly disciplines can emerge and develop in the latter half of the twentieth century and how the tools they generate and those they have yet to generate (the so-called holes in the bibliographic model) have come about.

It is possible to insert specific major titles in a lecture developed according to this option, but here again it is important to stress the concept of discipline shape and corresponding bibliographic shape or response rather than the specific details of any tools. Similarly, a handout is essential so that users will be able to refer to any specific tools that are mentioned without being distracted by taking notes.

An especially good way to lead a discussion about how a discipline grows and the parallel bibliographic structure that emerges to offer bibliographic control of that literature is through the use of a diagram. With this, it is possible to convey the idea of the different publications and reference books that appear over time. By determining the types of literature available in a field, it is possible to predict the types of reference sources one could expect to find. Thus, age of a discipline or subfield is crucial in this regard. The diagram can also illustrate the function of fact, finding, and hybrid reference tools. It is easy to point out which reference sources fit into the search strategy and should be used in order (finding and hybrid tools) and which reference tools do not fit into a search strategy (fact tools) and may be used at any point. (See

Table 9-1, where the arrow indicates the development of secondary sources over time. The corresponding finding tools that control these sources are used in the *reverse* order—top to bottom—to identify secondary material.)

Format option

By format we mean the section of question analysis that attempts to categorize a research topic according to whether the material is calls for is primary, secondary, or both. Another aspect of format has to do with the physical "container" in which information comes—book (monograph), journal article, newspaper, map, statistical table, and so forth. It is possible to construct an interesting and informative one-hour lecture around either or both of these concepts.

A word of caution about the crucial distinction between primary and secondary sources: Many if not most people do not have any notion, or at least not a clear one, of what is meant by a primary versus a secondary source. Underclass students who have not yet selected a major field of study will likely have heard those terms, but they will rarely be able to define them. And if they are able to express an even hazy idea of the distinction, they can seldom transfer it to a specific discipline. The definition of a primary source as "something written at the time" is the best you will probably hear from most people, whether undergraduates or—unfortunately—beginning graduate students. Until people have actual hands-on experience finding or generating primary source material, their notion of it will likely vary from vague to nonexistent. The concept is particularly slippery in the written humanities in which the primary source is itself a book, often a paperback at that, which is purchased and thought of by the individual as a textbook. The volume of criticism looks and feels just like the novel it discusses and is purchased at the same store or located on an adjacent shelf in the library. There is no tangible difference between the two; hence, the idea of their intrinsic difference escapes the average person. The concept of primary source will perhaps be somewhat more precise to those in the social and physical sciences because they, if students, may be enrolled in a laboratory, field-work, or experimental course and thus actually be generating primary data. In any case, an interesting one-hour lecture can center on the

Table 9-1 Control of Secondary Literature*

	Secondary Literature	Hybrid Tools	Finding Tools
Time for Generation ↑		Encyclopedias Histories	
	Textbooks Books (monographs) Anthologies Journal articles Conference papers		Bibliographies: ongoing single publications, local library catalogs Indexes and abstracts

Fact Tools	Guides
Handbooks Dictionaries Gazetteers Directories Biographical sets	Guides to the literature Guides to reference books

*The concepts in this table are adopted from William D. Garvey and Belver C. Griffith, "Scientific Communication: Its Role in the Conduct of Research and Creation of Knowledge," *American Psychologist* 26 (April 1971): 349–362.

distinction between primary and secondary sources and how that distinction is manifested in different disciplines. Add to this the key finding tools that will identify primary and secondary sources (or both) for the users' particular field of interest, and you will have a significant, and novel, lecture plan.

Format in the physical sense can also be discussed in the same lecture as the primary/secondary format concept. Here it might be worthwhile to concentrate on fact and finding tools that relate to only one physical format, for instance, to how to find journal articles that may themselves yield either primary or secondary information. Another way of approaching physical format is to take the concept of the journal as a major communication vehicle for current thought in a discipline and discuss the various fact and finding tools that deal with journals. Such a lecture might cover *Ulrich's International Periodicals Directory, Acronyms and Abbreviations, Union List of Serials/New Serial Titles*, or various Wilson indexes. At an advanced level, a single lecture on identifying and locating manuscripts might be especially useful for students majoring in any of the historical sciences. Depending on the disciplines involved, you can devise any number of creative lectures around characteristics of intellectual or physical format.

Mix-and-match option

Obviously, it is possible to take any of the preceding lecture options and combine them in a new pattern. An all-theory session, which could be adequately presented within 50 minutes, would, for example, begin with the various steps in question analysis, expanding on the final step—type-of-tool determination—with participants discussing what sorts of reference works they have used in the past and whether those were fact, finding, or hybrid. The lecture could conclude with a rearrangement of finding tools mentioned into search strategy order. Although a handout would not be necessary for such a one-shot, it would be desirable to provide one *after* the lecture, listing basic tools of each type with call numbers so participants have titles to start with as they attempt to adopt theory to circumstance.

Another variation on the mix-and-match theme is a lecture based on a subject of local interest. For instance, you may be asked to give a one-hour presentation to a group of library users who wish to do research on a particular regional or local topic, such as the history of a church or marriage patterns among residents in the nineteenth century. Such research requires primary sources and involves local archives, records, statistics, possibly master's theses or doctoral dissertations, and other nonstandard or not-well-controlled materials. This sort of lecture is an excellent opportunity to discuss basic search strategy briefly and then to explain how the standard recipe *cannot* be followed for the topic in question but must be modified so that local repositories and other resources are substituted at different steps. Diaries and oral history should logically be part of the discussion, as should the probability of locating relevant material in the files of local social and fraternal groups, not to mention in attics. The real goal of the local lecture is to get audience members thinking about hidden resources and ways to discover them.

The spectrum of possibilities for a mix-and-match lecture is nearly infinite, and you should explore all varieties, especially when you are requested to speak to an audience with undefined or diverse interests. Such an opportunity will allow you to experiment with concepts and presentation techniques and to decide from experience how effective a particular combination of ideas may be with a given group. Remember, however, that any time you give a "nonstandard" lecture, it is crucial to get at least verbal feedback from the audience and to make copious notes immediately afterward about how you feel the session went and how you could improve it the next time.

Whatever structure you choose for the one-shot lecture, you must make further decisions about whether the presentation should proceed from general to specific, whether (and if so, how) it should tie in to users' current needs, whether examples should be random (hoping thereby to "grab" all the participants at least some of the time) or all should pertain to a single topic or discipline, and whether activities are to be included. Ideas for such reinforcing activities are given throughout this chapter.

Hints for Presenting
One-Hour Lectures

1. Explain to the participants in every case why a particular concept or title is important for their work.

2. Be relaxed and friendly, injecting humor if possible where it "fits" into your presentation.

3. Plan ahead for some form of follow-up or evaluation; for example, arrange in advance with the faculty member who has requested a course-related one-shot to examine students' bibliographies submitted with research papers.

4. Until you have considerable teaching experience, you will find that it is difficult to speak slowly and articulately; so make a special effort to do so.

5. Similarly, you will probably lose your sense of the passage of time when you are giving a lecture; so make sure that a watch or clock is visible, and if possible jot down (or ask a colleague to attend your lecture and take notes) how long each segment of your presentation takes.

6. It is virtually impossible to cover more than 20 titles coherently in a one-hour time block; fewer than that if you are emphasizing theory.

7. It is extremely useful both for yourself and for your colleagues to keep a well-arranged archival file (indexed if possible) of all your lecture outlines, notes, and handouts, as well as evaluations. Be sure to date all materials and indicate the size and nature of the audience as well as your own subjective reactions to the group. Vow never to remove anything from the archive except to photocopy pages for use in planning a similar future lecture.

8. Be careful not to reproduce too many extra handouts thinking that you will use them for a repetition of the same lecture, since you will usually want to revise your presentation the next time you give it. Three or four extras are ordinarily sufficient, allowing one for the archival file, one for evaluation purposes or to accompany an annual BI report, and one to modify for future lectures (two if your handouts are on two sides of each sheet of paper and you cut-and-paste changes), and possibly one to give a user who misses the presentation and comes to you afterward.

9. In the event you make more handouts than you need, a way to make good use of them is to send them out to faculty members or other potential "customers" with a cover memo explaining the purpose and nature of the session and your willingness to provide such a lecture for other groups.

10. Consider the possibility of using a word processor to create, update, and maintain handouts and lecture outlines.

Such technology can be especially valuable if many different librarians offer lectures, permitting each person to assemble new handouts from citations input by colleagues. You might volunteer BI handouts when your institution is looking for practice material for those being trained to use word-processing equipment.

11. It would be a great help to you as an instructor and to your BI effort generally if, once you are comfortable teaching, you enlist a candid colleague to attend one of your lectures to make notes on both the content and style of your presentation. If this person will then share the observations with you and offer suggestions on how you might improve your effectiveness, you will undoubtedly benefit.

Preparing the One-Hour Lecture

If you have chosen any of the concept-only approaches for your one-hour lecture, preparation consists of making a detailed outline of the points you wish to present, in a logical order, and of the examples or anecdotes you will use to illustrate those points. It is particularly important to focus your thinking on the level and background of your audience. And don't worry about being too elementary, ever, in an all-concept lecture. Most people have never more than vaguely wondered whether there is any rhyme or reason to the organization of material in a library, or the organization of knowledge for that matter. People unfortunately expect to have problems finding information in a library, just as virtually everyone these days expects to encounter a bureaucratic hassle in any number of occurrences, for instance, clarifying one's eligibility for a certain tax deduction. But you cannot just talk in monumental generalities about the order of the research universe without also indicating ways in which your listeners can themselves profit from understanding how a library functions and where to tap in to a paradigm for specific types of information. Hence, consider how best to "hook" your particular group as you plan even an all-theoretical lecture—and remember to rethink both your approach and your specific comments every time you repeat that lecture so that each audience has a tailor-made presentation.

If, as is perhaps more likely, you have settled on a mixed approach for your one-hour lecture, hanging specific titles on a conceptual framework, then you might prepare it in a series of steps outlined below. As an example, we are assuming the common case of titles-in-search-strategy-order, centering on some specific research topic.

Step 1. Identify and become thoroughly familiar with the appropriate guide to the discipline(s) involved.[1] If the only existing guide in the field is poor or out of date, or if the topic you will be illustrating is too new or interdisciplinary to have been treated by the all-purpose guides, consult some of the sources noted in Finding Guides to the Literature, later in this chapter, to identify a guide that will be of help to you.

Step 2. Working with whatever guide you have found, and with any other descriptive material you may have collected, your next effort is to understand its model of fact and finding tools. Usually, just knowing what tools exist will allow you to sketch the bibliographic structure without further ado. If, however, the field is foreign to you, it might take some time to determine whether what appear to be "holes" in the paradigm are really that or whether the information that seems to be lacking is, in fact, satisfactorily conveyed by a tool in a related field. For example, if you are preparing a lecture on the search strategy and major tools for science fiction study and do not find a biographical directory of authors and scholars, it may be because these individuals are adequately covered in broader compendiums such as *Contemporary Authors* or the *Directory of American Scholars.*

"Holes" are usually, but not always, directly related to the comparative youth of a discipline. Yet sometimes a field lacks an obvious tool for other reasons, such as the inability of scholars to get funding for a monumental project or the absence of an adequate incentive or reward system that would incline practitioners to divert their energies to tool construction. You would always do well to consider the possible reasons for an apparent gap so that you can make the point to your audience that people will need to substitute another source or "do without" that particular type of tool. Especially good discussions of discipline structure can be found in *Literature and Bibliography of the Social Sciences, Sources of Information in the Social Sciences, Bibliography: Current State and Future Trends,* and *A Reader's Guide to the Social Sciences,*[2] but these tend to cover traditional disciplines only.

There are frequent "holes" or discrepancies in what one

would expect to be similar paradigms. Psychology, for instance, has a recent major encyclopedia (*International Encyclopedia of Psychiatry, Psychology, Psychoanalysis, and Neurology*); sociology, in many respects a sibling discipline, has no equivalent tool—to say nothing of the relative merits of *Psychological Abstracts* versus *Sociological Abstracts* in terms of ease of use of the printed tools. A different sort of discrepancy is found in cases such as the importance of almanacs for the study of pre–twentieth-century American literature or the fact that reviews are critical for film study but are of only minor use for the experimental social sciences. Collections of bibliographic essays—whether called *Annual Review of . . .*, *Year's Work in . . .*, *Advances in . . .*, *State of the Art in . . .*, or some distinctive title, exist in many, but not all, disciplines; political science and economics lack such a series, for example. These are but a few of the kinds of special contours you can anticipate as you prepare lectures in new fields.

Step 3. Select the few titles you plan to discuss in your lecture. Keep in mind the level and immediate research needs of your audience, and choose tools that reflect the general shape of the discipline's communication structure—providing, of course, that your intent is to expose students to the notion of search strategy. Mix broader with more specific tools of the same type; for example, discuss *Social Sciences Index* and then *Child Development Abstracts*.

Step 4. Check your institution's catalog to determine whether you have all the items you wish to discuss and, if so, where they are in the system.

Step 5. Having confirmed your institution's ownership of the particular tools you wish to present, explore your catalog and shelves carefully to find any appropriate items your library owns but that are not in the guide to the literature you have consulted. Use both the semantic approach (working from tracings of known tools to find unfamiliar ones by subject in the catalog) and the locational approach (browse both your reference collection and the general stacks for material classified adjacent to titles you are already aware of). If your institution's system is highly decentralized or if your topic is interdisciplinary, browse the stacks of other campus libraries as well as your own to determine the full range of relevant tools.

Step 6. Initiate orders for items your institution lacks that you have discovered are crucial to library research, and will strengthen your resources in the future. If you are not in a position to authorize book purchases, notify whoever is responsible for collection development of the significance of the purchase.

Step 7. Look at each title you are considering for your presentation. First, verify that your library has the item on its shelves. Frequently key titles get sent out for repair or are transferred just when you want to use them for a lecture (or the catalog record is wrong about holdings or location). Other times, a basic work may be missing; so you will have either to identify another copy or substitute another title that does approximately the same job in the search strategy. If at all possible, and especially for a group of undergraduates, avoid mentioning any reference tool that is not available.

Check each potential title against the annotations in the guide you are using. You will be surprised at the number of cases in which a publication has changed radically over time. This is particularly true of serial finding tools such as *Psychological Abstracts,* in which the scope of material included and/or the degree of indexing varies from year to year and can only be determined by closely examining the preface and the arrangement of recent issues. Even so common a title as the *Readers' Guide* has excluded, then included, book reviews and has changed important headings (such as Moving Pictures) to more colloquial terms in recent years. Do not overload your audience, but refamiliarize yourself with more details about each item than you ever intend to impart. (This process makes BI, along with database searching, an unequaled professional activity. In order to "do" BI well, you have to know the concepts and tools you present far better than you would need to otherwise. Continually establishing, or reestablishing, this rapport with theory and materials keeps you abreast of new developments in the world of reference and research librarianship in a way no continuing education course or workshop ever can.) The goal of BI is not to clone mini-reference librarians, but to create student sensitivity to the nuances of information gathering. Therefore, it is imperative that bibliographic instructors be so thoroughly acquainted with the material presented that they can readily extrapolate to other contexts.

Step 8. Compare and contrast tools, both to help you select the best ones to present and to determine what you want to highlight about those you do discuss.[3] Key aspects of any reference work are its scope, arrangement of or approaches to information, time lags (either coverage or publication date), revision frequency, indexes, and special features such as appendixes or chronological tables. At this stage you will also be determining relationships between one work and others that ostensibly do the same thing. Perhaps most important you will be deciding the place of each title in the search strategy outline you intend to present.

Make notes on all these points on oversize index cards, one card per item, possibly using different color cards for different types of tools or different lectures. Some people prefer to photocopy the entries from whatever guide they are using and paste them on their cards, supplementing the annotations with call numbers, additional points about the title, and examples to use with a class.

It is extremely helpful, especially for the first lectures you prepare, to jot down the logical connectives between items you discuss so that the context as well as the specific details are right in front of you as you speak. Other kinds of information you may want to record are shown on the Sample Card on a Reference Book for Instruction, later in this chapter.

Avoid imposing a librarian's perspective on students. Ask yourself about every title you select and about everything you decide to say about it, "Why would *these* students want or need to know this?" At first you will find it awkward to switch mind sets, but it becomes more natural the more lectures you do. Even if you are thoughtful about choosing tools, it is easy to mix extraneous facts (that the editor changes with each edition, for example) with essential ones (that there is no subject index). From a reference librarian's perspective, fine points about a tool may be crucial in indicating its appropriate use, but especially in a one-hour lecture for undergraduates, you are courting disaster to "tell all." Cut back on description and stress instead the role of each title in the research process.

Your observations about the books should be on a fresh card to reflect the user's perspective. Remember you are a teacher of *relevant* research methods and materials. Your intellectual stance should be that of user-advocate; you should be always comfortable explaining *why* some tool or procedure is important, rather than defensive because students have challenged—or yawned at—your presentation. You need not, of course, preface every tool with an explicit "why-you-want-to-know-this" statement, but that rationale should always be clear to you and implicit in your comments. You will find students' framework easier to deal with when you are lecturing on research procedures for a specific assignment; every title you present must have a direct and obvious bearing on the project at hand, regardless of what else you might prefer to discuss.

So what *should* you plan to say about any particular tool? There is no standard answer to that question, of course, but the cardinal rule is to keep your commentary to a minimum, saying only enough to describe the tool's nature and importance and (if you are also considering another title of the same type) what distinguishes it from similar tools. If use of the tool is obvious, you do not need to dwell on it, but you *will* need to expand on any idiosyncrasies of scope or arrangement that cause people problems. Any time you can relate a title to something you have said previously (the *Readers' Guide* today uses the same Library of Congress subject headings as does the catalog), by all means do so.

Step 9. Choose examples pertinent to your audience. The library users you are likely to meet in a BI lecture will at least have some interests in common deriving from their presence in that particular group. Some BI librarians believe firmly that all examples chosen from the tools to be presented in a single lecture should be consistent—that is, they should all concern the same specific topic (women in the work force) or author (Emily Dickinson) that students are studying. Following this approach allows you to compare tools in concrete terms and to demonstrate how coverage and headings vary from title to title as well as over time.

The competing belief is that it is better to choose a different example from each tool you cover, hoping that sooner or later you will mention a topic of interest to each student in your audience. This approach is most effective for relatively small groups, where you know in advance what topics students are working on, and so can "plant" interest-catching examples throughout your talk. Humorous or off-beat examples can heighten student interest and—in theory—retention. Every reference tool ever created, from telephone books and dictionaries to online catalogs and citation indexes, has either an unusual arrangement, bizarre entries, or both. It is easy to pick out entertaining examples to illustrate the scope and use of virtually anything. Take care, however, that the lecture does not become a stand-up comedy routine or an oral equivalent of the *Guinness Book*. A funny performance, even with an excellent handout, will leave students chuckling but not convinced about the usefulness of the tools presented for their (generally unfunny) needs. Worse yet, serious students and faculty members who attend your lecture are likely to be turned off entirely by what they may perceive as a sideshow act without substance. So, include humorous examples only when they make a point you intend to make anyway and do not rely exclusively on them in any single session. On the other hand, judicious use of unusual examples will often enhance your presentation, especially in contrast to fairly somber and straightforward concepts, such as question analysis, type-of-tool discrimination, and search strategy formation.

Here is a practical consideration in the choice of examples: If you plan to have copies of each tool for every member of your audience, it may be better not to predetermine the examples, but rather have each student look up his or her own specific topic in whatever volume is in hand. Doing this takes a little longer, but it also allows students to test each tool for relevance. Your role in such a situation is to be ready either to suggest an alternative heading or to explain why a topic may be beyond the scope of that particular tool.

Step 10. Sketch your lecture around the concepts and titles you have decided to highlight, keeping in mind your objectives for both the lecture and your overall BI effort, the time you have for presentation, the level of students to whom you will be speaking, and whether a research assignment is involved. Of these, time available is undoubtedly the most critical factor as you actually shape your lecture. Ask yourself whether you can spare the five minutes that would be necessary (at minimum) to give an in-class exercise or final quiz. Can you convey the notion of a particular type of tool by explaining a simple example (the *Readers' Guide* rather than *Poole's Index*), then mention that the other titles on the handout under that heading all work more-or-less the same way, and do the same job in the search strategy? Do you want to spend more time proportionately on concepts and less on specific titles, or vice versa?

What, if any, related resources are there on campus or nearby that you might want to mention? Such resources might include other whole collections, special services (maps, microforms, documents), or particular staff specialists with whom students might be in touch.

Step 11. Draft your final lecture outline, ordering together all the elements you intend to cover: introductory comments, theory, specific titles, quick tour as a summation, or whatever. Be clear about why you have chosen the sequence; every idea should be where it is for a reason that you are comfortable with and could explain to an observer. If you have not already done so, jot down at least phrases to remind yourself of logic, both on your note cards for specific titles and in your overall outline, so that you can move from theory to particular tools and back to theory with ease. Last, think about your introduction to the lecture, the two or three opening sentences concerning what you will cover and why it is important. If you are at a loss about how to make transitions from one major segment of your presentation to another, an approach that always seems to work is a rhetorical question on the model of, How would you go about finding a brief biographical sketch on each of the signers of the Declaration of Independence? (Don't worry about a conclusion; you will either have no time for one or will find yourself automatically reiterating whatever seems to be the most critical point you have made. If words escape you in the last few seconds, you can always say that you and your colleagues look forward to working with the students on their individual projects in the near future.)

Step 12: Prepare handouts and any other teaching aids. Unless you are giving an all-theory lecture, provide students with typed handouts listing all titles you will cover in the order you cover them. Basic information can be taken by a typist from your own note cards. It should include essential bibliographic data, call numbers, and special locations for each item. Space should be provided for students to take notes as you lecture or as they examine a given item. Including relevant LC subject headings for that type of tool is especially helpful. Since it is impossible for anyone to listen, look, take notes, and think attentively, it is not fair to expect students to perform all these activities in the course of your lecture, especially if they have to scurry to keep up with everything you are mentioning. They will get much more out of the experience if they concentrate on two of the four activities, knowing that they can fall back on a complete handout to refresh their memories. Many BI librarians would argue that it is essential to annotate the handout. However, the investment in time required to annotate a 15- to 20-title handout would probably at least double the effort involved in lecture preparation, and students are far more likely to be inattentive if they think the handout duplicates the lecture.

In addition to a complete list of all titles in sequence you will be discussing, a BI handout might include diagrams of concepts such as search strategy to be presented, or photocopies of pages from key tools. A column copied from *Library of Congress Subject Headings* is extremely helpful, especially if you do not plan to use transparencies, in helping students understand a new and rather difficult set of notations. Some BI teachers like to have copies of catalog cards to illustrate that part of their presentation, or samples of entries from difficult-to-use tools (such as *Comprehensive Dissertation Index*) in lieu of taking volumes to the lecture site. Consider the costs involved in larger handouts versus the benefits to students—and always try to arrange for duplication on both sides of each sheet.

Besides arranging for handouts, plan what, if any, other "props" you will need. The traditional practice is to take copies of all titles to be discussed to the lecture room, assuming it is not far and that library reference operations can stand the absence of important tools for the duration (that is why a duplicate collection of teaching materials is especially nice). If your group is too large to pass books around for individual examination, it is still useful for students to see an array of key materials and to be able to come up after the lecture to look at particularly intriguing titles.

Overhead transparencies and slides, if you are fortunate enough to have the expertise and equipment at hand to make professional-looking ones, are also favorite ways of supplementing a lecture. (The pros and cons of AV modes are discussed in Chapter 3.) Opaque projectors, although primitive, can help to explain particularly troublesome tools.

Still other aids you might wish to consider are oversize catalog cards or identical sets of cards for use in teaching filing rules, a "blown-up" and photographed entry from a complicated tool, or a slide/tape or videotape to explain a complex procedure. Some librarians have superseded copies of reference serials for use in BI, either handing out entire issues for students to peruse simultaneously, or else (and this can set a dangerous precedent) tearing pages from old issues and allowing students to keep them following the lecture.

Finding guides to the literature

If you do not know of a guide to the literature in a given discipline, consult the *American Reference Books Annual, Reference Sources,* the review summaries in the *Journal of Academic Librarianship,* and recent issues of the major library periodicals that separate reference materials from other publications: *Library Journal, Choice, RQ, College & Research Libraries* (especially the January and July issues, which serve to update Sheehy), *Wilson Library Bulletin,* and *Booklist.* If in the course of familiarizing yourself with the range of reference tools in the disciplines you will be discussing, you discover a source that ought to do a certain job in the search strategy, you will have to advise your clients how to proceed in your library without it.

Current Book Review Citations includes reviews cited in *Library Literature* and "catches" reviews of those same titles that may have appeared in the discipline journals themselves. Because *Choice*'s reviews are by faculty, they provide good insights into how practitioners in a discipline expect to use a reference tool.

Another helpful place to look for a list of tools for a given field is at the end of the article entitled "____ as a Discipline" in the excellent *International Encyclopedia of Higher Education.* Although the sources cited are not annotated, they do constitute a "mini-Sheehy," which serves to identify the major tools for each academic discipline. Similarly, a given article in a subject-specific encyclopedia, such as the *Encyclopedia of Philosophy,* may consider the development of the bibliographic structure of a particular field or subfield. Either your own institution's catalog or the *Library of Congress Book Catalog: Subjects* might identify a scholar's study of a discipline in which one chapter would logically discuss the origin and present state of bibliographic and factual control in the field. Unfortunately, the Library of Congress has yet to establish a specific heading phrase such as "____ as a Discipline"; so such a study is likely to get buried in the catalog limbo of "____—Study and Teaching," or, worse yet, be captioned with the discipline's name alone, without subdivision.

It might be well to contact the major association in the field to ask if an article or monograph has been published on its reference apparatus; the collection of such overviews that appeared in *Library Trends* and was later republished[4] is especially excellent if nothing more recent for your field is available. A call or note to LOEX[5] will quite possibly yield someone else's BI handout in your problem area. Disciplines that publish an annual volume of bibliographic essays will sometimes devote a section to new reference tools or a state-of-the-field in regard to bibliographic access. And don't overlook *Bibliographic Index* as a way of discovering guides that might appear there only under the discipline's name. If all else fails, consult the major finding tools in neighboring fields or perform a database search looking for the combined concepts of the discipline's name and reference or bibliography. DIA-LOG'S DIALINDEX, SDC's Data Base Index, and BRS's Cross Index serve as master indexes to each vendor's bases and would be particularly useful to try first.

All these tactics will seldom be necessary in order to locate a guide or a guide-substitute from which you can work in planning your one-hour lecture. But these are the possibilities in the event you are ever "stuck" on where to start.

Sample card on a reference book
for instruction

Kinds of information you may want to record include the following (for your own background if not for actual comments you wish to make to the audience): what Library of Congress subject headings have been assigned to the tool, where you found the item cited (for example, in which guide or under what circumstances you first became aware of the title), references to any reviews you may have read or collected about its coverage vis-à-vis that of a similar work, or anecdotes you recall from real-life reference questions where the tool proved useful. Save the back of the card for such data as when and for what group you discussed the work, plus after-the-fact memos to yourself such as "too complicated for sophomores" or "next time mention in conjunction with ____." Although every BI librarian's notes will be unique, the front of a sample note card might look something like that on the following page.

Ref.   CRIS: The Combined Retrospective Index Set to Jour-
Z   nals in History, 1838–1974. Washington, Carrollton
6205   Press, 1977–
.C92

COVERAGE: All articles from 1838 to 1974 in 243 English-language
                  periodicals.
SCOPE: History—political, military, cultural, local history.
ARRANGEMENT: Large classed arrangement including chronology, biog-
                  raphy, and subjects (in front of volumes); within catego-
                  ries articles are arranged by keyword in title; articles
                  with no keywords are first; articles chronologically sec-
                  ond, then keywords. Within a keyword grouping, arti-
                  cles are arranged by year article was written, then by
                  journal code.
INDEXES: author
ENTRY: Air Force Base, Maxwell AFB Alabama 36th Ann
                      CP Felice   1956   3   1   138

                  (An article may be listed in as many categories as nec-
                  essary and under several keywords.)
ADVANTAGES OF CRIS:
                  1. Replaces numerous separate searches in annual or
                     quinquennial volumes of several serial indexing
                     services.
                  2. Provides access to journals that were never covered
                     or were picked up years after journals began, e.g., *Pa-
                     cific Sociological Review* never in standard index;
                     Sociometry indexing began 1937 and picked up 1974.
TO USE CRIS MOST EFFICIENTLY:
                  1. Look at chronological, biographical, and subject cate-
                     gories to pick out relevant broad areas.
                  2. Look under all possible related keywords (syno-
                     nyms).

HISTORY—PERIODICALS—INDEXES

This chapter has elaborated the whys, wherefores, and hows
of the one-hour lecture because it is the essential building
block of all forms of bibliographic instruction. It is also much
easier to extrapolate principles from the one-hour lecture to
other modes than to do the reverse; hence, the reader can
adapt the thoughts in this chapter to another situation since
the considerations regarding content, planning, and presentation apply in all realms of BI.

Notes

1. When in doubt, or if you do not know if there is a special guide, rely on Eugene P. Sheehy's *Guide to Reference Books* (Chicago: American Library Association, 1976) and *Walford's Guide to Reference Material*, 3 vols, 4th ed. (London: Library Association, 1980–) as the standard universal tools that categorize and evaluate reference works.

2. Thelma Freides, *Literature and Bibliography of the Social Sciences* (Los Angeles: Melville, 1973); Herbert White, *Sources of Information in the Social Sciences* (Chicago: American Library Association, 1973); Robert Downs, *Bibliography: Current State and Future Trends* (Urbana: Univ. of Illinois Press, 1967); Bert F. Hoselitz, *A Reader's Guide to the Social Sciences*, rev. ed. (New York: Free Press, 1970).

3. If you have forgotten how best to scrutinize tools from the time you took general reference, you might want to reread the introduction to Sheehy's *Guide to Reference Books* for a succinct description of the procedure.

4. *Library Trends*, 15, nos. 3–4 (1967); republished as *Bibliography: Current State and Future Trends*.

5. LOEX (Library Orientation and Instruction Exchange), Library, Eastern Michigan University, Ypsilanti, MI 48197; 313-487-0168.

10
Planning Courses

Simply defined, a BI course is a series of one-shot lectures. But if that would suffice, a separate chapter on the subject would be unnecessary, because a librarian planning such a course could just repeat the steps covered in Chapter 9 for as many sessions as necessary. However, the concept of a BI course has underlying principles that should guide it, and it has a characteristic pattern all its own.

The order in which material is presented is crucial for the BI course in the same way that the sequence of topics in a one-shot lecture is critical. Also, the course permits the presentation of complex ideas, with one concept or one type of tool or specific title necessarily preceding another; for example, it is difficult even on the graduate level to present effectively in a single session the concepts of guides to reference work, bibliographies of bibliography, and comprehensive completed bibliographies. This is especially true if actual titles are also being described as the concepts are presented. Not only are all these related topics of great importance and deserve more attention than the five or ten minutes that can be devoted to each, but the simple learning factor of time to absorb the material is not generally present in a one-shot lecture. It would be, however, in a course in which the various topics can be handled in successive sessions. Even if they are handled in the same session, the following lecture can reiterate the major points that students must remember in order to proceed in their search strategies.

Another point is that except for the most theoretically oriented one-shot, most single contact lectures can convey only one or two skills or tools, can only present the notion that more is out there, that the librarian is approachable and has the willingness to work with the individual student in pursuit of additional material, and can only suggest that the concepts covered are transferable from discipline to discipline. In contrast, a course permits these same messages to be transmitted overtly to students because there is sufficient time to compare and contrast and generally comment on the utility of the ideas and titles described.

No specific quantitative criteria defines what is and what is not a BI course. It would be possible under precise circumstances to call a course a succession of just two one-shot lectures, if the materials covered in each had been carefully orchestrated to build the second upon the first. The nature of the discipline as well as the level of the students will in large part dictate the number of individual sessions that are necessary to constitute a meaningful course. For instance, in a relatively young discipline with good bibliographic control, such as psychology where library research is primarily conducted to identify relevant secondary source material, a complete BI course might involve as few as six contact hours. But in a field such as one of the historical sciences or one of the older humanities such as philosophy or literature, four times that many hours may be barely sufficient even for students at the same level of education because of their need to discover the full range of primary as well as secondary sources.

Everything said in previous chapters about possible modes of instruction and the ability to mix and match them is all the more powerful when it comes to the course, because with more than one presentation at the librarian's disposal, it is possible to combine the class lecture mode with, for example, printed guides or a brief pathfinder or programmed workbook assignment, possibly also a computer exercise. Use of audiovisuals and the possibility of inviting a guest lecturer or taking the group on a "field trip" to another library or to a special unit—for example, rare books—within the library also become feasible in the time span of several sessions. The creativity permitted when it is possible to mix and match modes, the flexibility in terms of the instructor's time, and the ability to draw on the talents of other staff members are major benefits of the course option.

This chapter discusses in detail the overall organization and development of a BI course of any length, with particular reference to the classroom lecture mode. This is not meant to exclude or downplay the benefits of involving other modes of instruction, but since we believe that the concepts covered in this book are most effectively conveyed by the lecture, in directing our attention to that mode, we can provide the most nearly complete picture of what the BI course can achieve.

Academic Sponsorship of a BI Course

In the realm of a "home" for a BI course, it is important to consider the various options, some practical in nature, some more political. If the library and the bibliographic instruction librarian want the course legitimized within the academic framework of the institution, and if the library itself is regarded as an academic unit able to generate courses, it is a relatively simple matter, with the agreement of the top library administrators, to establish the BI course under the aegis of the library itself. In some institutions this is happening today as a direct correlation to the growing emphasis on redeveloping basic literacy skills among incoming undergraduates. An academic institution committed, as, for example, is the University of Wisconsin—Parkside in Kenosha, to the principle that library research skills go hand-in-hand with writing, reading, basic mathematics, and study skills, can require a course taught by librarians to achieve this end. At other institutions, such as Long Beach State University in California, the library BI course is part of a larger "survival package" to which students are steered if they appear to be deficient in any of the basic skill areas. Both approaches tend to emphasize library concepts and skills for their use to the individual throughout life, not just as a means of surviving the academic years or writing required research papers more effectively.

In the more common situation, where the library is not itself a course-sponsoring entity on campus, there may be a possibility of offering the course under the name of an existing academic department, either as a required course or as an elective to some identifiable group, usually undergraduates majoring in a particular department or beginning graduate students. Of course, numerous and sometimes insurmountable political difficulties arise in having a course approved, let alone approved and required, by an academic department. Most of the difficulties arise from the apportionment of funds by the university administration or by a particular dean on the basis of credit hours generated and the problems of having a nondepartment instructor, that is, a librarian, generating credits, that is, money, in some departments and not others.

Another political difficulty has to do with the overall total of credit hours or semester or quarter hours required of any student in a program and what happens if a new requirement—a BI course—is added to their schedules. Does that mean they will take one less "regular" course within the department? If so, enrollment may decline in classes taught by regular faculty members. Still another difficulty has to do with the feeling of some faculty that credit in their discipline cannot or should not be given for a course the content of which is not that discipline, but rather concepts and research methods that relate to it. Other corollary situations, however, include the teaching of statistical methods or research design, which are not content but rather procedure and structure.

At any rate, if a course is offered for credit and the library would like to have it required, the best approach might be via an interdisciplinary academic department or program on campus, since its very hybrid nature means that students are bound to have particular difficulties in using the library's reference collections and in identifying primary and secondary source materials. Hence, this particular audience is much more ripe for such an innovation than one of the standard, established disciplines.

If a course is established within an academic department or on its behalf, but perhaps not structurally part of the curriculum of that field, it may again be either required or elective. Often the best way to achieve attendance at a required but noncredit BI course is to have faculty members who are teaching a credit course tell students that they are expected to attend the BI sessions and that attendance, in fact, is an assignment for the required course. The result may be either a concurrent but independent series of presentations by the librarian, or possibly the use of several of the course's regular class hours. For example, the librarian may meet the students in their regular classroom or in the library during the regular class period three different times in one week. This then becomes a BI course that is integrated into an existing course within the department.

If, on the other hand, a noncredit BI course is an elective, certain benefits accrue that either are not possible or are very infrequent when the same course is required. Assuming that the student body is in some way motivated to make more effective use of their library research time (for example, seniors needing to write theses or beginning graduate students new to the institution), noncredit courses can be successful. As a consequence, students, who are in fact "volunteers" for a series of lectures and who faithfully attend each one, truly want to be there and are, therefore, more likely to retain the information presented than are students who must fulfill a requirement they do not understand. Such a self-selected group will often be the best advertisement for the library generally and the library's BI program in particular, since these people find it useful themselves, they are bound to tell peers and acquaintances. Furthermore, in many cases it is not only more rewarding for the librarian to have a motivated group as an audience, but it is easier to choose relevant examples among the various titles that might be presented or examples of topics within a specific reference work just because the students will be more vocal about their actual needs.

It is especially important in designing the curriculum for a volunteer BI course to time its placement in the academic year so that the regular pressures that upset a student's routine—exams and term papers—do not lead to nonattendance at the BI course. It might, for example, be a good idea to meet twice a week or hold one 2-hour segment per week for the first half of the 12-week term, and not meet at all the second half when students are likely to be busier (and also likely to be using the information they have absorbed from the course in consultation with the librarian). It is also a good idea not to begin a BI course the first week of the term, when students are still settling into their schedules, especially if the librarian has to do all the publicity for the effort. It often takes a week or two to notify students of the BI opportunity and to find a time that is least likely to conflict with regular course work.

The number of sessions that can be given to a volunteer group must also be considered. Very often it is difficult for students to understand, when they are "donating" their time for this experience, that there is so much material to cover. So it might be useful to create a syllabus containing the minimum number of topics for the discipline and level of students, but also hand out a supplementary sheet of other important topics that cannot be covered in the streamlined volunteer course.

One excellent way to prove the value of BI to an academic department is to begin on an ad hoc, elective, volunteer basis, whether sanctioned officially by the department or just focused on the students in that field, with the department not directly involved in setting up or maintaining the course. Here it is especially important to have a method of evaluation planned so that not only the number of students reached, but also some idea of their comprehension before and after, can be ascertained and presented to the department as an argument for continuing and perhaps directly supporting the effort in the future.

In addition to the possibility of credit versus noncredit BI courses, whether offered through the library or through the university, is the cooperatively taught course in which both a faculty member, or sometimes a group of faculty members, and the librarian alternate or in some other way share responsibility for course content. Typically, this will be a research methods course that combines library research with experimental or field research or with an overview of methods or schools of thought. For example, in philosophy or literature one faculty member might lecture on formalist criticism, another on deconstructionist approaches to the text, and the third week the librarian might discuss bibliographies for that discipline. This sort of class can either be very effective or a total disaster, depending on the selection of topics and the academic department's commitment to offering such an overview.[1]

Despite the intrinsic problems of piggybacking in a course that is, in fact, the departmental "guilt offering," such an arrangement can provide an extremely valuable occasion for librarian instructors to demonstrate both their own concern for students' research effectiveness and also the broad and deep array of types of tools related to that particular discipline. Faculty members who are responsible for a course that has research as its primary content, or that involves an extensive research product on the part of the students, are usually very pleased to be approached by a librarian who is willing to supplement the course's lectures and demonstrations. This can, of course, end up with the faculty member abrogating responsibility and essentially turning over many of the course hours to the librarian. But even if that does happen, it provides a marvelous opportunity for bibliographic instruction in that students who have elected such a course for credit generally will attend the librarian's sessions and are sure to find a well-structured experience useful.

A typical research methodology course for a literature field sponsored wholly by the department consists of perhaps two parts "reference works," one part descriptive or physical bibliography (learning to transcribe title pages of seventeenth-century books, do a correct bibliographic collation, or determine a succession of printings of the same text based on watermarks and other intrinsic evidence), and one part an exposure to critical methodology.

An interesting variation on several of the above approaches to the BI curriculum is a collaborative effort with faculty in which the librarian presents one or even two hours of material each week and a third contact hour is provided by teaching faculty members in rotation, each presenting a specialty from the point of view of the major research tools and techniques employed. Another way of approaching this is to have faculty lecturers from an entire spectrum of disciplines so that students are exposed to the broadest possible range of approaches to humanities, social science, and scientific research.

Pros and Cons of the BI Course

Before proceeding to the unique elements in preparing and presenting a BI course, let us look at the advantages and disadvantages of this mode. The primary advantage of the BI course is flexibility—more than any other method of instruction, it can be tailored to meet user needs. Educators sometimes refer to "teaching for failure," and this is a particular strength of the course mode—that is, addressing the content of the course to particular frustrations or problems library users have had in the past. For instance, most people, at one time or another, have had difficulty finding material using the subject approach to a card catalog, or they have had a scrambled citation to a periodical article or have felt that they were wasting time in what should have been some straightforward research. The flexibility of the BI course allows the instructor to respond to particular difficulties that users have experienced. Other modes, because they lack a long time frame for interaction between instructor and BI audience, cannot respond so effectively to user experience.

Another definite advantage of the course mode is that it permits two or more librarians to collaborate closely in planning and presenting the bibliographic instruction program. Different instructors and different librarians can be responsible for certain lectures or certain components of each lecture.

The course format can also give students a sense of the library, and of library research, as a coherent and comprehensible system that they can manipulate and be comfortable with. The best one-shot lecture in the world is likely to leave students glassy-eyed and amazed, even if also enthusiastic about the library, but it does not have the reiterative effect that a course permits. A course can also foster an understanding of search strategy and the various other theoretical constructs with which much of this book is concerned. By permitting a slow and careful exposure to the various components in the search strategy, the course gives students a much better sense of the whole world of information storage and retrieval than does a single isolated presentation.

Evaluating the effectiveness of a BI course is much easier than evaluating any other mode. Both the instructor and students have time to assess their progress and to straighten out any confusions that may arise. Learning can be reinforced from lecture to lecture or from lecture to the corresponding assignment or term project that may be part of the curriculum.

Still another advantage is that the course is the most familiar way in which students of any age or background have learned in the past. Therefore, they will not find the concept of a course in library research at all threatening, nor do faculty have to relinquish their own class time in order for the BI sessions to take place.

All the factors favorable to the one-hour lecture also pertain to a series of lectures, except that they are more intensified because of the additional exposures between users and instructor. Hence, the possibility for personal interaction between instructor and library users is increased, as is the opportunity for reinforcing exercises.

Disadvantages of the course mode are that the BI instructor especially needs good teaching skills and the ability to design and follow a curriculum and meaningfully evaluate it. The course requires a regular, adequate teaching space and any necessary equipment. This can be a problem if there is not enough space for a regular room assignment. Scheduling sessions is often a problem because the instructor's time needs to mesh with the students' or users' free times and also with the instructor's other job commitments, such as reference desk duties. (When dealing with a volunteer group of students, you may have to coordinate their free times with your own in order to schedule sessions that are convenient for all concerned.) The course format of instruction requires adequate and continual administrative support in terms of preparation time, support staff to assist the instructor throughout the teaching process, and reasonable help from colleagues who understand the importance of instruction and are willing to rearrange their own schedules to allow the instructor to meet BI commitments.

The BI course is immensely time-consuming to prepare, which some may see as a distinct disadvantage, but which may also be regarded as a golden opportunity for becoming personally and professionally current. Some administrators look down on the BI course because it has a relatively limited audience, permitting a few users to gain a great deal of information at the apparent expense of those who are not part of the group. Furthermore, it is impossible for one person to undertake more than two, or at the most three, courses simultaneously; so in order to reach a sizable number of library users with this sort of in-depth BI mode, many more librarians must necessarily be involved.

Faculty cooperation, or its lack, can be a treacherous problem in creating a successful course whether for credit or not. Only if the library itself is the sponsoring academic unit can this problem be totally averted. Good public relations are required no matter what the auspices of the BI course. If the library administration does not recognize this, perhaps that is an indication that so large a task should not be undertaken.

Another disadvantage to the course is the time involved for the staff to prepare teaching materials, such as making transparencies for slide/tapes and duplicating handouts and other aids.

Situation Factors for the BI Course

Audience size is one of the most critical aspects in planning an appropriate BI curriculum. Usually, however, librarians have more control over the number of students and any prerequisites for the class than they do for the one-shot lecture, which students usually attend in prearranged groups.

Other important aspects with which the BI planner must be concerned are the level of user sophistication in the library and the common background, if any, shared by users. Users' background will determine whether the BI course is kept to general concepts, tools, and skills, or whether it can move from the general to the specific within a certain discipline. User knowledge should be well understood, and if it is not apparent, it should be tested so that a syllabus can be designed that takes it into account.

Another factor is where the BI course fits in the total curriculum of the institution; for instance, are the students for whom the course is designed also writing senior honors papers or preparing for preliminary examinations? The number of contact hours and the length of each session must be determined at the outset so that the course outline can be prepared to make the best use of all available time.

Where the course will be taught and the equipment available are also critical to success. Not only is adequate space and comfortable seating necessary, but consideration must be given to the presence of a blackboard, the availability of sufficient outlets and any other equipment, and the proximity of that equipment and elevators. The expectations of faculty members and any preexisting scheduling problems are the final situational factors you should investigate before agreeing to undertake a BI course.

After having thought through and noted the various givens in the BI environment, you should focus on the content of the course you are designing. How should you combine orientation, specific types of tools, concepts (and of concepts, which ones in particular), specificity for a particular discipline or discipline group, and larger library research issues, such as the impact of automation on library research or the presence of a computer network.

Write one or two general or overall objectives for the entire BI course and several terminal objectives for each particular session. The best time to draft these objectives is either after you have targeted an audience and their situation, or after you have assembled a list of topics you wish to cover, but perhaps before you have decided what goes into each particular session. (Refer to Chapter 2 on objectives for a fuller discussion on their nature and intent.)

Overall Course Planning

Step 1. With a calendar, determine how many sessions you will have with your BI group. How often will you meet each week? What is the length of class sessions? Note any weeks or days in which the course will not meet, for example, during fall or spring break or on a holiday. Also try to anticipate from the beginning what sessions will be field trips or what sessions will be in collaboration with someone else so that you can make arrangements. A library conference or other professional commitment may intrude on one or more sessions of your curriculum. How do you intend to handle this? You can double up sessions at some point or continue past what would ordinarily be the last meeting date to make up time lost when you are not able to be present and a class has to be cancelled. Also consider enlisting colleagues as guest lecturers.

Step 2. Make a list of all the topics you would like to cover and that meet your stated objectives. Many people wonder what one would cover in a 10-session, 20-session, or even 30-session BI course. We have never had any problem with this and even have difficulty restricting the topics to the time available, even if it is an entire semester with more than one session a week. All the previously mentioned topics are critical enough and complicated enough to take an entire one-hour session within a larger course, but you will still want to plan for parts of sessions to be devoted to in-class exercises, student reports, quizzes or examinations, or guest lecturers. Determining potential content for a BI course is the single most important decision you will make in planning. See the list of possible topics below.

Possible topics in a BI course

Orientation:
　To the building.
　To the collection.
　To technical services processes.

General theoretical topics:
　Question analysis.
　Type-of-tool recognition.
　Search strategy formation.
　Discipline growth.

Specific families of fact and finding tools:

Indexes and abstracts.	Computerized bibliographic
Encyclopedias.	databases with demonstration.
Handbooks.	Almanacs.
Dictionaries.	Fact books.
Bibliographies.	Quotation books.
Gazetteers and atlases.	Book and film reviews.
Guides to the literature.	Manuscript sources.
Dissertations.	National bibliography.
Periodical directories,	Library catalogs.
union lists, periodical	Citation indexes.
abbreviation books.	

Special and auxiliary kinds of formats:

Government docu-	Manuscripts.
ments.	Archives.
Maps.	Microforms.
Film.	Special collections.
Vertical files.	Records, tapes.

Nature and future of libraries:
Card catalog/filing rules.
How to find a book.
Concept of classification.
Interlibrary loan.
Organization of the public catalog.
Library networking—OCLC, RLIN, WLN.
Online catalogs.
How to determine subject headings.

Step 3. Determine the characteristics of the discipline or discipline family on which you will concentrate (assuming that your audience is subject specific). If you are a subject specialist, you will already be aware of the important concepts and tools to be conveyed to students in your field. If you are not, you will have to consult guides to the literature for that particular discipline. (See Chapter 9 for the best way to use a guide to the literature in preparing a lecture.)

Step 4. Decide if you want to include other resources on your campus or in your area, such as an oral history collection, the rare books and manuscripts division, the map room, special libraries in the area, or the Human Relations Area Files. Also decide whom you might ask to guest lecture on a particular topic, either for a short segment within a single session or for an entire session.

Step 5. Organize your topics, field trips, and guest speakers into a logical order that fits the sessions available. One way to do this is to write down on separate slips of paper the possible content of any given session, and then arrange and rearrange these elements while looking at a calendar to decide what fits best in what time slot. You will probably have a longer list of potential topics than you have time to accommodate. The best way to pare down this list to manageable length is to consider whether some of the topics you would like to cover, and which you know should be covered for that discipline or particular audience, can in fact be omitted because users at that level have no immediate need for the information. For instance, dissertations and how to identify and obtain them may not be of any immediate interest to beginning graduate students and are almost certainly not a top priority to discuss with undergraduates, who (even if they know of the existence of relevant dissertations) probably do not have time to obtain data for any given project. Similarly, if you are at a small college library, you may want to avoid discussing the more erudite indexes that would lead students to periodicals and journals your institution does not own. Waiting for photocopies or interlibrary loans will only frustrate them in the long run.

Consider whether each topic will itself take an entire session or whether two topics can be logically and meaningfully combined into a single presentation. Try to fit together concepts or tools that are actually used together, but if you must have a miscellaneous session or two, it should combine easy and difficult concepts or tools. For example, a major topic such as trade bibliographies could be discussed in the same session with such a straightforward but unrelated subject as the handbooks that decode abbreviations. It is a good idea to avoid such unusual juxtapositions if at all possible, but in almost every sample BI syllabus, certain "leftovers" end up together toward the end of the course.

When scheduling content into specific time blocks, consider the flow of your objectives for the course and the progression of theory and specifics from session to session. Try to achieve an interesting mixture of types of presentation; for example, try to balance tours or physical orientation to special collections with lectures that are entirely theoretical, and others with an exercise on specific difficult tools.

We strongly advocate presenting material in search strategy order (this assumes that you will have discussed the nature and intent of search strategy in the first or second session and be building on it throughout the course). By discussing specific types of tools and specific titles of each type in the same order you are recommending for efficient research, students will get the idea of an appropriate method for their own research. If students have a research assignment for a course they may be taking concurrently, and if the BI sessions proceed in search strategy order, students will be able to pursue the necessary research for their other class while doing the assignments for your course.

Another possibility for course organization is to begin with varieties of reference tools with which students are already familiar, for example, encyclopedias or dictionaries, in each case expanding from the few titles they already know to helpful ones in other disciplines, explaining how each is representative of that particular type of material. Conversely, you can organize the course to move from more difficult or unusual types of tools to the more common and ordinary ones, thereby seizing attention immediately. Students gain confidence as they master the more difficult tools first and later see how the more seemingly ordinary ones complement and flesh out a general research procedure. Presenting complicated tools first allows people to deal with difficult material while they are fresh. This second method—moving from the difficult to the more common—is actually effective in sessions aimed at faculty, since once faculty members become "hooked" on the tools and on your competence in presenting them in a meaningful fashion, they will be likely to continue to attend sessions even when it might seem that they already know those particular materials.

Another method is to move from the most recently published tools to older more established ones. Again, this works best with faculty who have themselves performed significant research in the past and who will appreciate being informed of new developments in the reference control of their discipline.

Step 6. Decide what types of reinforcement you want to incorporate in your course. Such common tactics as brief quizzes, in-class activities, or short oral reports on individual research projects can be effective, as can homework assignments, projects, readings, and major tests. Be sure that you allow enough time in an early session to explain what the course requirements are and how they will be evaluated. Also allow time during any session in which you will plan to return homework or assignments to make general comments about the strengths and weaknesses of the students' performance. As you plan specific activities for students, relate these assignments to students' particular needs. For example, allowing them to do a theoretical search strategy in their own disciplines is a good way to force them to think through the paradigm they will be dealing with most frequently.

Step 7. Decide whether you will assign any reading or require students to purchase a textbook. If you intend to have materials on reserve, decide at this stage what they will be and how many copies you need to make available. Similarly, if you intend to assign textbooks, decide exactly what pages will be assigned in conjunction with what sessions of the course. If you find a textbook you like, you may be able to cover some topics primarily through reading assignments. We are not aware of any good library-skills textbooks that incorporate the theories underlying search strategy and search strategy itself with the skills necessary to perform research in a library. General library-skills texts, such as Gates's *Guide to the Use of Books and Libraries,* 4th ed. (New York: McGraw-Hill, 1979), are a possibility, but you should evaluate the alternatives carefully in selecting one. You can always do without a textbook and substitute assignments built around class handouts and specific projects you assign students that will enable them to use the material you have described for a real research topic. Another good way to reinforce student learning is to require students to keep a handwritten journal every time they undertake research in the library. This forces them to think through exactly what they did and how it worked out and to reflect on ways in which they might change their research habits for a similar topic in the future.

Step 8. Determine what means of evaluation, if any, you will build into your course. The three major reasons for evaluating are to ascertain the extent of student learning, to determine apparent teaching effectiveness, and to assess the means and methods of instruction. Evaluation could involve some form of measurement of student learning from a baseline, usually a pretest, administered at the beginning of the course. (Evaluation is discussed in Chapter 2.)

Whether the BI course is being offered for credit may determine your evaluation procedures. Obviously, if you must assign course grades, you will need a meaningful basis on which to do so. (You should investigate the practices at your institution for courses in similar disciplines, for example, education, to see how students are evaluated. For example, do instructors rely on multiple-choice tests, essay tests, take-home research examinations, or term projects?) If your course is not offered for credit, you still need to evaluate it for your own information in order to improve the program and to satisfy the administrative needs of the library director, who will want some information on the effects of all the human and financial resources that have been devoted to such an effort.

Step 9. After you have carefully outlined the content of each session and thought through the logical connectives between sessions and the assignments and evaluations you intend to use, the last step is to proceed for each session as you would for the one-hour lecture. (See Chapter 9 for a thorough discussion of all the practical points involved for each individual session.)

Hints for Planning a BI Course

1. Allow a certain amount of time and subject flexibility in your curriculum to tailor specific sessions to student's own interests. Unfortunately, it is impossible to know students' background and precise research needs before meeting them; so in the first class session you might distribute a brief questionnaire on which students indicate research interests and other information you would find useful (for example, languages they read). Having a profile of the specific individuals in your audience will help you to better choose the specific titles you discuss in any single session, as well as the specific examples you mention from any given work.

2. In general, we recommend combining within a given session the concept of a particular type of tool—that is, what it is generically and what kind of job it does in the search strategy—and a discussion of specific titles of that type, moving from basic to more specific or erudite ones. For example, within a single session it is possible to convey the idea of a periodical index, perhaps by having students practice indexing a brief article from a news magazine (as outlined in Chapter 9) and then discuss typical periodical indexes, moving from the

Readers' Guide to other Wilson indexes to specific discipline indexes for whatever fields the students are working in. This method allows you to cover elementary as well as the more specialized tools in the same hour and to make a point of their similarity. If your group regards the *Readers' Guide*, for instance, as too elementary for their needs, you can explain that it is the prototype from which the others spring and, therefore, is worth studying.

3. If this is your first experience planning a BI course, and if your colleagues have no BI or general teaching experience, we strongly urge you to contact educational specialists at your institution to help with curriculum planning (but only after you have decided on the content you want to convey). These people can help you with test design and other evaluative aspects of the overall course. And don't forget about the regional and national clearinghouses, such as LOEX at Eastern Michigan University in Ypsilanti, Michigan, from which you can readily obtain samples of other librarians' BI curricula, possibly in the same discipline or discipline area that you intend to teach. Seeing what other people have done, what concepts and tools they have included, and in what order can be an immense help in establishing your own sequence of sessions. You may find the examples deficient or faulty in some major way, but your approach will be stronger because you have thought through the alternatives. If at all possible attend BI meetings at conferences—state, regional, or national—to talk with people who are facing the same sorts of problems and decisions.

4. After you have designed the curriculum and are at the point of typing the syllabus and the assignment sheet for the students, look at it again. Is it appropriate for your potential audience and their situation? Will it translate your overall objectives into measurable information transfer? Look for an overall sense of unity, logic, and balance, with an appropriate emphasis on concepts and types of tools of interest to users in your audience. We do not assume that the readers of this book are all library science students, but it is, nonetheless, worthwhile to note some of the common problems in curricula design encountered by the library science students we have taught so that you can be aware of them in your own planning. Among the common pitfalls are a lack of a sense of order between successive sessions, difficulties combining general tools and specific ones of the same type, and a problem including information about automation as it affects libraries

and library users. Library science students tend to think in terms of their general reference and bibliography courses and to rearrange the tools that they themselves have come to recognize for whatever group of students they have defined, even though the audience might have only marginal interest in certain types of materials. General courses covering types of material and a range of titles usually lack scientific works and examples and stress instead the social science or humanities reference works. Basic library survival skills and concepts, such as the notion of a union list or the serial record for a given institution or the availability of interlibrary loan, ought to be included in any general BI course, but were often omitted by students we taught. Library science students would often have trouble viewing their curriculum from the user's point of view rather than from the library science point of view, and hence would overload certain sessions with library jargon or esoteric tools of little potential use to their audience. Another problem had to do with the academic orientation of the curricula that library science students designed, when, in fact, many of them had specified a public or public school library audience. They had difficulty translating the specific concepts and types of tools they intended to discuss for that audience.

The planning and execution of particular sessions within a BI course are discussed in Chapter 9. Just as the single, or one-shot, lecture is the building block of all bibliographic instruction, the BI course is the only method certain to immerse students in the theory and in the research methods they will need, whether for general library research throughout their lives or for specific advanced academic work. Costly as a course is in terms of staff time and financial burden on the library, the returns on the investment are extraordinary and certainly worth the commitment. As in any other educational process, the carefully constructed course is preferred over the single intensive workshop or over private reading and study; we advocate the supremacy of the BI course of whatever length over any other mode of instruction.

Note

1. Mary W. George and Mary Ann O'Donnell, "The Bibliographic Research Methods Course in American Departments of English," *Literature Research Newsletter*, 4 (Winter 1979): 9–23.

Part IV
Implementing
a BI Program

We are frequently asked three types of questions by library administrators contemplating a BI program or by librarians who have designed what they think would be an effective program, but who then wonder how to go about institutionalizing their ideas. Part IV covers common questions regarding the administrative climate of bibliographic instruction, with all the ramifications that top and middle managers need to be aware of, alternative ways for getting started once a program has been designed, and the relative costs of various BI modes.

11
Administrative
Climate

Bibliographic instruction is frequently a grass roots undertaking on the part of reference librarians, and they often speak of political situations that either further or frustrate their well-intended efforts. Politics is, of course, a key component of any planned change in a complex organization, and we know of no long-term BI effort that has continued to grow and flourish, without significant support from the library administration. In this chapter we discuss the many significant and subtle ways in which the library and the institution's administration can foster the development of a BI program. We describe the typical academic library environment, that is, the academic library as a component within the college or university. We assume that the BI effort is directed toward particular academic programs or departments in the course-integrated or course-related mode. ·

The administrative climate for bibliographic instruction in an academic setting involves three distinct groups of people: the university or college administrators, particularly those in offices such as the vice-president for academic affairs, the provost, the dean in charge of curricula, or deans of various academic schools or colleges; the department chairpeople of any academic units for which BI has been designed; and the library's top managers, particularly the director and deputy director or associate/assistant director for public services. It is important at the inception of a BI program for the planners to decide who within the library should be talking to whom outside the library. Contacts should be made by peers, with communication taking place between department chairpeople, deans and other college or university administrators, and middle- and upper-management library administrators. Whether these sorts of contacts occur early in the program or only after BI has proven itself to have a positive impact on education, these one-to-one relationships must be established for the program to survive. An outstanding case of BI program survival based in large part on the willingness of the director to take the case for BI directly to university officials involved the University of Wisconsin-Parkside in Kenosha in the late 1970s, when the director, Joseph Boissé, received a 10 percent budget increase for the library while academic departments were cut by the same amount. Boissé believed that the library was largely rewarded in this instance because of an active bibliographic instruction program, which had already proved its importance to college administrators.[1]

Conversations and commitments with regard to bibliographic instruction made at all levels must, of course, be carefully planned and orchestrated so that the library director is not promising a vice-president something that the BI librarians involved cannot ultimately deliver. To quote from the handbook published by the Association of College and Research Libraries: "A BI program has goals, objectives, and continuity. It comes into existence when responsibility for planning and development has been delegated by the library into a specific unit of the library organization."[2] Communication needs to be frequent and in all directions so that library administrators are regularly informed of faculty contacts made by the BI librarians and so that BI librarians are aware of the thinking conveyed by university and college administrators directly to the library administration.

Let us examine in some detail the impact of planned change as brought about by bibliographic instruction on two key groups within the library organization—top library administrators and middle managers.

Top Library Administrators

In terms of the long-range planning of the library, the library director and whatever other top administrators are most closely concerned with public service and budgeting must be comfortable from the outset with the place of bibliographic instruction in the overall mission of the library within the institution. BI must be an integral part of the library philosophy and reason for being, or the program will die after a few years of initial enthusiasm on the part of the librarians most directly involved. If a library has a written mission or goal statement, it should be examined to see if the objectives of the BI program are clearly reflected in it. If not, BI planners should suggest and push for an amendment that will establish BI as a library priority.

Top library administrators must also set an example for intellectual and moral support of a BI program. They must be committed and excited about the effort to the extent of making a strong case for it whenever called upon to do so. They must be convinced that bibliographic instruction is a good idea in the abstract and that it is an appropriate and effective means of accomplishing the library's mission at their institution. At small colleges where there may only be a handful of professional librarians, it is essential that the director express commitment regularly to the program as a top priority for public service; otherwise, one or two (that is a large percentage) librarians are bound to be indifferent if not hostile to the change in emphasis. Furthermore, library administrators must be regularly informed of all thinking and any decisions made by the BI planners and must concur in any major aspect of the program. For instance, when a particular type or group of students or faculty is targeted for BI and the scope and mode of instruction are chosen, the top library administrator must agree that these decisions are appropriate. A particularly startling example of library priorities changing to accommodate the bibliographic instruction program is the case of Earlham College in Richmond, Indiana. Long a pioneer in course-related bibliographic instruction throughout the entire undergraduate curriculum, this library decided to reduce the extent of their in-house cataloging in order to channel more resources into the instructional program.[3]

Library administrators can further the BI effort, once they have made sure that it fits into the library's stated mission and that staff at all levels are aware of this commitment, by establishing some form of staff training, whether in-house or at continuing education workshops, to develop appropriate BI skills. Likewise, it is for the top administrators to write the charge and establish appropriate committees of staff members to work on various modes of BI or to share experiences and short-term planning with one another. A support group among BI librarians is essential, and if one is not formally established, they are likely to set up an informal or underground network to share their experiences and new ideas. It is advisable to sanction such a group by appointing a task force or committee with clearly defined goals and responsibilities and to ask them for a timetable so that all concerned will know the rate at which the BI program is to develop.

The budget impact of a bibliographic instruction program is immense, whether or not separate line items are so designated. Major costs are discussed in detail in Chapter 13, but here it is appropriate to mention the implications of staff time and training, equipment, materials, photoduplication, space, and—especially—the cost of not doing something else so that existing resources can be reallocated to bibliographic instruction. Administrators must realize that they cannot simply hand the BI planner a finite amount of start-up money, but that a successful program will draw continually on the budget even if the modes involved can be repeated year after year. To keep a program fresh and to do the public relations, publicity, and evaluation that are continual elements of a program using any mode, it is necessary to earmark funds from year to year for the program to grow and, once it has grown to the full extent, to maintain its vitality.

Sources of special funding for a bibliographic instruction program need not come only from the library's existing budget, but, with the efforts of the library administration, might come from a subsidy supplied by the institution for salaries, equipment, photoduplication, or whatever. Similarly, the library director might persuade the academic departments best served by the BI program to contribute funds toward the BI librarian's salary, especially if an academic department itself is receiving funds based on the generation of credit hours where the actual teaching is done by a library staff member. In the short range or medium range, grant proposals can be written for funds to start, expand, or modify a BI program.

Problems can arise, of course, when the soft money runs out or if the BI librarian ends up reporting to a department chairperson or someone else outside the library structure because some funding has come from this outside source. Questions such as to whom do librarians report and what are their benefits in terms of faculty perquisites, for example, sabbaticals, need to be ironed out whenever responsibility for funding shifts outside the library's own budget.

Some top library administrators regard bibliographic instruction as a sort of budget vacuum chamber, which if left on its own would continually attract and drain off money with no bounds in sight.[4] Some long-term budget implications are the result of the so-called snowball effect, that is, the impact on the library's budget of needing to hire additional BI librarians to undertake the increased workload generated by the program. Similarly, it may be necessary to hire new professional staff at a higher salary level and to expect previous BI experience. Some libraries, most notably a project in the middle 1970s at Brown University, Rhode Island, have undertaken to teach faculty and graduate teaching assistants the major library concepts and tools that they in turn can convey in the ordinary classroom situation. As far as we know, this sort of effort has not caught on at many institutions and hence cannot be relied on as a method of reducing a library's overall expenses. A commitment to continuing education will also have a budget impact, although less so than employing additional staff.

A critical corollary to budget considerations of BI is that library directors must realize that the birth, maturation, and flourishing of a fully developed bibliographic instruction program, even if it is aimed only at a particular segment of the college or university community, is a phenomenon to be measured in years, not months. Tom Kirk, director of the Berea College Library in Kentucky, said in 1980 that it takes at least ten years to establish a bibliographic instruction program at any higher educational institution and that the larger the institution, the more time it may take beyond ten years.[5] Carla Stoffle said in 1981 that workbooks take approximately five years to perfect and establish as a regular part of the college curriculum.[6] Thus, library administrators need to think about investing library resources over time in BI just as they invest money in the future for any library project or commitment.

BI falls in the category of long-range planning even though the first contacts with students may occur soon after the program is initiated. A special instance of the need for long-range planning is in adapting the design for a new library building to accommodate user-oriented services, and BI in particular, in terms of the modes that the institution has selected. Layout of services, availability of classroom areas, and sufficient materials and equipment must all be planned into any new facility. Personnel considerations go beyond the budget impact of salaries. Decisions about whether to require all public service librarians or all librarians to be involved in the BI program must come from the top. Some administrators may start adding ability to carry out instruction as part of all vacancy announcements, but other aspects of personnel can foster the climate for BI. Among these are including instruction as a component of every librarian's or every public service librarian's annual review for merit evaluation or promotion. If merit increases are clearly tied to active participation in BI as one of the library's priorities, it becomes clear to every staff member exactly what the importance of the program is in the overall scheme of things.

BI librarians invariably work many hours beyond the stated work week since it takes approximately 15 hours to prepare a 50-minute lecture the first time it is given, and somewhat less for each successive repetition. Since virtually all BI librarians start out with a full-time job commitment, usually in reference, attention needs to be paid to the energy and compensation levels of BI librarians. If salary cannot be increased directly as a result, benefits such as time for attending BI conferences or a somewhat reduced work load on occasional weeks when BI activity is particularly heavy might be appropriate measures and can only be sanctioned by consultation with top administrators.

Incentives built into the classification and promotion system for librarians who participate in BI are also crucial to reward staff for devoting their time, energy, and expertise to professional programs. BI, unfortunately, does not fit into traditional promotional and review schemes for the library's professional staff, which tend to evaluate positions on the basis of the number of people supervised, place in the chain of command, or extent of responsibility for particular areas of decision-making. These factors must be taken into account at an early stage in the library commitment to BI. Not to do so will only hasten the burn-out factor and the migration of excellent BI librarians to other institutions or to positions outside BI that have more responsibility and that further their careers. We strongly advocate granting short (one or two months) mini-sabbaticals to BI librarians for the express purpose of developing some aspect of the overall program, such as printed guides or slide/tape presentations. It does not seem just to expect BI to occur as an overload based exclusively on the enthusiasm of a small core of professionals.

Some of the ramifications to the library system as a whole that the astute top administrator must come to expect when a BI program is undertaken are discussed below.

Staffing patterns

Bibliographic instruction can be a separate unit within the library system, housed in a single department or actually shared by several units, but it must be determined to whom it should report. Often BI is an add-on responsibility for the reference department, the bibliographers, or some combination of the two. The combination of teaching with selection responsibilities and outside professional contacts or reference is unbeatable in terms of synergy—of reinforcing one activity with others. Unless, however, additional people are brought in for the project or unless existing commitments are significantly reduced or present duties are rearranged to make work significantly more efficient, you are simply overloading already overworked people. Another staffing pattern consideration is to draw on BI talents among technical services staff members. Another is the joint funding of an additional professional librarian between, for example, the reference department and an academic discipline. The difficulties with this option lie in the hiring procedures and who has ultimate responsibility for individuals' performances. Clerical support will also need to be increased as BI grows so that additional support staff will be assigned to the unit housing BI to do the many important background tasks connected with any mode of instruction.

Impact on other public services

Any successful BI program has an immediate impact on interlibrary loan, circulation, shelving office, database search requests, and so forth, as students become aware of the range of services they can expect from the library. It is possible for interlibrary loan to increase or decrease, depending on its previous situation. For example, if many interlibrary loan requests were made for materials already owned by the library because students were unable to use the card catalog well and BI remedies that problem, the interlibrary loan business might shrink. It is impossible to predict the impact on these auxiliary services in advance of the program, but the library administrator must be aware of these ramifications and realize that no public service can avoid feeling the impact of a successful BI effort.

Serials, government documents, bindery, microforms, map collection, and other such services should all have increased activity as a result of the BI program, insofar as these materials are discussed. Staff in these units, if they are not directly involved with the BI effort, will need to be aware of the impact and be willing to assist the BI librarians in planning for it. This kind of encouragement can only come from the top administrators, whose responsibility is to coordinate the many different factors and personalities that make a library "work."

Space limits

Any BI program needs space, and BI needs, as well as any other future space needs, must be considered when planning a new library building. If, however, the space in the library is inadequate for teaching, the top administrator may have to contact university or college administrators to obtain regular classrooms and equipment so that BI can take place outside the four walls of the library. Similarly, the BI librarians will need to have at least semiprivate office space for their preparations and for consultations with students; if this is not available in the library, it may be arranged elsewhere on campus.

Definition of success

Finally, it is the responsibility of library administrators to determine in advance what constitutes success for a BI program. If a trial period is arranged, it should be several years in duration because otherwise there will be no effective way to measure the impact of the program. Some appropriate means of evaluation may be suggested by library administrators so that they can present the case for expanded support of BI in cost-benefit terms to the university or college administration. The library director and appropriate other administrative staff should discuss evaluation at the beginning of the program to ensure that whatever form of evaluation is decided on will meet the needs of the library administration as well as the educational feedback needs of the librarians themselves.

In short, it is the responsibility of the library director to foster the appropriate intellectual and financial climate and to support the emotional climate so that a BI program can flourish.

Middle Managers

The role of middle managers in establishing and continuing a BI program cannot be overstated. Middle managers serve a double function; on the one hand, they are involved in the institutionwide considerations that are the primary responsibilities of top management (see above), and, on the other hand, they work with BI librarians to formulate and further each step of the actual program. If there is no middle manager, or if that person is weak and/or unable to understand the goals of BI as articulated by the library administration or by the BI librarians themselves, that program is doomed to frustration if not total failure. The middle manager in question is usually the head of the reference department in a large library or an assistant or associate director for public services in a smaller facility. The middle manager is responsible for the personnel, planning, cost estimates, and general provision of resources to make a program work.

The middle manager alone can make sure that strong people are channeled into BI. Even if the library director has indicated that new people brought into the system must have teaching experience or the skills necessary for BI, the middle manager too must make sure that criteria actually appear in vacancy announcements and that all applicants are screened and interviews conducted with BI in mind. Ongoing training, whether in-house or by means of outside courses and workshops, to enhance the BI skills of staff must be furthered by the middle manager. Likewise, personnel evaluations of those involved with BI must seriously take into account the actual contribution of the individual to the objectives of the overall program. Where it is possible to do so, merit increases and other rewards should be tied to BI performance for those assigned that duty.

Support for the BI program from the perspective of the middle manager means personal interest and commitment that is obvious day by day to BI librarians. It also means providing BI staff with a climate in which they can excel, giving them a large degree of independence in their contacts and decision-making premised on the understanding that any time a serious problem arises, the BI librarians will immediately apprise the middle manager. It means giving staff the freedom to create a program and to succeed and perhaps to fail. It is difficult for BI librarians, especially those just beginning to become involved in that activity, to work in a vacuum. They require not only a support group of colleagues and peers, but also someone above them—the middle manager—to whom they can take novel ideas and who will listen thoughtfully and react candidly. And, on those occasions when a certain aspect of the BI program seems to fail, it is critical that the middle manager sit down with the BI staff to consider why it is failing and to change whatever tactics may be necessary to ensure success in the future.

BI librarians also require from their superiors a strong sense of loyalty and propriety so that when a problem arises, they can discuss it freely. The wisdom based on experience that the middle manager can bring is an excellent ingredient to the BI effort; overeager BI librarians often need to be reminded that it takes time, patience, and repeated attempts to make any program successful. In connection with the moral support is the middle manager's responsibility to encourage the BI librarian to publish, to participate in national, regional, and local organizations, clearinghouses, and conferences, and generally to learn about programs elsewhere.

Good morale can be fostered by the middle manager. It is important for that person to recognize that there may be some resentment or professional jealousy on the part of staff suspicious of a BI program. These people are bound to feel "dumped on" because they will be picking up occasional extra duties so that the BI staff can meet commitments. They may feel jealous about the BI librarian's involvement in conferences, whether as participants or speakers. Staff may well be angry about group pressure to do BI, even if they believe in it, because they feel they lack the time or expertise to devote to it. There may be ill feelings about the apparent "glamour" of BI—the very obvious positive reaction on the part of faculty and students to those who have provided instruction and the fact that BI librarians will become much more knowledgeable and expert in reference work than they were previously. Staff may resent being asked considerably more complex questions than they are used to, questions generated by bibliographic instruction; if they don't know the answer, and especially if to find the answer they must consult with the BI librarian, who now knows how to handle such questions, further bad relationships will develop. These possible negative effects on library personnel of a successful BI program are intended only as a warning to those just beginning, and particularly to their middle managers. It is unlikely that all these problems will appear or that any of them will appear immediately. It is good, however, to be aware of the troubled waters that may be stirring among other staff so that steps may be taken from the planning stage to assure the widest possible understanding and cooperation.

Other forms of support include the following: arranging for appropriate staff to assist the BI librarian in the many tasks involved in any mode of instruction; capitalizing on the skills of existing staff even when that means reassigning duties in order to assure that good individuals are involved in the BI program and that those with the appropriate skills are available; and generally using politics in a good sense to maneuver people into a situation where they are willing to undertake some BI responsibility or where they assume duties previously handled by someone who will now be doing BI. A basic decision will be whether only those who volunteer will be involved or whether others, such as library school students, may become part of the program.

One way for the middle manager to encourage hesitant staff to become involved in BI is to suggest that they first prepare a one-hour lecture in a subject area where they are already comfortable or, failing that, that they work with someone else and jointly prepare and deliver a lecture. Some people who are opposed to BI are nonetheless happy to serve as guest lecturers on topics with which they have expertise, for example, microforms, serials, documents, or maps. These individuals will generally, in the course of preparing their guest lecture, come to be sympathetic to the BI staff because they will realize how much time is involved in putting together a good presentation. They will also become aware, if they are not already, of the widespread ignorance of most students with regard to any library concepts or skills.

Problems with scheduling can appropriately be handled by an astute middle manager; for example, reference desk schedules may need to be rethought to permit those doing BI to have several hours in succession when they are not on duty in order to prepare for a lecture, actually give it, and recover from it. Obviously, this cuts down on the flexibility available for desk staffing, but if the middle manager is aware of this from the beginning and can work with everyone to achieve an equitable new arrangement, this need not be a stumbling block.

Scheduling is also affected when anyone on the staff is sick, on vacation, or absent for any reason, since BI librarians will not be able to pick up extra hours because of their teaching commitments (again, assuming that they are involved with the lecture format). Time must also be allowed for faculty and student conferences, for general exploration of campus resources, and for handling more complex reference questions that are invariably generated by a good BI program. In libraries where the professional staff is unionized, the middle manager will have to make some early decisions with regard to handling overtime involved in BI.

The planning responsibilities of middle managers with regard to BI include meshing of unit and personnel goals with BI objectives. Middle managers must understand the types of statistics that need to be collected and the best way to analyze them to help monitor the program. They must be aware of resources other than personnel that are required—adequate space and equipment, sufficient copies of titles used in teaching, or duplicates of the various discipline guides so that BI librarians are able to check them out and do some work at home, the relative cost of materials and staff time, and careful consideration of the long-term impact of a successful program and how the demand can be handled in the future.

Overall Organization of a BI Program

Several times in this chapter, we have mentioned alternate staffing arrangements. Now let us look at the relative merits of each. In the library, with only one or at most a handful of professional librarians, the responsibilities of BI will either be shared equally by all, or the director will determine who has primary responsibility for the program and will change job assignments accordingly. In a large academic or research library, where departmental divisions are more pronounced, BI personnel can be drawn from a number of possible areas. These include the following:

Creating a separate department for instruction.

Keeping BI in the reference unit.

Drawing on subject specialists or bibliographers.

Involving technical service librarians.

Utilizing the institution's audiovisual staff.

Integrating the central library BI effort with that in special or branch libraries at the institution.

Separate department

Advantages of a separate BI department are that it may provide more flexibility in terms of scheduling and staff skills since it may involve several people, each of whom has a background that will enhance the total effort. An especially attractive advantage is that it allows staff to concentrate on the job at hand without continual distractions and interruptions caused by other duties. Likewise, a separate unit will have a certain visibility on an organization chart and signs for staff office space. This visibility will provide a sort of "corporate clout," which it would lack if BI appears to be just another responsibility of, for example, the reference department. Staff development, at least for those involved in the BI department, is ongoing and exciting as each person contributes his or her best efforts and insights to the others and as they brainstorm on a daily basis.

Two drawbacks of the separate BI department must be mentioned. One is that although those involved in BI may develop excellent reference skills, they would not in all likelihood have regular reference duty, which means that such skills will be hidden from all but the students whom they meet. Also, expertise in collection development will be enhanced, but unless it is somehow fed back into the system, it will not profit the organization. A second, and we believe a much more critical, drawback for the separate department is that it hinders BI staff from a continual realization of student and faculty needs to be found only at the reference desk. No user survey and no BI evaluation can ever completely substitute for the one-to-one interaction over the reference desk. For this reason alone, one should consider carefully the creation of a separate BI department.

Reference unit

Another possible BI structure, and the one that is no doubt most common, is to assign bibliographic instruction to the reference unit, thereby expanding the responsibilities of reference librarians. By adding and rearranging the duties of the reference department, the middle manager increases overall expertise and public service in that area. Although it is exhausting to be involved with BI on a full-time basis, it is invigorating to include BI along with its corollary responsibilities of reference desk service and collection development. Everyone in the reference department invariably benefits, actively or passively, from the inclusion of BI, because reference skills are improved via the preparation of the BI librarians and their interaction with colleagues and with users at the desk. Collection development, both of the reference collection and the general stacks, will also improve as BI librarians become aware of lacks in certain areas and generate orders to fill them. The constant interaction with users, together with the flexibility involved in adding BI as a reference responsibility, make this our favored organizational pattern, and it is one that many middle managers favor because the visibility and satisfaction of users with reference is bound to increase when reference librarians take active roles in instruction.

The disadvantages of reference as the home for BI were discussed earlier in this chapter when staff morale was considered. This is a very real and inevitable problem, but that should not in itself outweigh the advantages of incorporating bibliographic instruction into the reference department.

Subject specialists or bibliographers

Some libraries assign BI to subject specialists, bibliographers, or those in collection development who have a particular expertise. They assume that these people are the most familiar with the literature and reference fact and finding tools in their field, that they have already established faculty and student contacts, and that they are recognized by users as knowledgeable about library research methods. Therefore, the argument goes, it is a natural extension of their duties to have them actively involved in instruction, thereby using their education and experience to benefit the library as a whole.

Undoubtedly, public relations will improve, and any comparable resistance on the part of faculty will be overcome, when the specialist/bibliographer is also the BI instructor. A problem arises, however, in that most bibliographers are not fully aware of how inadequate is student and faculty knowledge of the use of simple reference tools. Specialists are more used to working one-to-one via office appointments with people who have a complex topic. One way to overcome this usual lack of reference experience is to assign the bibliographer regular hours at the reference desk or to ask the person to take part in a term-paper clinic or other one-to-one tutorial program sponsored by the library and to which users come at the beginning of their research. This permits the subject specialist to become aware of the range of problems that users have and, hence, to be more sensitive in designing a program to actual needs.

Using high-level bibliographers to do undergraduate BI, especially BI in the one-shot lecture mode, might be very cost ineffective, since their advanced training will not very often be involved in that level of instruction. On the other hand, it might be very effective to use the bibliographer for graduate BI or faculty seminars, in which they can speak as educational and intellectual equals with those whom they instruct.

Some librarians feel it will improve job satisfaction for subject specialists and bibliographers to be involved in BI and not to spend so much time passively involved with book selection and collection development, with only the occasional intense tutorial initiated by a user. Much can be said for that argument, but to require personnel to do BI, however good their background, without also exposing them to the day-to-day reference desk environment will probably result in instruction skewed toward a more sophisticated set of tools and skills than users are actually ready for.

Technical service staff

Technical services personnel can be important components of the BI program because of their subject background, their languages, and their general interest and expertise, especially regarding the organization of the catalog and of materials within the collection. If the objectives of a program include an understanding of the way in which material is classified and arranged and some information about the catalog, technical services librarians could fit in very well. We know of no BI program staffed exclusively by technical services personnel, but in several instances catalogers, for example, have been involved in planning and executing a program.

Audiovisual staff

In some libraries, particularly community colleges, it would be possible to organize bibliographic instruction within the

AV unit on campus, whether or not that unit is already part of the library system. Particularly if the mode of BI is audiovisual, involving the production of videotape lectures or slide/tape orientations to the various libraries on campus, it may be appropriate to center the effort in the existing AV unit.

Integrating the program

A coordinator may be able to work with a diffuse and diverse BI program on a very large campus, serving as the focal point between the library administration and the BI librarians, who may be in numerous special libraries as well as the central facility. Such a coordinator might chair a BI task force or support group that would monitor developments and attempt to collect evaluations, statistics, and other data from all units doing any form of instruction. Having a single contact person is important so that there is a recognized figure to call when instruction is wanted or someone to contact for additional information about BI efforts. The coordinator would act as a referral point for faculty interested in instruction to pass a request along to the appropriate special librarian.

Another responsibility for a BI coordinator in a large system would be to formulate an overall program involving different modes appropriate to different groups and to keep the objectives of every effort on campus in line with overall institutional objectives for instruction. The coordinator would also logically provide certain types of training, as well as encouragement, to librarians in the field who are attempting to set up an instruction program with their existing staff. The coordinator could be hired specifically for such a position, or could be someone designated by the library administration to accept these responsibilities on either a permanent or a rotating basis.

Notes

1. Joseph A. Boissé, "Library Instruction and the Administration," *Putting Library Instruction in Its Place in the Library and in the Library School*, ed. by Carolyn A. Kirkendall (Ann Arbor, Mich.: Pierian Press, 1978), pp. 1–12.
2. *Bibliographic Instruction Handbook* (Chicago: Association of College and Research Libraries, 1979), p. 27.

3. Thomas G. Kirk, "Problems in Library Instruction in Four-Year Colleges," *Educating the Library User*, ed. by John Lubans, Jr. (New York: Bowker, 1974), p. 87.

4. Richard M. Dougherty, "Getting a Larger Slice of the Budget Pie for Library Instruction," *Reform and Renewal in Higher Education: Implications for Library Instruction*, ed. by Carolyn A. Kirkendall (Ann Arbor, Mich.: Pierian Press, 1979), p. 24.

5. Thomas G. Kirk, "Conference Synthesis and Prognostication for the Eighties," conference wrap-up at Tenth Annual Conference on Library Orientation for Academic Libraries, May 8–9, 1980, Ypsilanti, MI.

6. Carla Stoffle, presentation to students in Library Science 608, Special Topics: Bibliographic Instruction, University of Michigan, May 7, 1981.

12
Alternatives for Getting Started

"How did you get your students?" is the most frequent question from librarians new to bibliographic instruction. Of course, there is no one answer to that question. Each of us has a unique set of experiences, and no two people have the same story. Circumstances, goals, and personalities will always differ; so there can be no set formula for starting an instantly successful program. However, in this chapter we discuss several common "openers" for those launching a bibliographic instruction effort of any kind.

Establishing Contacts

Once you have outlined the objectives and chosen a mode for your BI program, you must decide how best to establish contacts with your intended audience. Since it is unlikely that you will be able to work from the start with your entire target group, it is good to look for an appropriate, readily convened, and interested subset of the target group and begin with those people. For instance, in the college setting, certain academic departments or schools might be approached at the start and others deferred until your program is more fully developed. In the public library, certain civic groups might be indicated by their prominence, or groups with special needs (the unemployed, children in a basic skills program) might be given first priority.

The best possible way to start is to draw on or establish personal contacts with key people in your focused audience. For example, if you already know a library board member, the president of a local hobby or service club, or senior faculty members in an academic department, approach them with a substantive proposal for BI for their group. It is politically wise to deal with individuals who are active in high-profile endeavors—leaders in the community's employment skills program rather than in the garden club. In the elementary or secondary school setting, the key contacts might be teachers in whatever subjects are currently popular and hence are receiving the most tax support or media attention. In the rest of this chapter, we concentrate on the academic library situation, but these suggestions can be easily transferred to other areas of librarianship.

Faculty Support

A continual preoccupation of BI librarians in colleges and universities is how to initiate and sustain faculty cooperation. This concern derives in part from librarians' desire to prove that they are peers of the teaching faculty, especially if they are in a common union and must go through the same tenure and promotion screening as do teaching faculty. More important, however, since faculty are the most visible and influential members of the academic community, they are the people who can make or break a BI program. Faculty do, after all, control the raw material of BI, namely the students whom academic librarians want to reach.

Close working relationships with faculty are obviously essential for course-related and course-integrated modes of instruction, but they are also necessary for the success of other modes as well. Faculty who think highly of the library and respect its efforts to offer instruction on research concepts and methods are likely to urge students to take advantage of a volunteer BI course or to assign students to watch a videotape or make use of printed guides prepared by the library to explain the use of complicated tools. If a BI course is given for academic credit through an existing department rather than through the library, faculty support must remain constant in order for the course to be repeated.

Wherever faculty support for library efforts is already flourishing, you will find it much easier to discover student strengths and weaknesses and to learn directly from teachers what research skills students will need to perform satisfactorily in courses within a given department. Furthermore, faculty members are aware of the interests of their students and have control over specific assignments for which BI is appropriate.

Faculty feedback to library and institutional administrators is crucial for the continuance of a BI program, and faculty who attend BI presentations significantly increase their students' attention (and retention) by spontaneously commenting on how central certain concepts or tools are for themselves. Remember, too, that you really must rely on faculty for any evaluation of a one-shot lecture since there is usually no time to spare during the presentation. The faculty member may be willing to give a quiz in the next regular class session following your talk or to allow you to assess students' research papers (or at least the bibliographies of those papers) so that you can determine the impact of your lecture.

The most effective entrée to an academic department will vary with circumstances, but it might well include contacting a faculty member with whom you are already acquainted or going directly to the department chair or to the individual who heads the department's curriculum committee. Sometimes getting introduced to key secretaries—who in any event should be cultivated for the insights they can throw on the department's politics and priorities—is an effective move, since they can suggest which faculty members would be most interested in your program.

To determine which courses have library research components, and hence would be good candidates for instruction, try to talk with students who request substantial help at the reference desk on term papers. Another method is to peruse the college catalog to discover courses requiring major projects that demand library research. If your institution publishes a detailed description of requirements for all classes and faculty expectations of student performance, by all means study it as an indication of where to begin with BI.

Another possibility to consider is the informational meeting held every fall at most institutions for new faculty members, graduate students, or departmental majors. If at all possible, have yourself invited to this orientation session to say a few words about the library and, not incidentally, to make a pitch for the availability of bibliographic instruction. Letters or phone calls to individual faculty members (especially to new people on campus), followed by appointments at which you discuss the library's collection and services, including BI, are another rewarding tactic. Ask faculty with whom you have already worked to mention your program to their associates. Under no circumstances should you worry about those few people who, invariably and inevitably, will be indifferent or uncooperative. Every difficult faculty member has numerous colleagues who will be delighted to have you assist their teaching efforts and who will quickly take you up on any offer.

Whether or not your BI courses are for credit, it is often wise to deal with the faculty member who advises the students you would like to reach. This same person may be teaching a required course on which the BI class can piggyback, that is, students must attend the BI sessions as a requirement for another course. Advanced students may have a regular time when they meet together informally to study as a group for a comprehensive exam, and getting in touch with such a group is another way to form a class. If you discover from the course catalog that certain courses concentrate on study skills or research methods, you might approach those professors.

Today most colleges and universities have some sort of program to improve the general literacy and study skills of minority students. These students can be an excellent first group for a BI course directed toward their needs. It is likely that the addition of a basic library skills component will be favorably received by the institution's administrators and that support, either from internal or external sources, may be forthcoming as a result.

Advertising

Ways of advertising BI include mentioning it as a public service program in all general library publicity and in any presentations you give to community groups. Whenever term paper clinics or one-to-one tutorials are offered, suggest to the participants that it might be useful to identify other individuals with the same interests so that material can be covered more efficiently with a small group. The effectiveness of word-of-mouth publicity cannot be overstated; the so-called locker room effect invariably occurs as "satisfied customers" tell others about your work. Other forms of promotion are flyers distributed to potential participants, via a library, departmental, or campus newsletter, or advertisements in local media. News stories or interviews describing BI as a major new library service can be especially valuable in calling attention to your program.

Among the possible innovative sessions to capture student and faculty attention, and thus serve as lead-ins to more comprehensive instruction, are to focus on changes in the library's catalog (the impact of the second edition of the *Anglo-American Cataloguing Rules* and of computerized catalogs), to discuss the effect of library networks on resource sharing, or to demonstrate various bibliographic databases.

Sessions on the online catalog are bound to intrigue all regular library users, especially if public-use terminals are available. People are curious about the contents and capabilities of online cataloging, as well as about the relationship of the online catalog to the traditional card catalog. By offering special interest lectures dealing with the online catalog, you will both establish your own reputation as a teacher and your library's willingness to reach out to explain changes caused by new technologies. Discussing innovations in the catalog allows you to develop teaching skills on a familiar topic, at the same time solidifying faculty and student contacts that you can draw on subsequently when you attempt discipline-specific instruction. Moreover, after getting people "hooked" with information about the catalog, you can "plug" other features of the library and the availability of other BI topics or modes.

Similarly, lecture/demonstrations of bibliographic database systems—including Boolean logic, the scope of various databases, and online sessions—make outstanding one-shots. The ideal method of organizing a database lecture is to work with a homogeneous group so that the bases considered are all relevant to the audience. Use of a demonstration or teaching password or free time made available by the database vendor will significantly reduce the costs of such a session. Ask participants in advance to jot down their current research topics so that you can prepare demonstration searches that will result in citations actually needed by someone in the audience. Also, by using "real" research problems, you will be able to show off the versatility—as well as the limitations—of database searching in a particular discipline, and the individuals who best know the subject field will be able to evaluate the appropriateness of the items retrieved on the spot. (An interesting tie-in between database searching for an individual faculty member and subsequent library instruction for that person's classes has been tried at Temple University in Philadelphia, where publicity regarding the BI program is inserted in the envelope containing database search results. This alerts faculty to the possibility of instruction on the printed tools that correspond to the database that has been searched for them.)

Whatever you can do to help users realize that librarians do more than acquire and organize information and provide answers to random reference questions will further the cause of BI and will help you get started. Likewise, the more BI librarians become active in discipline associations, the more they will assert their credibility as experts at understanding and assisting with library research at an advanced level.

We know of no BI program that has failed for lack of participants; the reverse situation is usually true. People are so eager for instruction once the opportunity is brought to their attention that the audience is self-renewing. The suggestions in these chapters should, however, help those who are wondering whose door to knock on first. Actually, whose door is not so important as having a well-designed proposal to present when the door is opened.

13
Costs of a
BI Program

Economic realities being what they are in the 1980s, costs have a serious impact on all aspects of library operations, not least of all on "new-fangled" programs such as bibliographic instruction, which lack the long and sacred tradition of cataloging and collection development. Public service, of which BI is a prominent part, is the most endangered area of library operations at many institutions because it seems possible to reduce or eliminate it without harming "vital" services or the collection. However you may feel about funding priorities at your institution, it is important to recognize that BI *is* costly. The purpose of this chapter is to discuss the nature of those costs and how they vary from mode to mode of instruction. Whether you have an established BI program that may be partially or entirely cut, or whether you are starting a program knowing that its funding future is shaky, you will want to consider the factors outlined in these pages so that you make reasonable and responsible choices in an uncertain climate (see Table 13-1).

Key Economic Principles

The following four key economic principles affect the relative expense and return of the various modes of BI: supply and demand, utility, opportunity cost, and cost/benefit ratio.

Ironically, a good BI program tends to create a greater demand for public service at a time when staffing levels in that area may be shrinking. Reference questions typically increase

Table 13-1 *Relative Costs of BI Modes*

	Material Costs	Staff Costs	Update/Repeat Costs
PRINTED MATERIALS General	Paper Printing: inexpensive duplication or elaborate printing Graphics Number: size of "run" affects the cost Display rack Space: floor space, heat, light for display rack or tables	Initial preparation: usually lengthy, especially if written annotation; time can be considered less expensive if partially allocated to staff development Graphic skills Layout skills Typing or typesetting Duplicating: multilith, print, and collate Collating	Update: revise Repeat: make more of same Reprinting Typing
Commercially available or borrowed from a clearinghouse	Purchase (from vendors) Printing (if borrowed) Collection development (to buy titles or finding tools cited but not owned by the library) Display rack or promotion to show that they are available	Time to obtain: identify, request/order, prepare for mailing back, time to compare; obtain copyright permission or pay royalty Adapt for local use: check card catalog; add call number; substitute for volumes not owned; typing if borrowed Graphic skills Layout skills Collection development when holes exist in the collection	Typing Reprinting Staff time varies with extent of revision Staff time to reorder

AUDIOVISUAL			
Transparencies	Equipment: need equipment to create AV materials; need equipment to show AV materials, e.g., screen and overhead Transparencies: color and overlays are extra cost; can hire outside agency to do; can have simple sheets to write on Crayons for transparencies	Staff skills to make transparencies Staff skills to show transparencies Planning for effective presentations Requires an accompanying presentation	Update: same cost as original Repeat: storage; filing/cataloging system; electricity when reuse
Slide/tape	Equipment to make slide/tape: camera; film, take many more slides than use; developing film Equipment to show slide/tape: projector and screen; caramate; tape/cassette recorder; cassettes Space to show: table for caramate; use room only for presentations, not used for something else; may have to remodel to accommodate either of the above, buy a table, etc. Storage space Security Maintenance and service contract for equipment Buy commercially available	Graphics Layout Photographer Technician for developing film Script writing Security Professional speaker Catalog slides Staff time to plan, prepare, execute Train to use equipment Time to compare, select, and order	Repeat: electricity Update: replace slides and edit tapes

Table 13-1 (cont.)

	Material Costs	Staff Costs	Update/Repeat Costs
Videotape	Color vs. black and white Equipment to make videotape: camera; film; editing equipment; screen/monitor Equipment to show: videotape machine; monitor Maintenance and service contract Security and insurance Space to show—separate room Buy commercially available	Graphics Technician to tape, edit Script writing Rehearsal Staff time to create, plan, prepare, execute Train to use equipment Time to compare, select, and order	Repeat: only cost of electricity Update: retake film, edit, match sound, splice in track
POINT-OF-USE			
Printed (place next to tool or as handouts next to tool)	Usually brief—one page or less See costs listed above for general printed materials	Preparation time See costs listed above for general printed materials	See costs listed above for general printed materials
Audiovisual	See costs listed above for AV slide/tape	See costs listed above for AV slide/tape	See costs listed above for AV slide/tape
PROGRAMMED INSTRUCTION			
Workbook	Buy published copies for students Buy or borrow one copy Paper Wear and tear on collection: replace; rebind Printing: test drafts; copies of workbooks locally Binding	Staff time varies: create from "scratch" and devise own questions; design editions to pretest; adapt model; standardized questions or unique sets of questions Correct answers Give feedback to students or faculty Typing Graphics	Repeat: cannot reuse same workbook—have to reprint Update: two days/year according to Mimi Dudley to write new annotations or update edition information; costs depend on size and quantity of rerun

Computer-assisted	Hardware Software package, if purchased Computer time Space for terminals Terminals	Programmer Preparation time for content Time to test Teach users to operate equipment Troubleshooting Train staff to use	Repeat: electricity and computer time for same or new individual Update: reprogram; rewrite content; change books; change sequence; change test questions and test answers
SINGLE LECTURE	Varies widely Space: special classroom for that use or appropriate conference room or other area Handouts Media costs from above if use transparencies, etc. Cards for notes Could utilize aspects of other modes if use	Preparation time for librarian—15 hours/1 hour lecture first time through Support staff: check bibliographies; pull books and mark examples; type handouts; copy, collate and staple handout	Repeat: staff time to present and assemble book, AV, etc.; handouts Update: revise own notes and review order and content; retype handout and reproduce; media revisions
COURSE	Varies: multiply single lecture considerations by number of contact hours	Several first time preparations Evaluation, design, and execution Planning sequence of course Multiply single lecture considerations by number of contact hours	Repeat: lower costs if same staff member repeats than if others do; if several sections of same course have only extra staff time costs for extra presentations and handout costs Update: multiply single lecture considerations by number of contact hours
TUTORIAL (E.G., TERM-PAPER CLINIC)	Publicity	Staff time: few people reached per staff contact hour, therefore more hours needed	Not applicable

as a result of BI, as do interlibrary loan requests. This situation must, however, be put in the broader context of the library's mission within the community. More effective library use as a consequence of instruction yields better—that is, more cost-effective—use of public resources, and so can be justified in that sense. Also, most BI modes use professional staff time more efficiently than does traditional reference service. In the classroom, for instance, BI librarians are active 100 percent of the time; at the reference desk they are idle for "nonproductive" minutes every hour.

The economic principle of utility refers to the relative value to the individual of a particular good or service, in this case, the knowledge and skills gained from bibliographic instruction. Some people argue that utility cannot be measured in monetary terms and, therefore, that utility cannot be determined for a particular mode. However, the utility of BI seems no more difficult to calculate than it is for any service in society. A successful BI program will enable individual participants to decrease the time spent doing research and increase both the accuracy and the thoroughness of their findings, and the individual should be able to quantify these results in personal terms.

Opportunity cost pertains to alternatives that are foregone when a particular choice is made. For every BI mode there are opportunity costs, since each mode has different strengths and weaknesses (see Chapter 3), and limited resources mean that the choice of one mode will preclude others, at least initially.

The cost/benefit ratio, again rather subjective, can and should be considered as a significant factor in selecting the best possible BI mode for a given institution and audience. Actual costs versus impact can at least be approximated and then periodically reviewed so that library administrators have a sense of the worth to their users of the BI program.

With these four principles in mind and by referring to Table 13-1, you can begin to weigh the *relative,* if not the real, costs involved as you deliberate before choosing a specific BI mode or modes. Rather than attempt to assign actual costs for each potential mode at the outset, you might narrow the modes from which to select by rating the three factors across the top of the table as relatively low, medium, or high at your institution. Then, when you have focused on some possibilities, draw up sample cost sheets to facilitate a closer comparison.

Part V
Impact and
Conclusion

These are exciting times for those involved in bibliographic instruction. Despite the economic realities discussed in Chapter 13, despite the problems that are common to the beginning of any worthwhile endeavor, bibliographic instruction does have an impact on various groups in society and an important role to play. That impact and role, as well as trends now developing that will affect BI throughout the decade, are discussed in Chapter 14.

14
Benefits and Trends

What are the impact and role of bibliographic instruction on various groups in society? What trends of the early 1980s will affect instruction in the future?

Benefits

The benefits of library instruction accrue to the user who receives the instruction, the library staff who give it, the library as an institution, the larger community of which the library is a part, the various disciplines, and society in general. We have discussed at length the influence that effective bibliographic instruction, at the appropriate time and the appropriate level, can have on the user—providing self-confidence in doing research and speeding up that research and its thoroughness incalculably. Likewise, librarians involved in any mode of library instruction enhance their own professionalism by expanding their skills, knowledge, and perceptions of their role. Public relations generated by a solid library instruction program redound to the good of the library as an institution; BI becomes a vital public service on a par with reference or circulation in terms of helping users connect with information they need. The institution or community with which the library is tied benefits from library instruction insofar as the students or citizens so instructed become wiser consumers of information, better able to investigate topics and make informed decisions based on the best and most current available information. Academic disciplines and faculty who purvey them are immeasurably enhanced by subject-specific bibliographic instruction programs in that the students instructed are more knowledgeable and better able to teach library research methods in the future. They will be more influential within the associations in their disciplines, affecting decisions regarding bibliographic control. And society in general benefits from more self-sufficient citizens who are able to understand their own research needs and pursue them vigorously.

BI should be a comprehensive concept, implemented at all levels from childhood through adult education. It can serve as an opportunity for librarians in all types of facilities to institute certain concepts and skill levels in early childhood education, elementary school, secondary school, and throughout the educational system in the United States, so that at each level students may be assumed to have a basic command of the concepts and skills they were exposed to at the previous level. Given the difficulties of basic literacy in this country at this time, it may seem a pipe dream to assume that library use skills can be satisfactorily taught in a sequential manner throughout the curriculum when we are questioning our ability to teach reading, writing, and arithmetic successfully.

The goal remains, however, that BI could be programmed so that we could safely assume what students would know as they enter college or graduate school. We are far from achieving this goal, but it is certainly one worth looking at and working toward. Several years ago, Evan Farber of Earlham College made the cogent suggestion that if basic library concepts and skills were added to the Scholastic Aptitude Test, educators and students in the United States would take note of that lack in the system and begin to do something about it at the secondary level. The problem is not the principle of testing, but exactly what we would be testing for, and until BI librarians are able to agree on that, the suggestion remains only a suggestion. It would be fascinating, were it possible logistically or politically, to inventory the bibliographic expertise of scholars in particular disciplines to learn what they use more frequently, what they are aware of, and where they *think* the gaps exist in the paradigms for their fields. No doubt BI librarians would be horrified to discover faculty ignorance of particularly prominent and valuable tools that we use every day, but the survey would have the result of pointing up problems that are only passed on from generation to generation since the faculty member who is unaware of a particular tool can never suggest its use to a student.

Trends

Among the contemporary trends and disciplines that have a direct impact on the future of library instruction are many cited by Tom Kirk.[1] For instance, secondary schools in the course of their accreditation reviews are concerned about the literacy of high school students, and that can be tied in directly with the use, misuse, or nonuse by those same students of the high school library or media center or of the public library. Similarly, various discipline associations accredit graduate schools or undergraduate programs for their discipline, and it is becoming customary for a more vigorous, rigorous review of the library and its resources and services to take place during accreditation visits. This would be an ideal time or an ideal reason to initiate a bibliographic instruction program to improve the expertise of students and faculty alike.

Interest is also growing in the concepts that underlie bibliographic instruction and in the discipline structures discussed earlier in this book and how they relate to real life research in those fields. Another trend has to do with technology, with librarians' decisions now and in the future about whether to have numerous public access terminals to permit users to do their own database searches or their own OCLC or RLIN searches, for instance. Obviously we do not intend to have an online catalog that users cannot themselves use, but how does one instruct those people in the scope and basic search protocols? The answer to that question will be a real and important BI challenge in the near future.

The proliferation of reference-type publications since the 1950s has increased the necessity of library instruction, since faculty educated prior to that time are unlikely to be familiar with the extent of the fact and finding tools that exist and their availability online or with the various microformats that reproduce sources for their fields.

The very proliferation and unsettling nature of reference publishing is a strong argument in favor of faculty update seminars, such as those that have been so successful at the University of California at Berkeley, which acquainted and reacquainted faculty with resources in the library. As physical access to materials becomes more and more difficult because material is sent to storage, disintegrates, is put on microfilm, or subscriptions are cut back, and so forth, it is more and more imperative that users be aware of the entire scope of finding tools that will help identify the whereabouts of items within a library system.

Lifelong learning is another factor that promotes bibliographic instruction and has an impact on it. More and more people are returning to school for substantive subjects involving research, and these are particularly ripe candidates for certain modes of instruction. Here in particular public libraries may be able to assist academic facilities in working with groups of older and special students, since they are more used to serving patrons of a variety of ages and capabilities.

The future of scholarly journals will have an impact not on just library instruction, but on the whole finding tool paradigm for any field. If journals are no longer printed but are available for online scanning or on-demand offline printing only, with just abstracts published, then we will have to rethink the impact of journals on the various disciplines and the importance of browsing. Videodisc, cable, and satellite technologies must also be studied to determine what exactly will be collected and how it will be controlled. Will we be receiving cable or satellite transmissions of bibliographic data in the future? How will hard copy be transferred from point to point? What sorts of materials will be converted to videodiscs and other microformats?

How the BI librarians of the future should be educated in terms of library school preparation, subject background, and continuing education once they are practicing forms a debate that will influence the people coming into bibliographic instruction in the middle and late 1980s, and through them will have an impact on BI in the future. We cannot stress enough the importance of conveying the underlying theoretical frameworks in the basic library school degree programs, whether or not students decide that BI is for them. Other matters such as AV and teaching techniques can be well conveyed via continuing education workshops, but no library school should graduate students who cannot do an acceptable search strategy in the abstract on any given topic.[2]

What will be the role of bibliographic instruction librarians in terms of not just identifying and retrieving information and showing others how to do the same, but in educating people on how to interpret and judge that information? Librarians ordinarily leave interpretation to the individual, and the person who has difficulties is referred to a scholar or specialist in the discipline. But perhaps in the future BI librarians will be doing more interpretation themselves from the vantage point of how information reflects discipline growth and structure and what the existence of a particular communication "means."

We look forward with excitement to these and the other developments that will affect bibliographic instruction in the years to come, and all those connected with BI should be resolved to turn promising trends into firm realities.

Notes

1. Thomas Kirk, "Past, Present, and Future of Library Instruction," *Southeastern Libraries,* 27 (Spring 1977): 15–18.
2. Sharon A. Hogan, "Training and Education of Library Instruction Librarians," *Library Trends* 29 (Summer 1980): 105–106.

Selected Bibliography

The following items are among the most helpful and most frequently cited in any discussion of bibliographic instruction. The listings under Additional Readings proved useful to the authors in clarifying observations in this book.

Bibliographies

Lockwood, Deborah L., comp. *Library Instruction: A Bibliography.* Westport, Conn.: Greenwood Press, 1979. 166 pp.

LOEX News: The Quarterly Newsletter of the Library Orientation-Instruction Exchange. Ypsilanti, Mich.: Center of Educational Resources, Eastern Michigan University, 1974– .

Rader, Hannelore B. "Library Orientation and Instruction—[year]," annually in *Reference Services Review* (Ann Arbor, Mich.: Pierian Press, 1976–) and in the proceedings volumes of the Annual Conference on Library Orientation for Academic Libraries, published in the Library Orientation Series, also of Pierian Press, 1971– .

Taylor, Peter J., et al. *The Education of Users of Library and Information Services: An International Bibliography.* Aslib Bibliography, no. 9. London: Aslib, 1979. 135 pp.

Guides

Bibliographic Instruction Handbook. Chicago: Association of College and Research Libraries, 1979. 69 pp.

A Comprehensive Program of User Education for the General Libraries. Austin, Texas: The General Libraries, University of Texas at Austin, 1977. 101 pp.

Organizing and Managing a Library Instruction Program: Checklists. Chicago: Association of College and Research Libraries, 1979. 30 pp.

Renford, Beverly, and Hendrickson, Linnea. *Bibliographic Instruction: A Handbook.* New York: Neal-Schuman, 1980. 192 pp.

Rice, James. *Teaching Library Use: A Guide for Library Instruction.* Westport, Conn.: Greenwood Press, 1981. 169 pp.

Collections of Articles

Henning, P. A., and Shapiro, J., eds. "Library Instruction: Methods, Materials, Evaluation." Special issue of *Drexel Library Quarterly* 8 (July 1972).

Henning, P. A., and Stillman, M. E., eds. "Integrating Library Instruction in the College Curriculum." Special issue of *Drexel Library Quarterly* 7 (July–October 1971).

Lubans, John. *Educating the Library User.* New York: Bowker, 1974. 435 pp.

Lubans, John. *Progress in Educating the Library User.* New York: Bowker, 1978. 230 pp.

Marshall, Albert P., ed. "Current Library Use Instruction." Special issue of *Library Trends* 29 (Summer 1980).

Additional Readings

Adams, Mignon. "Individualized Approach to Library Learning Skills." *Library Trends* 29 (Summer 1980): 83–94.

Bibliographic Instruction Program. Kenosha, Wis.: University of Wisconsin at Parkside, 1976. ERIC Doc. ED 126 937. 62 pp.

Biggins, Jeanne. "A Study of the Administration of Library Use Instruction Courses by Committee." Masters thesis, Syracuse University, 1978. ERIC Doc. ED 171 241. 51 pp.

Biggs, Mary M. "On My Mind— 'The Perils of Library Instruction.' " *Journal of Academic Librarianship* 5 (July 1979): 159, 162.

Davis, Jinnie Y., and Bentley, Stella. "Factors Affecting Faculty Perceptions of Academic Libraries." *College and Research Libraries* 40 (Nov. 1979): 527–532.

Dickinson, Dennis W. "Library Literacy: Who? When? Where?" *Library Journal* 106 (April 15, 1981): 853–855.

Dubin, Eileen. "An In-Depth Analysis of a Term Paper Clinic." *Illinois Libraries* 60 (March 1978): 324–333.

Duvall, Scott H. *Library Instruction: Two Teaching Methods.* Provo, Utah: Brigham Young University, 1975. ERIC Doc. ED 112 898. 52 pp.

Elkins, Elizabeth A., and Byman, Judith A. *Developing Printed Material for Library Instruction.* Workshop presented at the Annual Meeting of the New York Library Association, Lake Placid, NY, October 1976. ERIC Doc. ED 171 258. 27 pp.

Freides, Thelma. *Literature and Bibliography of the Social Sciences.* Los Angeles: Melville, 1973. 284 pp.

Garvey, William D. *Communication: The Essence of Science: Facilitating Information Exchange among Librarians, Scientists, Engineers, and Students.* Oxford: Pergamon Press, 1979. 332 pp.

Glogoff, Stuart. "Using Statistical Tests to Evaluate Library Instruction Sessions." *Journal of Academic Librarianship* 4 (January 1979): 438–442.

Hernon, Peter. "Library Lectures and their Evaluation: A Survey." *Journal of Academic Librarianship* 1 (July 1975): 14–18.

Hoselitz, Bert F., ed. *A Reader's Guide to the Social Sciences.* Rev. ed. New York: Free Press, 1970. 425 pp.

Hughes, Phyllis, and Flandreau, Arthur. "Tutorial Library Instruction: The Freshman Program at Berea College." *Journal of Academic Librarianship* 6 (May 1980): 91–94.

Kirk, Thomas. "Library Administrators and Instruction Librarians: Improving Relations." *Journal of Academic Librarianship* 6 (January 1981): 345.

Knapp, Patricia B. "The Library's Response to Innovation in Higher Education." *California Librarian* 29 (April 1968): 142–149.

Kuhn, Thomas S. *The Structure of Scientific Revolutions.* 2nd ed., enlarged. International Encyclopedia of Unified Science, Foundations of the Unity of Science, vol. 2, no. 2. Chicago: University of Chicago Press, 1970. 210 pp.

Lewis, James M. "Answers to Twenty Questions on Behavioral Objectives." *Educational Technology* 21 (March 1981): 27–31.

Lubans, John. "Objectives for Library-Use Instruction in Educational Curricula," in his *Educating the Library User*, pp. 211–220. New York: Bowker, 1974.

Lubans, John. "Library-Use Instruction Needs from the Library Users'/Nonusers' Point of View: A Survey Report," in his *Educating the Library User*, pp. 401–409. New York: Bowker, 1974.

McInnis, Raymond G. *New Perspectives for Reference Service in Academic Libraries.* Westport, Conn.: Greenwood Press, 1978. 351 pp.

Montemayor, Aurelio M., and Stillman, Garry. *Integrating Library Skills into Bilingual Bicultural Classrooms, or Preventing LESA Future Shock.* San Antonio, Texas: Intercultural Development Research Association, 1978. ERIC Doc. ED 165 462. 7 pp.

Morris, Jacquelyn M., and Webster, Donald F. *Developing Objectives for Library Instruction.* Workshop presented at the Annual Meeting of the New York Library Association, Lake Placid, NY, October 1976. ERIC Doc. ED 171 257. 31 pp.

Patterson, Margaret C. "Library Literacy: A Cumulative Experience." *Literary Research Newsletter* 2 (October 1977): 180–186.

Phillips, Linda L., and Raup, E. A. "Comparing Methods for Teaching Use of Periodical Indexes." *Journal of Academic Librarianship* 4 (January 1979): 420–423.

Phipps, Shelley, and Dickstein, Ruth. "The Library Skills Program and the University of Arizona: Testing Evaluation and Critique." *Journal of Academic Librarianship* 5 (September 1979): 205–214.

Rice, James. "Testing and Evaluation," in his *Teaching Library Use: A Guide for Library Instruction,* pp. 97–129. Westport, Conn.: Greenwood Press, 1981.

White, Carl M., et al. *Sources of Information in the Social Sciences: A Guide to the Literature.* 2nd ed. Chicago: American Library Association, 1973. 702 pp.

Yaple, Henry M. *Programmed Instruction in Librarianship: A Classified Bibliography of Programmed Texts and Other Materials, 1960–1974.* Occasional paper, no. 124. Urbana, Ill.: University of Illinois Graduate School of Library Science, 1976. 25 pp.

Index